# Date Due

| | | | |
|---|---|---|---|
| | | | |
| | | | |
| | | | |
| | | | |
| | | | |
| | | | |
| | | | |
| | | | |
| | | | |
| | | | |
| | | | |
| | | | |
| | | | |
| | | | |
| | | | |
| | | | |
| | | | |
| | | | |
| | | | |
| | | | |
| GB | PRINTED | IN U. S. A. | |

# BARTH'S TRAVELS IN NIGERIA

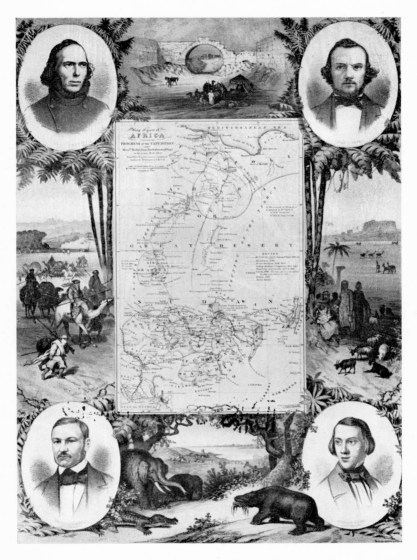

An illustration from Petermann's Royal Folio, 1854, with portraits of Richardson, Overweg, Barth and Vogel.

WEST AFRICAN HISTORY SERIES

General Editor: GERALD S. GRAHAM

*Rhodes Professor of Imperial History, University of London*

# BARTH'S TRAVELS IN NIGERIA

Extracts from the journal of
Heinrich Barth's travels in Nigeria,
1850–1855

Selected and edited,
with an introduction,

by

## A. H. M. KIRK-GREENE

LONDON
OXFORD UNIVERSITY PRESS
IBADAN ACCRA
1962

*Oxford University Press, Amen House, London, E.C.4*

GLASGOW NEW YORK TORONTO MELBOURNE WELLINGTON
BOMBAY CALCUTTA MADRAS KARACHI LAHORE DACCA
CAPE TOWN SALISBURY NAIROBI IBADAN ACCRA
KUALA LUMPUR HONG KONG

Preparation and publication of this series
has been made possible by the generous
financial assistance of OVERSEAS
NEWSPAPERS GROUP, Accra, Freetown,
Lagos and London.

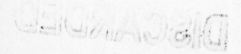

PRINTED IN GREAT BRITAIN

For
HELEN

# PREFACE

Of Africa's eminent explorers, none has been so neglected by posterity as Heinrich Barth. Stanley in Central Africa, Speke and Baker on the Nile, Livingstone in South–Central Africa, Park and the Landers on the Niger, Mary Kingsley in West Africa, have all received a large measure of recognition; Barth alone seems to have been ignored. Not a single biography has yet been written in English, and the century since his death has produced barely half a dozen worthwhile commentaries on his African travels.

Nor is it merely a question of biographical study; Barth's own works are involved, too. The English edition of his monumental *Travels and Discoveries in North and Central Africa* has become a collector's piece. It is seldom found outside libraries, not only for the reason of its very limited publication, but also because its format (five volumes in octavo, almost 3,500 pages) has dissuaded many Africanists from exposing such a library set, despite its scholarly merits as a travelling companion, to the hazards of a tropical climate or the frequent *déménagements* inherent in life in Nigeria. 'Barth's work', one of the Vice-Presidents of the Royal Geographical Society said a few years ago,[1] 'for those who study the area between Lake Chad and Timbuktu, is still, for many purposes, the standard work. Unfortunately, the book is now extremely difficult to get hold of . . .' an observation made all the more poignant by the story of how a complete set of the *Travels and Discoveries* has recently been thrown on the refuse heap.[2]

It is in an attempt to remedy both these faults — the lack of appreciation of Barth's real achievements as an explorer-scholar and the ever-growing difficulty of obtaining a copy of his works — that this 'essential Barth' has been compiled. Prefaced by a biographical monograph, these excerpts from his

[1] *The Geographical Journal*, Vol. CXXIV, September, 1958, p. 339.
[2] *West Africa*, December 26, 1953, p. 1211, where Maboth Moseley describes some of the incidents experienced in collecting Africana.

Nigerian diary aim at presenting a balanced cross-section of personal narrative, geographical description, ethnological observation and historical reconstruction. As with all anthologies, readers will lament the pruning of their favourite passage, the absence of their most treasured anecdote; moreover, on account of the strictly Nigerian context of this volume, there is no place for tales of Timbuktu or detailed descriptions of Barth's Saharan crossing and his adventures in Kanem, Mandara and Bagirmi. This book sets out simply to describe some of Barth's journeys in those regions of nineteenth-century Central Africa that today are recognized as Northern Nigeria.

Two final prefatory remarks. First, I have been guided by the belief that in a compilation of this nature no words can replace the phraseology of Barth's own journal, which, though written in a style that is neither exemplary nor particularly absorbing, remains an integral element of the *Travels and Discoveries*. It is for this reason that, apart from setting the stage in Chapter 1, I have avoided paraphrase and summary, and have aimed at reproducing original extracts, uninterrupted by cuts or brackets or frequent footnotes, and linked them with the minimum of editorial continuity passages. Secondly, so great is the difference in format and pagination of the English, American, German and French texts, that I have thought it more helpful to locate quotations from Barth's *Travels and Discoveries* by giving the actual date of the entry in his diary in preference to the customary context of volume and page number.

A. H. M. KIRK-GREENE

Zaria, 1958 —
California, 1959

# CONTENTS

# LIST OF PLATES

# LIST OF FIGURES

# LIST OF MAPS

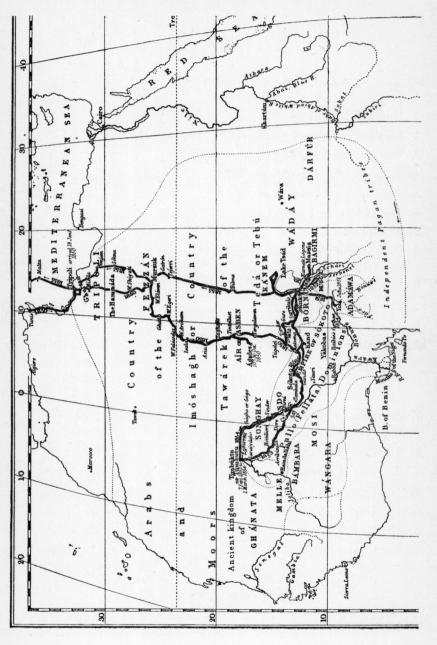

MAP OF AFRICA, 1857, SHOWING THE ROUTES OF DR. BARTH'S TRAVELS, 1850–1855

# INTRODUCTION

## 1. HEINRICH BARTH: THE MAN[1]

### EARLY YEARS

Heinrich Barth[2] was born in Hamburg in 1821. The date is variously given as 18 April, 19 May, or 16 February — the earlier date is preferred by a few contemporary and most subsequent scholars. He was the third child of a Thüringian peasant, Johann Christoph Heinrich Barth, who in 1801, on the death of his parents, had been taken from Wilmersdorf to Hamburg. His mother was Charlotte Caroline Zadow, a Hanover girl whom Johann Barth had married in 1814. Both were of orthodox Lutheran belief and brought up their children to observe a rigid discipline and morality. Barth's mother was domesticated and strict, with neither the time nor inclination for intellectual matters. His father, a self-made man, had built up a good Hanseatic trading business in Hamburg: it may be that its overseas connexions kindled in the young Barth the wanderlust that so marked his adult years. From his father he inherited a capacity for intense industry and a great love of orderliness, while from his mother he acquired a strong self-reliance that led at times to introspection.

Educated at first in private schools, in 1832 Barth entered the Johanneum School, Hamburg, under the direction of Dr. Friedrich Karl Kraft. That the academic discipline seems to have at once caught Barth's imagination is evident in the posthumous

[1] For textual authorities, see 'A Note on Principal Source Materials', at the end of the Introduction.

[2] In German, the name is pronounced to rhyme with 'part,' with a slightly more guttural 'r' and a more staccato 't'. In English, it has been the custom to rhyme the name with 'bath', a practice recently commended by Mr. E. W. Bovill of the Royal Geographical Society (*The Geographical Journal*, September 1958, p. 338).

recollection of a fellow pupil who described[3] how Barth subjected not only his mind to a strict training, but also his body,
building up a naturally weak constitution by cold baths and
physical exercises, even in mid-winter. Other school friends have
recalled a certain self-sufficiency, a quality doubtless of great
value in his subsequent trials in the Sahara and Sudan, but at
that age a trait that could not fail to make him unpopular with
his class-mates. Gifted with an astonishing memory and outstanding linguistic talents, so that he was fluent in English by
the time he was fourteen, Barth found his early interest in
Arabic called 'the summit of absurdity' by his schoolfellows.
They judged him rough and awkward, recalling him as a
boy who indulged in none of the fun and carefree joys of school
life, slow to laugh and appearing to his comrades an unbending
pedant. It is significant that Barth had no intimate friend in
his youth (other than Dr. Danzel,[4] who died early), for even as
a child he was self-contained, complacent, a teacher's pet rather
than a popular student.

### AT THE UNIVERSITY

In October 1839 Heinrich Barth enrolled at the University
of Berlin, a city rich in museums and architecture, and in men
of learning like Müller, Curtius, Humboldt and Gerard.
Among the other internationally recognized scholars then in
the faculty of the University, three in particular exercised a
profound influence upon Barth: August Böckh, professor of
archaeology, Jakob Grimm the historian, and Karl Ritter,
professor of geography. At the end of the second semester
Barth broke off his studies, taught himself Italian, and set off
for a year's travel in Venice, Florence, Rome, Pompeii and
Sicily. In a letter sent to his family from Rome in November,
1840, Barth wrote, 'I now find it quite easy to wander around
for nine hours at a stretch, nourished by nothing more than a

[3] *Vossischer Zeitung*, 29 November 1865, quoted by Schubert.
[4] It is interesting to find that the copy of Barth's doctoral dissertation, acquired by
the Smithsonian Institution, Washington, D.C., and now owned by the Library
of Congress, is inscribed by Barth to W. Danzel.

few drops of wine and a snack.' The self-discipline he was to practise in Africa had already begun. On his return to Berlin, Barth entered the law school.

In 1842 he received disastrous news from home. On 24 May, a serious fire in Hamburg destroyed half his father's possessions, and the whole of his own valuable library, among which he had spent so many of his schooldays. That vacation he again spent in Europe, this time travelling in the Rhineland and Switzerland. Writing to his father, of whom he was always particularly fond, he said, 'I have an immense force inside me, the most altruistic striving towards the great and the true and the beautiful. To be of use to mankind, to inspire and motivate them . . .' He returned to Berlin to complete his Ph.D. dissertation and on 31 July 1844[5] he defended his thesis *Corinthiorum commercii et mercaturae historiae particula* before L. von Winter (later Lord Mayor of Danzig), R. Bergmann and G. Koner.

Barth passed the next six months at home with his parents, on the curious yet characteristic understanding that their affection for him would not interfere with his studying ten hours each day. His inclination now lay towards a teaching career, but learning that it was advisable not to take up university lecturing for three years after gaining his higher degree, he gave up his idea of teaching in Bonn and set forth on what he called his *Studienreise*, his grand tour of 1845–47. Provided with letters of recommendation from Böckh, a generous purse of £2,000 from his father, and a copy of the Koran — this he always carried with him, partly for language study and partly to gain an insight into the wisdom and customs of Islam — Barth planned an extensive journey around the Mediterranean coast. First he travelled to London, where he busied himself in perfecting his Arabic, in studying the British Museum's treasures of classical antiquity, and in securing the important protection of the British consuls along the Barbary Coast. It was on this occasion that he first met Chevalier.

---

[5] The date usually quoted is 28 June, but the published thesis has *rite obtinendus die XXXI M. Julii MDCCCXLIV, hora XII.*

Christian von Bunsen, Prussian ambassador to Great Britain and a renowned Egyptologist, who a few years later was to play such a prominent part in securing Barth's appointment to the Central African expedition.

On 7 August 1845 Barth first set foot in Africa, crossing from Gibraltar to Tangiers. Moving thence to Algiers and Tunis, with a side trip to Malta (one German commentator[6] regrets that Barth did not leave all his diaries and coins there, as they were stolen from him in the subsequent Bedouin attack), he crossed the Libyan desert to Egypt. It was at Kaf, in Tunis, that a Hausa slave said to Barth, 'Please God, you shall go and visit Kano''.

During the journey up the Nile to Wadi Halfa and over the desert to Berenice, Barth was attacked on 7 June 1846 by Bedouin brigands. They apparently believed his large red chest to be full of gold; in fact, it contained one of the newly-invented daguerreotype machines. Barth lost most of his papers, sketches and photographs and was fortunate to escape with his life. It is recorded that he defended his tent with a sword in his hand until he was knocked out by a well-aimed sling-shot. He received two rifle wounds: one bullet went through the right leg and the other penetrated his left thigh.[8] From the way in which Barth minimized the gravity of this incident, it is reasonable to suppose that he wished to prevent his father from worrying about his safety.

Barth returned to Germany on 27 December 1847: 'the youth had become a man', writes his biographer, Gustav von Schubert, an army officer who was later to marry Barth's younger sister. Barth, it may be noted, took himself seriously in the role of elder brother, for his brother-in-law tells us that the first letter he received from Barth warned him that 'if you make my sister unhappy, I will shoot you dead'.

Barth was now determined on an academic career, in Berlin if possible. In January 1848 he wrote to his old tutor, Böckh, to whom he had dedicated his dissertation, and after considerable

---

[6] Koner.          [7] Quoted by Barth in the Preface to his Journal.
[8] It remained there for the rest of his life.

correspondence was finally taken on as *Privatdozent* in the Department of Archaeology at the University of Berlin in October 1848. During the year he helped Ritter to read the proofs of his *Vorlesungen über die Geschichte der Erdkunde* and worked hard on the preparation of the first volume of his own *Wanderungen durch die Küstenländer des Mittelmeeres, ausgeführt in den Jahren* 1845, 1846 *und* 1847, which appeared in June 1849. The second volume was never published, although extracts from it were later reproduced in one of the Berlin geographical journals. As a lecturer, Barth was not a success, his content being too heavy and his delivery lacking enthusiasm; indeed, so few undergraduates turned up to his lectures on ancient colonial commerce and comparative geography that he regretfully cancelled the course. It was perhaps this disappointment in the academic career he had looked forward to, coupled with the blow to his pride that made him eagerly accept the offer to join an expedition to Central Africa that was being planned by Her Majesty's Government in London.

In passing, it should be noted that all that area of West Africa that is now recognized as the Western Sudan was, a century ago, without any definitive name and was referred to variously as Central Africa, Guinea, the Sokoto Empire, the Kingdom of Zamfara, Zegzeg, Nooffee or simply *Beled es Sudan*, the Land of the Blacks, or Negroland.[10]

## CENTRAL AFRICAN EXPEDITION

The leader of the expedition then being mounted for the exploration of Central Africa was James Richardson, who had travelled widely in the northern Sahara a few years earlier and had written:[11]

Since my return from a first tour of exploration in the Great Sahara, I had carefully revolved in my mind the possibility of a much

---

[9] Schiffers quotes a rumour of disappointed love: *Die Grosse Reise* (Minden, 1954), p. 9.

[10] See, for example, 'Who Coined the Name "Nigeria"?' A. H. M. Kirk-Greene, *West Africa*, 22 December 1956, p. 1035. *The Times* of 16 August 1851 talked of Barth's entry into 'Nigritia'.

[11] *Narrative of a Mission to Central Africa*, James Richardson, 1853, I, p. 1.

greater undertaking, namely a political and commercial expedition
to some of the most important kingdoms of Central Africa . . . two
objects, one principal, if necessarily kept somewhat in the
background — the abolition of the slave trade; one subsidiary, and
yet important in itself — the promotion of commerce by way of the
great desert; appeared to me, and to the distinguished persons who
promoted the undertaking, of sufficient magnitude to justify considerable sacrifices.[12]

Chevalier Bunsen, a scholar as well as an ambassador, had
his attention drawn to this African project by the German
cartographer, August Petermann, who was at that time working
at the London Observatory. Eager to ensure German scientific
participation in this expedition, Bunsen asked Professor Ritter
to recommend a scientist, for Richardson had expressed how
gravely he felt the want of a broader education, particularly
with reference to the making of astronomical observations.

Ritter at once suggested Barth:

. . . he is a young man about 33 years of age, a classical scholar,
understanding modern languages, and speaking besides French,
Spanish and Italian, also English and Arabic, who has at his own
expense made a scientific journey of four years around the coasts
of the Mediterranean.

Bunsen authorized Ritter to go ahead and put the proposal to
Barth. This he did on 5 October 1849, adding the condition
that Barth would be expected to contribute £200 for his
private needs on the expedition. Confident that his generous
father would provide this sum, Barth did not hesitate. His only
stipulation was that 'the exploration of Central Africa should
be made the principal object of the mission, instead of a
secondary one as had been originally contemplated'.[13]

But Barth's father, too mindful of the hazards of his son's
recent experience in the desert and probably not unaware of
the fate of would-be explorers of the Sudan over the past fifty
years, 'entreated me to desist from my perilous undertakings
with an earnestness which my filial duty did not allow me to
resist'[14] and refused to allow his son to participate in such a

[12] Thus the original punctuation.          [13] Barth, in the Preface to his Journal.
[14] ibid.

dangerous venture. With a heavy heart Barth was obliged to break the news to Ritter that he must withdraw his acceptance. Ritter arranged that his place should be filled by another pupil of his, Adolf Overweg, a geologist and astronomer, whom Petermann had come across in his work at the observatory.

Fortunately for posterity, a legal undertaking is less easily broken than paternal opposition: Her Majesty's Government, acting with providential firmness, insisted that Barth had already foreclosed the contract by his verbal acceptance. This time Barth had less difficulty in persuading his father to let him go, for Bunsen's hints of a professorship with a salary of 800 thalers[15] on Barth's return calmed Johann Barth's fear that his son's academic career might be endangered. 'Mr. Bunsen', runs a subsequent memorandum in the Foreign Office, 'seems to have been instrumental in procuring for him [Barth] the promise of a professorial chair at Berlin on his return, without which promise his father would not let him go.' Bunsen was also able to influence the British Government into allowing two German scientists to accompany the expedition instead of one. In the event, it was probably as well that Overweg was appointed a member of the expedition, for despite his other qualifications, Barth had no particular competence in making astronomical observations.[16]

The three explorers met for the first time in London at the end of November 1849. On 30 November a document was drawn up. At the insistence of Bunsen, no formal declaration that the Germans had entered British service was made; although this provision ensured their independence of action, outside their contract of reporting all geographical discoveries to the Foreign Office, in the long run it caused them considerable moral and financial embarrassment.

The principal items of this contract allow us a proper understanding of the legal position of the three participants. In brief, they were as follows:

[15] 1 thaler (dollar) was then worth about 3/-, and three marks equalled a thaler.

[16] In a private letter to H. Berghaus, Humboldt subsequently criticized the accuracy of Barth's astronomical observations, regretting his ignorance in this field.

(1) The choice of route, the method of advance, and the time of withdrawal, were the responsibility of Richardson, though he was permitted to consult Barth and Overweg on these matters.

(2) Richardson should retire after reaching Lake Chad,[17] leaving behind whatever instruments were required for the return journey.

(3) Richardson should help Barth and Overweg in the promotion of their scientific work. The British Government made an immediate grant of £100 for Barth and Overweg, and supplies worth a further £100 were to be dispatched through the vice-consul in Murzuk and the Sheikh of Bornu.

(4) Should the two doctors on reaching Lake Chad wish to separate from their leader to make a journey towards the east, either towards the Nile or in the direction of Mombasa,[18] Richardson was authorized to draw a further £200 through the vice-consul in Murzuk. Should the travellers proceed further, then they were empowered to obtain yet another £200 from the English consul in Zanzibar or from the English consul in Cairo.

(5) Richardson was authorized to make gifts on behalf of Her Majesty's Government, and to pay the guides, escorts, and lodging fees.

(6) In case of separation, the contents of the medical chest were to be divided.

Simultaneous instructions were issued by Lord Palmerston to Richardson in his capacity as leader of the expedition. These elaborated the high character and scholarship of his two

[17] He planned to return to the Mediterranean through Kordofan and Egypt.

[18] It is not widely appreciated that the expedition seriously envisaged the possibility of a trans-African trek. R. M. Prothero, in a letter published in *West Africa*, 31 January 1959, claims that the original idea for a transcontinental journey came from Karl Ritter. There are a number of references to the project in the pages of Barth's diary, and Lord Palmerston's dispatch of 7 October 1851 addressed to Barth allowed him either to push his ' further researches eastward toward the Nile or southeastward toward Mombaz ', or to turn west to Timbuktu. For obvious reasons, physical and financial, Barth chose Timbuktu.

German companions and added that in the light of Richardson's previous experience in Saharan travel, it would not be necessary to 'spell out' all the instructions of the mission. Lord Palmerston did, however, emphasize that, in addition to the political and scientific goals of the expedition, the British Government was anxious to explore the possibilities of trade treaties.

### SOME REFLECTIONS ON THE ORDER OF MARCH AND THE INTERNAL ORGANIZATION OF THE EXPEDITION

The *Travels and Discoveries* contain within their 3,500 pages, interesting details of the day-to-day living and minor organizational problems of the expedition. On trek Barth wrapped in his tent his large pack, his firearms, and the table and planks on which he used to lay his bed. 'I will mention here, for the use of future travellers', he writes, 'that I always wore not only my azimuth, but even my chronometer in my belt, and found this an excellent precaution against accidents of any kind.'[19]

Barth had wished at first for a donkey, and on his expedition to Agades, he rode (and came off) a bullock;[20] he was saved from injury by falling on his musket, and vowed he would never again ride a bullock. Consul Warrington gave him a Ghadamsi saddle and pillows and a Stambuli carpet, for comfortable riding.[21]

Normally he rode a camel; his favourite, named Bu-Sefi, carried him all the way from the Mediterranean to Lake Chad.[22] In Nigeria, he owned a number of horses, one of which he named 'Blast of the Desert'.

The caravan that left Tripoli consisted of sixty-two camels, arranged in four strings, one of them with thirty-three beasts fastened head to tail.[23] Of this trans-Saharan caravan, Bath notes how:

the lazy Arab mode of letting the camels go singly, as they like, straggling about right and left, strains and fatigues the traveller's

---

[19] 26 February 1850.    [20] 4 October 1850.    [21] 27 March 1850.
[22] A fine example of Barth's affection for Bu-Sefi is to be found in the diary entry of 25 March 1851.
[23] 29 June 1850.

attention; but his mind is stimulated and nerved to the contempla-
tion of great distances to be traversed when he sees a long line of
camels attached one to the other and led by a man at a steady pace
without any halt or interruption.[24]

In describing how he set out from Kukawa for Timbuktu,
Barth gives a good idea of how his personal caravan, consisting
of two servants, three freemen, two redeemed slaves, four
horses and four camels, travelled.[25]

One of the discomforts that they soon experienced was the
*pennisetum distichum* (*karengia*),

which, together with the ant, is to the traveller in Central Africa his
greatest and most constant inconvenience. It was just ripe, and little
bur-like seeds attached themselves to every part of my dress. It was
quite necessary to be always provided with small pincers, in order
to draw out from the fingers the little stings which, if left in the skin,
will cause sores.

Another was the white ants. They destroyed Barth's leather
bags when he was in Yo in September, 1851, and on his
journey to Timbuktu two years later 'made great havoc with
the whole of my luggage'.[26]

Barth undertook a number of long, strenuous marches,[27] often
of twenty miles and on occasions up to thirty, such as the
appalling twenty-six-mile trek through the wilderness of
Gundumi,[28] or that between Wurno and Kano, when at one
point 'I felt so much exhausted that I was obliged shortly after
to remain secretly behind, protected only by my faithful servant,
el Gatroni, when I lay down flat on the ground for a few
moments.'[29]

At Tripoli he bought 'a strong, spacious low tent . . .
Tents intended for travellers in hot climates should be well
lined and not too high . . . All the tents are also to have top ropes,
which can alone secure them in a tornado such as is common in
these climates.'[30] He considered the Government issue too light
to withstand the wind or to exclude the sun. When the three

___

[24] 19 June 1850.      [25] 25 November 1852.      [26] 8 October 1850.
[27] Schiffers, op. cit., p. 12, estimates that Barth covered nearly 10,000 miles on foot
and in the saddle during his five years in the Western Sudan.
[28] 31 March 1853.      [29] 7 October 1854.      [30] 26 February 1850.

travellers were together they generally pitched two of their five tents on short stops, or four of them at longer camps. Richardson had what he called a ' double Bornu tent ' which, though nothing but a species of gauze cottonwork, kept out the rain. During the journey the tents wore out, and needed frequent patching. Barth mentions that when they were in Agades,

the tent, a common English marquee, blended as it was with cotton stripes of all the various fashions of Negroland, constantly formed a subject of the most lively scientific dispute . . . [the local people] not having seen linen before, were at a loss to make out of what stuff it was originally made.[31]

When they arrived in Bornu the Shehu also showed great interest in their tent. The expedition presented him with a large double tent, and pitched it outside the palace for him.[32]

Barth generally slept in his tent, though on the way to Yola and again when journeying to Timbuktu, he at times lived in a mud hut. He was not always a welcome visitor, having from time to time to use force to obtain accommodation.[33] He related how on one such occasion when he was refused hospitality by the head-man of a village, two black clouds passed over the sun without, however, any rain falling: a hut was at once made available.[34]

Barth normally wore what he described as a half-Arab, half-Sudanic dress. Before crossing the frontier of Nigeria, he bought a black Sudan tobe, which he wore over a white one, with a white burnous on top, and stained himself with indigo so as to give himself 'an appearance more suited to the country.'[35] He also had a pair of richly ornamented Ghadamsi shoes 'which formed my greatest finery.'[36] For a while in the Sahara he wore a *tailelt*, the speckle-coloured tobe and narrow-ankled trousers so favoured by the Tuareg.[37] Unlike Clapperton, Barth did not enter Kano wearing full uniform; yet, even after four wearying years in the Sudan, he was able to produce a black

[31] 16 October 1850.    [32] 10 May 1851.
[33] For example, 19 June 1853 and 21 July 1853.
[34] 11 July 1853.    [35] 9 October 1850.    [36] 10 October 1850.
[37] 20 October 1850.

dress suit so as to fulfil the wish of the Gogo inhabitants to let them see European clothes.[38]

There are many references to food in the diaries. Breakfast usually consisted of *zummita*, 'a cool and refreshing paste'.[39] At first he was unable to derive satisfaction from sorghum though he

afterward became accustomed to the various preparations of sorghum and pennisetum, particularly the *asido* or *tuvo*, and found that no other food is so well adapted for a hot climate; but it requires a good deal of labour to prepare it well and this, of course, is a diffi-cult matter for a European traveller, who has no female slave or partner to look after his meals.[40]

In their original baggage the mission had ten large iron cases filled with dry biscuit. These proved a sorry disappointment to the Tuareg thieves who smashed one of the cases and found that 'instead of heaps of dollars, a dry and tasteless sort of bread came forth from the strong enclosure.'[41] For a while the party was reduced to couscous and onions, so that we can sympathize with the pleasure expressed by Barth in eating meat again after a diet of 'raw and bitter dishes of guinea corn, the more so as I had no tea left to wash this unpalatable and indigestible paste.'[42] Barth found that cakes made from the pounded fruit of the *magaria* tree 'may be safely eaten in small quantities even by a European to allay his hunger for a while till he can obtain something more substantial.'[43]

Overweg was a keen shot (wild-fowling, indeed, led to his death) and he often shot duck for the pot. On one occasion Barth notes how this

made us support with some degree of patience the trying spectacle of a long procession of men and women, laden with eatables, passing by us in the evening toward the camping-ground of the Chief, while not a single dish found its way to us; and though we informed them that they were missing the way, they would not understand the hint and answered us with a smile.[44]

[38] 5 July 1854.    [39] 15 July 1850.    [40] 17 September 1850.
[41] 27 August 1850.    [42] 27 November 1850.    [43] 29 December 1850.
[44] 8 January 1851.

In Bornu, Barth records how every time he had his coffee pounded, he was suspected of preparing gunpowder, as this was the way it was prepared in neighbouring Bagirmi.[45] We have further glimpses of Barth's menus from his comments on the foodstuffs available in the markets of Kano and Kuka,[46] and in his occasional references to palatable local foodstuffs such as the *senasin* which, 'a kind of thin pancake prepared from this sorghum grain, is the lightest and best food for a European in this country.' Every reader can feel with him in his accounts of more memorable meals . . . 'this was one of those rare occasions, during my travels in Negroland, on which I dined with a truly European appetite.'[47]

With the death of two out of the three original members of the expedition,[48] it is relevant to notice Barth's comments on health. He himself was seriously ill on a few occasions,[49] notably at Yo and again during the long attack of dysentery that laid him low at Wurno on his way back from Timbuktu in 1854. Barth writes, on the occasion of his servant being attacked by guinea worm, 'I always dreaded it more than any other disease during my travels in Central Africa.'[50] He was a firm believer in the tamarind fruit, which in his opinion constituted 'the best and surest remedy for a variety of diseases, on account of its refreshing and cooling character.'[51] He relates the following incident as an example of the risks which European travellers might incur by issuing medicine to ignorant patients for self-administration at home:

Ibrahim told me one day that he wanted some cooling medicine and I gave him two strong doses of Epsom salts to use occasionally. He

[45] 1 December 1851.          [46] Chapters XXV and XXX.          [47] 5 January 1852.

[48] The only accounts of Richardson's death are those given by Barth in his diary and letters. For a discussion of Overweg's death, the different eyewitness accounts and the discovery of the grave many years later, see 'The Death and Burial of Adolf Overweg', A. H. M. Kirk-Greene, *West African Review*, March 1959.

[49] Vogel was desperately ill with yellow fever ('black vomiting') in February 1854. Overweg remained comparatively fit until the rainy season in Kukawa began to wear both him and Barth down. They made it a rule to try to pass the rains anywhere but in the baleful environs of Chad.

[50] 11 August 1850.          [51] Chapter LI.

then complained the following day that he was suffering from worms; when I told him that the Epsom salts would not have the effect of curing this complaint, but that worm powder would, he begged me to give him some of the latter; and I gave him three doses to use on three successive days. However, my poor friend, though an intelligent man, thought it might not be amiss to take all this medicine at once, viz., four ounces of Epsom salts and six drachms of worm powder, and the reader may imagine the effect which this dose produced upon a rather slender man. Unfortunately I had just taken a ride out of the town; and he remained for full two days in a most desperate strait, while his friends, who had sent in vain to my house to obtain my assistance, were lamenting to all the people that the Christian had killed their companion, a pious pilgrim.[52]

Like 'all the people who travel along the Niger', Barth was attacked by rheumatism, which left him quite lame for two or three days on end.[53] On his final return to Bornu he suffered a very serious attack.[54]

There are a number of passages in which he analyses the essential loneliness of travellers in the Sudan, and in shrugging off the wanton offers so frequently made to him he notes that:

it would be better for a traveller in these regions, both for his own comfort and for the respect felt for him by the natives, if he could take his wife with him; for these simple people do not understand how a man can live without a partner. . . . But as it is difficult to find a female companion for such journeys, and as by marrying a native he would expose himself to such trouble and inconvenience on the score of religion, he will do best to maintain the greatest austerity of manners with regard to the other sex, though he may thereby expose himself to a good deal of derision from some of the lighter-hearted natives.[55]

A little later he was to declare that the offer of women by their husbands 'could scarcely be taken as a joke.'[56]

Two quotations from Barth's unpublished correspondence give a very good picture of his general conditions of living. Writing from Wurno in 1853, he states:

---

[52] Chapter XXX.          [53] 1 September 1853.          [54] 21 January 1855.

[55] Schiffers has a graphic sketch of what he terms Barth's *Stunde der Versuchung* at Agades (23 October 1850).

[56] 3 January 1851. Barth seems to have overlooked the cultural element in this gesture of traditional hospitality, not unknown in many countries.

all of us enjoy the best of health and spirits, and the state of my means
is also satisfactory—especially if my hope of finding some relief at
Timbuktu should be realized . . . my little party is provided with
straw hats, which are excellent but only when worn over the *shashia*
and a large turban. My health is excellent, being kept up with coffee,
in which, thank God, I am still able to indulge; tamarind water is
also a capital beverage. Without comparison, a thousand times
better than lemonade. When I feel a little sick, I add to the tamarind
an onion, a strong dose of black pepper and, when I can procure it, a
little honey—this forming the most useful medicinal drink in these
countries and one that cannot be too much recommended to travellers in this quarter.

In another letter, written to his relatives from Timbuktu, he
notes ' what I have most suffered under [sic] latterly is the total
absence of milk, which, with coffee, has been my only food for
a considerable time past. Oh, if I could but once more partake
of the pleasures of your table! This hope keeps up my spirits
sometimes.' Barth repeatedly mentions milk,[57] advising travellers not to take too much of it.[58] A serious illness of his at
Timbuktu he ascribed to the possibility of drinking poisoned
milk.[59]

There are many references to religion in the *Travels and
Discoveries*, outside the apologia in its preface. Nearly everywhere
that Barth went, strenuous efforts were made to convert him to
Islam. He records such instances in Kano and Bornu; the Yola
incident may be quoted as characteristic of them all:

I had a visit from two very handsome and amiable young Fulbe,
and, in my rather morose mood [Barth was very ill at the time],
refused their urgent request, made in the most simple and confidential way, to say the *fatha*, or the opening prayer of the Koran, with
them. I have always regretted my refusal, as it estranged from me a
great many people; and, although many Christians will object to
repeat the prayer of another creed, yet the use of a prayer of so
general import as the introductory chapter to the Koran ought to
be permitted every solitary traveller in these regions, in order to
form a sort of conciliatory link.[60]

[57] 12 March 1851. See also 28 August 1853, for Barth's shortest sentence: ' Milk is
plentiful.'
[58] Richardson considered it ' the most refreshing thing that can be drunk in the heat
of the day.'
[59] 14 January 1854.          [60] 24 June 1851.

In Timbuktu, where Barth's life would have been in danger if
he had been known to be a Christian (especially as he was taken
for the son of Major Laing)[61] he posed as a Syrian *sherif*.
When his companions began to remark how strange it was that
he did not pray with them in the courtyard, he thought it wise
to join in the repetition of the *fatiha*. There are many penetrating references to the tenets and trends of contemporary Islam
in the Sudan, among them the humorous and honest note on
the contempt in which the Fulani of Masena held the Christians,
'sitting like women in the bottom of their steamboats and doing
nothing but eating raw eggs.'[62] Richardson, a pious man, was
probably disturbed by Barth's spiritual broad-mindedness, for
there is an entry in his diary that ' I'm glad that Barth borrowed
my Bible and is reading today. Overweg was the first to propose
prayers on Sundays when we are staying long together in one
place.'[63]

When Barth writes that on his approach to Timbuktu he was
'obliged to assume the character of an Arab',[64] he was following
the custom long practised by travellers in West Africa of
adopting a Muslim disguise. Barth took the name of Abd el
Karim, Richardson was already known as Yakub from his
previous Saharan expedition, and Overweg was inevitably
called Tubib on account of his title of doctor; Vogel became
Abdul Wahid, while his two Royal Engineer companions were
known as Abdullah and Milud. In accordance with a long-
standing Hausa tradition, faithfully carried through to this
day,[65] Barth accumulated a number of other nicknames.
'My liberality of making presents of needles,[66] and nothing but
needles, procured me the title among these witty people of the
Needle Prince.'[67] Having to spend a night in the bush on his

---

[61] Major Laing set out on his second search for the River Niger in 1826. He reached
Timbuktu, but was murdered on the return journey.

[62] 11 April 1854.                [63] 17 November 1850.                [64] 2 August 1853.

[65] See, for example, 'Nicknames in Northern Nigeria's History', A. H. M. Kirk-
Greene, *West Africa*, 21 January 1959 and subsequent correspondence.

[66] Barth acknowledged his gratitude to Beke for the idea of carrying a plentiful
supply of needles to serve as currency and gifts.

[67] 28 March 1852.

journey through Gwandu, he found on his return from Tim-
buktu that he had earned the name of 'the Man who spent a
Day in the unsafe Wilderness.'[68]  It is said that in Bornu the
Kanuri called him 'the Man who goes through Fire', and 'the
Overbearing One' when he refused to sell his horse to the
Shehu.  Elsewhere he was known as 'Father of Three', because
of his habit of wearing stockings, thin leather slippers and thick
overshoes, in sharp contrast to the local custom of bare feet.[69]

Like so many travellers after him, Barth was called on to
perform various services for which he was in no way qualified:
he was taken, among other things, a rain-maker, an angel, a
charm-writer, a Turkish spy (because of his telescope, the
constant entries in his memorandum book, and his stockings),
and a rural doctor-cum-veterinary surgeon

pestered with applications, having generally from 100 to 200 patients
in my courtyard every morning . . . the people even brought me
sometimes animals to cure; and I was not a little amused when they
once brought me a horse totally blind, which they thought I was
able to restore to its former power of vision.[70]

On one occasion he was expected to dispense blessings — the
sudden change from two hundred threatening shouts to a plea
for his benediction allowed Barth one of his humorous tales
against himself:

all of a sudden they dropped their spears and thronged around me,
requesting me to give them my blessings; and the circumstances
under which I was placed obliged me to comply with this slight
request, although it was by no means a pleasant matter to lay my
hands on all these dirty heads.[71]

Despite Barth's insistence on giving alms, which gained him
no small favour, it may be seen by reading between the lines
that Overweg was the more popular, probably because he
seems to have been more of a handyman. Overweg 'lost a
great deal of his time in repairing, or rather trying to repair,
their watches and things'.[72]  Barth however was referred to
contemptuously as *Abd el Karim faidanso bago*, a useless man . . .
' although I sacrificed all I could in order to give from time to

[68] 10 June 1853.          [69] 19 July 1852.          [70] 26 February 1853.
[71] 25 July 1853.          [72] 6 August 1851.

time a new impulse to their favour by an occasional present.'[73]

It is interesting to try to discover what books Barth took with him, for he talks in his diaries of 'my small library'. We know that the Koran was his constant companion. On the inner front cover of the first volume of his diary he wrote in Arabic 'Abd el Karim Barth el Inglisi', and on the inner back cover 'In the name of God the Merciful'. On Overweg's death Barth kept as a token of friendship his copy of the New Testament in Greek,[74] given to him by Bunsen in November 1849. Another favourite book of his was *Herodotus*, inscribed by Barth himself: 'This Herodotus was my steadfast companion on both my great journeys, round the Mediterranean in 1845–47, when he joined up with me in Alexandria, and in 1848–55 through Central Africa. Thus he is immortally dear to me, despite being so soiled.' There is also a hint that among his baggage was a copy of Lander's narrative. When he joined Vogel, he described his pleasure at finding among his baggage Perron's *Voyage au Waday*, with an introduction by Jomard, and Sir William Hooker's *Flora Nigritia*. Richardson, it may be noticed, planned to read the whole of the Bible in Hebrew on the back of his camel, and relaxed in the evenings by reading Milton's *Comus*, 'a great relief in drawing my mind off African subjects'; he regretted that he had forgotten to bring a copy of Shakespeare's works with him.

In Katsina Barth

received information of a large 'Christian book', bound in leather, with edges and lock made of metal, in the possession of a Pullo in the town; but no one could tell me whether it was a manuscript or print; and although I offered to pay for a sight of it, I never succeeded in my object. It might be one of those heavy books which Clapperton, when dying, told Lander rather to leave behind than take with him to England.[75]

In Wurno, he whiled away the days of his enforced delay by reading Abdullahi's *Tezen el Aurekat*, and caught no more than

[73] 6 August 1851.

[74] This is presumably the copy from which Barth read 'the Greek text of the Evangelists' aloud to the Kel es Suk (2 July 1854).

[75] 23 January 1851.

a tantalising glimpse of Sultan Bello's *Infak el Misuri*. The learned El Bakay showed him in his library at Timbuktu an Arabic edition of Hippocrates, which had been a present from Clapperton to Sultan Bello of Sokoto, who in turn had passed it on to El Bakay as an acknowledgement of his erudition. Another unusual find was the life of Bruce, published by Murray in 1835, which Barth discovered among the wild Kel es Suk and which he suspected as being the property of Davidson: 'it was almost complete, only ten leaves being wanting, and I bought it for three strips of indigo-dyed cotton. It had been used as a talisman, an Arabic charm having been added to it.'[76] On returning to Gwandu from Timbuktu, he was greatly saddened to find that a fire in the town had destroyed all the books that he had left there.

The Government had insisted on the expedition being armed. At first, this seemed unnecessary, since Richardson had travelled to Ghat a few years earlier without arms. But as Barth points out,

On that occasion he had gone as a private individual, without instruments, without presents, without anything; and we were to unite with the character of an expedition that of a mission ... it may be taken for granted that we should never have crossed the frontier of Aïr had we been unarmed; and when I entered upon my journey alone, it would have been impossible for me to proceed without arms through countries which are in a constant state of war, where no chief or ruler can protect a traveller except with a large escort, which was sure to run away as soon as there is any real danger.[77]

Barth took with him a double-barrelled shotgun and a revolver, with extra ball cartridges for supplying to his various escorts.

In addition to the boat, to be christened *Lord Palmerston* and launched on Lake Chad after an adventurous journey across the Sahara,[78] the Government provided a number of scientific instruments. Unfortunately, the minimum and maximum thermometers were so upset by their journey that even Overweg

[76] 14 June 1854.        [77] Preface to Barth's Journal.

[78] For the full history of the *Lord Palmerston*, which does not receive just treatment in Barth's diary, see 'What Became of the Boat?', A. H. M. Kirk-Greene, *West Africa*, 23 May 1959.

could not repair them, and on their first Tripoli expedition the only aneroid barometer was damaged by Overweg (Barth makes it quite clear that the fault was nobody's except Overweg's). This explains why the estimates of altitude, made no more accurately than by the boiling water system, were over-generous in the heights of, for example, the Mandara and Alantika Mountains. Barth's care over scientific observations was characteristic of his self-discipline in everything: 'attempting to water the horse, I found the water was excessively warm; unfortunately I had not got my thermometer with me, but resolved to be more careful in future.'[79] Another testimony to this is his meteorological registers, fragments of which are published as an appendix to his *Travels and Discoveries*. He seems to have endured both the hottest (111° on 5 June 1851) and the coldest (41° on 25 November 1852) days when he was in Bornu. In the Sahara on the way home, however, the thermometer rose to 114° at 2 o'clock 'in the best shade I could find', and by sunset had dropped only to 105°.[80]

The meticulous way in which Barth kept his diaries is evident to every reader. He was impatient of laxity or inaccuracy in others:

Some geographers think this [recording the names of villages *en route*] is a matter of no consequence—for them it is enough that the position of the chief places be laid down by exact astronomical observations: but to me the general character of a country, the way in which the population is settled, and the nature and character of those settlements themselves, seem to form the chief and most useful objects of a journey through a new and unknown country.[81]

Overweg comes in for a lot of criticism:

He was deficient in that general knowledge of natural science which is required for comprehending all the various phenomena occurring on the journey into unknown regions. Having never before risked his life on a dangerous expedition, he never for a moment doubted that it might not be his good fortune to return home in safety, and he therefore did not always bestow that care upon his journal which is so desirable in such an enterprise.[82]

[79] 13 January 1851.          [80] 27 June 1855.          [81] 6 June 1851.
[82] Preface to Barth's Journal.

| Date. | Hour of Day. | Degrees in scale of Fahrenheit. | Remarks. | Date. | Hour of Day. | Degrees in scale of Fahrenheit. | Remarks. |
|---|---|---|---|---|---|---|---|
| 1851. May | | | | 1851. June | | | |
| 23 | sunset | 90·5 | | 6 | sunrise | 73·4 | |
| 24 | sunrise | 77 | | | noon | 93·2 | At 10 p.m. frightful tempest, with much rain. |
| | noon | 98·6 | | | | | |
| | sunset | 97·7 | | | | | |
| 25 | sunrise | 79·7 | | 7 | No observation. | | In the evening thunder-storm in the distance. |
| | noon | 96·8 | | | | | |
| 26 | noon | 97·7 | Sky thickly overcast; a few drops of rain. | 8 | sunrise | 73·4 | |
| | sunset | 93·2 | | 9 | sunrise | 75·2 | At four o'clock in the afternoon a tornado, with a short but heavy shower. In the night another storm, but no rain near us. |
| 27 | sunrise | 78·8 | | | | | |
| | noon | 104 | | | | | |
| | sunset | 93·2 | In the evening lightning. Sky not clear. | | | | |
| 28 | sunrise | 84·2 | | | | | |
| 29 | No observation. | | | | sunset | 82·4 | |
| 30 | noon | 99·5 | | 10 | sunrise | 71·6 | In the afternoon a storm, with but little rain. |
| | sunset | 87·8 | | | | | |
| 31 | sunrise | 75·2 | | 11 | - - | - - | Sky cloudy. |
| | noon | 99·5 | In the afternoon the sky became thickly overcast, and a little rain fell. | 12 | 2 p.m. | 82·4 | Atmosphere humid and rainy, felt quite chilly, sun did not come forth till after noon. |
| | sunset | 90·5 | | | | | |
| June 1 | sunrise | 78·8 | In the evening a thunder - storm, towards the south and the north, came down upon us, accompanied with heavy rain. | 13 | sunrise | 69·5 | |
| | noon | 98·6 | | | noon | 89·6 | In the afternoon thunder-storm towards the south. |
| | sunset | 99·5 | | | | | |
| | | | | | sunset | 75·1 | |
| 2 | sunrise | 79·7 | | 14 | sunrise | 79·7 | |
| | noon | 98·6 | Tornado near us. | | noon | 91·4 | About 2 p.m. a tornado, with a little rain later in the afternoon. |
| 3 | sunrise | 74·3 | | | | | |
| | noon | 104·9 | | | sunset | 77·0 | |
| 4 | sunrise | 74·3 | | 15 | noon | 95·1 | 8 p.m. a tornado, but not much rain. |
| | noon | 98·6 | | | | | |
| 5 | sunrise | 75·2 | Weather extremely sultry; at 2 p.m. a heavy thunder-storm, with much rain. | | sunset | 77 | |
| | | | | 16 | sunrise | 77 | |
| | | | | | noon | 90·5 | |
| | | | | | sunset | 80·6 | During the night tornado with rain. |
| | 2 p.m. | 111·2 | | 17 | sunrise | 75·2 | Fine clear morning. |
| | sunset | 101·3 | | | noon | 91·4 | 7 p.m. heavy thunder-storm. |

FIG. I. An extract from Barth's Meteorological Register for May/June 1851

Elsewhere he condemns Overweg's calculations as 'very vague'.[83] 'His memoranda are in such a state that, even for me, it will be possible, only with the greatest exertion, to make anything out of them, with exception of names'.[84] 'Mr. Overweg, at a later period, visited the town of Boso, but without accurately surveying the line of the river and without stating exactly the character of the point where it joins the lagoon.'[85] Overweg further displeased Barth by his behaviour in the presence of pagans at Adishen,[86] just as he had earlier caused Richardson to record in disgust the part he had taken in a local wedding celebration.[87] Barth, however, was critical of all who made mistakes, as various remarks in his diary show.

Bath usually sent his mail to Europe by the hand of the leader of the frequent caravans crossing the desert to Tripoli, which generally took just over two months. The first mail that he received in Nigeria was an unexpected package delivered while he was on his way from Kano to Bornu in March 1851: 'this was a most fortunate and lucky day for me', he wrote. It had been brought by an Arab travelling with a caravan from Murzuk and contained in addition the sum of two Spanish dollars. By return of post, as it were, Barth bundled up a number of letters to Kano, the writing of which he declared 'freshly imbued [me] with the restless impulse of European civilisation.'[88] Among the papers that Barth received were copies of the *Athenaeum*, 'probably the first which were introduced into Central Africa and which gave me great delight',[89] and the Maltese news-sheet *Galignani*.

Barth's dispatches did not always reach their destination. He recounts one amusing incident at Gwandu where

in consequence of the violent rains through which he [the messenger] had had to make his way, and the many rivers and swamps which he had to cross, the whole envelope of the letter containing the lines addressed to my friend in Sokoto had been destroyed, so that the

---

[83] 27 April 1851.          [84] 7 May 1851.          [85] 19 September 1851.
[86] 23 December 1851.
[87] *Narrative of a Mission to Central Africa*, James Richardson, 1853, II, p. 48.
[88] 15 March 1851.          [89] 6 August 1851.

latter, receiving only the English letter, and not knowing what to do with this hieroglyphic, at length returned it to the bearer, who had since used it as a charm.[90]

Again, the parcel of letters that he dispatched from Timbuktu to the British consul at Ghadames failed to reach Europe because of the consul's transfer to the Crimea: 'thus my family was thrown into the deepest grief in consequence of the rumour of my death.' Those who have experienced the distance and solitude of a cultural exile will know how to sympathize with Barth's description of his behaviour on receiving mail from home, 'revelling in the midst of my literary treasures which had just carried me back to the political and scientific domains of Europe.'[91]

Of Barth's countless observations on botanical, geological, geographical, historical, genealogical, etc., matters, no mention will be made here, as they are readily apparent on every page in the diaries. There are, however, two matters connected with the conduct of the expedition that deserve attention.

One is the question of servants. Mohammed Belal, the son of a freed slave from Gobir, whom Barth took on in Tunis, was quickly replaced by Mohammed el Gatroni, 'our best and most steady servant'.[92] He remained with Barth throughout the five arduous years and Barth always speaks most highly of him. He also had with him for much of the time two liberated slaves, Abbega, a Marghi youth of some seventeen years of age, and Durogu, a very intelligent Hausa boy aged about fifteen, who had been freed by Overweg; these were the two Nigerians whom Barth brought back to Europe with him in 1855.[93] One of Abbega's sons is the remarkable octogenarian Mai Maina, today (1961) chief of Askira in Bornu.[94] Then there were a number of boys who did not stay long with Barth: one was

[90] 17 August 1854.    [91] 6 July 1852.    [92] 7 July 1850.
[93] The story has been told at length in 'Abbega and Durogu', A. H. M. Kirk-Greene, *West African Review*, September 1956.
[94] Mai Maina's autobiography was published by the Northern Region Literature Agency, Zaria, Nigeria, in 1958. The book is in Hausa, but an English version, in the form of an edited summary, is to be found in two articles, 'Link with Lugard', A. H. M. Kirk-Greene, *West Africa*, 14 and 21 December 1957.

Mohammed, a liberated Tunisian slave, 'a clever but spoiled
youngster . . . a protégé of the British consulate in Tunis',[95]
who was 'at times a most insolent rascal'[96] and laughed in
Barth's face when he refused to be converted to Islam. By the
time they had reached the southern edge of the Sahara, Barth
was only too willing to get rid of Mohammed as soon as he
reached Kano, for this 'impudent and dissolute Tunisian half-
caste servant' had become 'quite insupportable'.[97] Then there
was Ibrahim I, who refused to accompany him beyond Tripoli;
Ibrahim II, 'though much more prudent, was not at all trustworthy, which was more to be regretted as he had travelled all
over Hausa and even as far as Gonja and might have proved of
immense service'. The young Mohammed e' Zintani was one
of a series of local boys whom Barth was always anxious to
employ so that he could pick up the dialect from them. Another
was Mohammed ben Ahmed, a Tubu boy whom Barth had
taken on in Gumel at two dollars a month, but who had left him
there. Later he followed Barth to Bornu, 'begging my pardon
and entreating my compassion, and after some expostulation I
allowed him to stay without hiring him, and it was only on
seeing his attachment to me in the course of time that I afterwards granted him one dollar a month'.[98] There was also
Mohammed ben Habib, another Fezzani lad, 'weak in mind
and body',[99] whom, with his fellow countrymen, Barth described
as 'as limited in their intelligence as they were conceited in
their pretensions as Moslemin'.[100] It is pleasant to recall that
on his final journey home through the Sahara, Barth stopped off
at the village of his faithful servant Mohammed el Gatroni and
was entertained to a breakfast which included the luxury of
grapes;[101] while Abbega and Durogu were later given a holiday
in Europe.

The other point to be emphasized here is Barth's friendly
nature, so evident in the number of passing friends he made
with young Africans. One thinks immediately of the two

[95] 24 August 1850.       [96] 12 August 1850.      [97] 8 November 1850.
[98] 11 May 1851.          [99] 25 November 1851.    [100] 4 March 1852.
[101] 8 July 1851.

camel drivers, Ibrahim and Sliman,[102] and their colleague Musa, 'grave but cheerful',[103] on the Saharan crossing; the penetrating, but sympathetic description of the dandy Sarkin Turawa of Gazawa,[104] a fief of Maradi; the Tubu whom he picked up in Asben;[105] the friendship he established with the sons of the Emirs of Kano and Zaria;[106] the young men of Yola;[107] the Shuwa lad he took on in Bagirmi;[108] the Fulani boys in Timbuktu, Zen en Abidin and Kungu — the latter spoke affectionately of Abd el Karim to Lieutenant Hourst some forty years later;[109] and the group of children at Humbutudi.[110]

## FINANCES

This is perhaps the place to examine the finances of the expedition, whose inadequacy is so often mentioned in the diaries[111] and so pointedly emphasized in Petermann's reports to the British public in the *Athenaeum*. The separation of the travellers just before they entered Nigeria was brought about 'on account of the low state of our finances'.[112] On arriving in Kano, Barth's own debts which he was obliged to liquidate, totalled 112,300 cowries,[113] made up of 55,000 cowries for transport of their merchandise from Tinteggana to Kano (the merchandise itself largely consisting of their cash in cowries), 8,300 as his share of the presents and passage money, 18,000 to Gajere for the mare and bullock that he had bought, and 31,000 for the presents he had had to buy for the Emir of Katsina. Barth notes that a camel carried 100,000 cowries.

On his arrival in Kukawa in April 1851, he was confronted by a similar financial crisis when he had to pay off Richardson's servants and debts, as well as establish himself in the capital. By

[102] 6 June 1850.          [103] 26 June 1850.          [104] 18 January 1855.

[105] 2 March 1851.         [106] 18 February 1851.       [107] 24 June 1851.

[108] 5 March 1852.

[109] 24 March 1854. Hourst's account of his Niger expedition was translated into English by Mrs. A. Bell in 1898, under the title of *French Enterprise in Africa*.

[110] 12 June 1851.

[111] For example, Chapters XXV and XXVIII for only the first three months in Nigeria.

[112] 10 January 1851.         [113] 3 February 1851.

September the situation had not improved: 'the scanty supplies which had reached us were not sufficient to provide for our wants and were soon gone. We were scarcely able to keep ourselves afloat in our credit and to supply our necessary wants'.[114] Barth thought that the Kanuri looked upon Overweg as being in their employment, because of the gifts that the people continued to make to him out of charity.[115] When he set out with the Bornu army against Mandara, 'my means were scanty in the extreme and did not allow me to have a mounted servant'.[116] When the time came for him to leave Bornu towards the end of 1852, he found that the money matters of the expedition were in a very confused and desperate state and 'totalled, besides a large debt due to the merchant Mohammed es Sfaksi, a debt of 500 Spanish dollars to the Waziri of Bornu'. 'Indeed', Barth bitterly notes, 'we might now have been able to achieve a great deal if it had been our destiny to remain together; for in the beginning almost all our efforts were paralyzed by the smallness of our means, which did not allow us to undertake anything on a large scale'.[117] Barth was obliged to give away more than three-quarters of the money they had received to pay off the mission's debts, and many of the articles of merchandise had to be given away 'in order to reward friends who for so long a period had displayed their hospitality towards us and rendered us services almost without the slightest recompense.'

In Zinder Barth was delighted to receive a valuable consignment of one thousand dollars in specie, 'which were packed very cleverly in two boxes of sugar so that scarcely anybody became aware that I had received money', and of this he spent 775,000 cowries on 'all sorts of articles which I expected would be useful on my farther proceedings [to Timbuktu], such as red common bernuses, white turbans, looking-glasses, clothes, razors, chaplets'.[118] A little later, in Katsina, he spent 1,308,000 cowries in providing himself with cotton and silk cloths from

[114] 6 August 1851.
[115] P-L. Monteil puts forward, on somewhat naïve grounds, the theory that both Barth and Nachtigal were duped by the institutionalized hospitality of Bornu: see *De Saint-Louis à Tripoli par le Lac Tchad*, 1894, pp. 337–339 and *passim*.
[116] 25 November 1851.          [117] 23 August 1852.          [118] 20 January 1853.

Kano and Nupe 'in order to pay my way, by means of these favourite articles, through the countries on the middle course of the Niger, where nothing is esteemed more highly than these native manufactures'.[119] On his return from Kano, exhausted after his Timbuktu experiences, he was once again destitute.

Some idea of the plight of the mission can be gained from Barth's letter to Dr. Beke, written from Kukawa soon after his arrival there in April 1851:

> for we poor Germans, who, in order to go on with *the scanty means* — £200 from London to Mombas or Sennar by the way of Central Africa, with which we have been supplied by government — sacrifice our own property (not to mention our lives), have not been regarded as members of the mission or as gentlemen, but almost as servants. The consequence is that Mr. Richardson's death has not only stopped the proceedings of the expedition for a short time, but has threatened even to put an end to it altogether . . . Instead of finding preparations made for our journey around Lake Tshad, I found the whole expedition in despair and everybody about to return. . . . Instead of meeting with fresh supplies for myself, I found debts of over 300 dollars; and in order to maintain the honour of the government in whose service we are travelling, I have felt it my duty to exhaust my own private credit to pay off a part of the debts incurred by the mission, from which I myself have to demand 91 dollars.

Petermann made repeated appeals for further funds for the expedition in the *Athenaeum*.

Originally, Barth and Overweg had each contributed between £150 and £200, an expenditure that was in some measure offset by the initial grant of 1,000 thalers (£150) from the Geographical Society of Berlin. To this was added a further £150 as a personal gift from the King of Prussia. On Richardson's death in Bornu in 1851, it had been arranged with Her Majesty's Government that Barth should not assume the status and pension rights of a British agent (in accordance with the stipulation that Bunsen had earlier insisted on), but that on his return a corresponding indemnity should be made to him, and the government would repay him the actual public costs of the expedition. Back in October 1848, Richardson had

[119] 2 February 1853.

informed Lord Palmerston that 'the whole expenses from beginning to end could not, if the expedition be well conducted, exceed £500 for the two years — the reasonable and more probable limit of the time to be occupied'. After Overweg's death in 1852, King Frederick William IV had, at Humboldt's request, sent £150 from his private purse, to which Prince Adalbert had added 300 thalers; Bunsen had optimistically sent another large sum, collected from scientific societies in Germany, to Mombasa, to await Barth's expected arrival across the Sudan and Central Africa.

The total expenditure on the expedition according to Barth, 'including the payment of the debts left by the former expedition and £200 which I contributed myself', came to £1,600 for the five years, a modest enough sum when viewed against the expenses of previous Saharan missions. Bunsen therefore proposed to the British Government that Barth be paid a retrospective annual payment of £600 *per annum* for the five years, and the reimbursement of £1,600 for the mission's expenses. At the same time, in answer to Barth's application for a subsidy towards publishing his diary, Her Majesty's Government agreed to make an *ex-gratia* payment of £1,000 upon the completion of volumes I to III, and to pay a further sum in the same proportion, but not exceeding £1,000, when the final volumes were published. In return for this subsidy, the Treasury stipulated that they be furnished with 50 copies ' for the public service'. In a minute to the Foreign Office dated 20 December, 1855, the Treasury compromised on a lower figure of £5,280, calculated at £500 *per annum* for the four and a half years after Richardson's death, and a reduced lump sum for the book. In Germany, Barth was granted a government pension of 1,000 thalers for two years, subsequently increased to 1,500 thalers and extended to 1861. For publication rights, Messrs. Longmans Green of London offered £500 and Justus Perthes of Gotha the equivalent of £750 (16,500 marks). These were, as one German biographer[120] has pointed out, reasonable and satisfactory payments.

[120] Banse.

For Barth, the next ten years were not altogether happy; they were marred first by his querulous misunderstandings with the British Government and the Royal Geographical Society, and secondly by his failure to obtain the academic honour that he felt to be his due following his eventual return to Germany.

In 1854, when he was still in Africa (though whether he were alive or not was at that time uncertain) there had been intimations of the 'German problem' in Petermann's *African Discovery*.[121] This nine-page open letter, which accompanied his royal folio volume, was addressed to the President and Council of the Royal Geographical Society. It drew attention to the attack on the expedition, 'an attack which is as unwarranted and uncalled-for as the statements it contains are untrue and offensive and in which, it appears to me, the honour and interest of the Society are as much involved as that of the expedition and the persons connected with it'.

The offensive remarks to which Petermann referred had been published, as an account by Dr. Norton Shaw of the proceedings of a Royal Geographical Society meeting held on 9 January, in the *Nautical Standard*. Petermann described the report as a 'scurrilous and offensive publication', objecting in particular to the hostile innuendo in the comment that

it might be presumed that their [Barth's and Overweg's] labours would have been placed at the disposal of the English Government, and the results would have been accessible to English geographers and other promoters among our countrymen. But this has not been the case . . . the information respecting this expedition seems to be of a private character, if we may judge from the manner it is dealt with and the closeness with which it is preserved from English geographers.

121 *African Discovery: A letter addressed to the President and Council of the Royal Geographical Society of London by Augustus Petermann*, published by E. Stanford, 6 Charing Cross, on 18 March 1854. This took the form of a covering letter, published as a pamphlet, to Petermann's *An Account of the Progress of the Expedition to Central Africa by order of Her Majesty's Foreign Office under Messrs. Richardson, Barth, Overweg and Vogel in the Years* 1850, 1851, 1852 *and* 1853, which appeared separately on the same day.

Then came another jibe: 'In connection with Lake Chad and other African names, it may be observed that the Germans are adopting various ways of spelling them, because they find it difficult to say "cheese".' Even if such aspersions were true, as Petermann pointed out, it might well be asked whether such a 'silly and foolish remark' became the dignity and character of a person reporting the proceedings of the Royal Geographical Society.[122]

This was all before Barth's return,[123] but his personal clash with the Royal Geographical Society was soon to come. This Society had followed his travels with considerable interest and his dispatches to the Foreign Office were read from time to time at the meetings of the Society. The same dispatches were summarized by Petermann in his *Geographische Mittheilungen* and in the *Athenaeum*. But the Council of the Royal Geographical Society had complained to the Foreign Office that 'it has been a subject of frequent remark that the proceedings of Dr. Barth's mission in Africa were published by Mr. Petermann in Germany before they were known in England, or at least before they were communicated to the Society'. It does not appear that the Royal Geographical Society had any particular role in the establishment and support of the expedition, but having followed its progress carefully, and in its position as one of the country's leading learned societies, its Council seemingly felt that the Society had certain claims on Barth's geographical discoveries since he was a member of an English expedition. Barth, on the other hand, maintained that he was bound to do no more than report such discoveries to the Foreign Office, and that if anything beyond this—such as access to his diaries— was contemplated, the German geographical societies were entitled to first consideration.

During the course of this argument there appeared in the

[122] Rear-Admiral Henry Smyth was President of the Royal Geographical Society in 1855 and Dr. Norton Shaw its secretary.

[123] Petermann also crossed swords with Sir Roderick Murchison, who succeeded Rear-Admiral Henry Smyth as President of the Royal Geographical Society, on the role of the Society in the *Pleiad* project (Baikie's 1854 expedition to the Niger and the Benue).

press an unfavourable report of Barth's leadership on the expedition. At once he ascribed this to the machinations of the Royal Geographical Society, and at a meeting held in his honour in Berlin on 13 October 1855 he rashly allowed himself to say:

If in England a few mean-minded individuals, seeking to exploit national enmity under the guise of scholarly questions, have given vent to their feelings in contemptible utterances against the leadership of an English expedition by a German, such an attack must urge me all the more to present as quickly as possible my achievements before the English public in order to justify myself as well as the respected English statesmen, above all Lord Palmerston, who honoured Germans with their trust.

In vain did Rear-Admiral Henry Smyth, in the name of his personal friendship, urge him to retract this regrettable remark.

The situation was not improved by further unfortunate incidents. In a somewhat impolite note, Barth declined a courteous invitation from Dr. Norton Shaw to dine with certain members of the Council of the Royal Geographical Society and to address the Society. Then followed an incident in connexion with a public lecture. It had been announced that Barth would read a paper at a meeting of the British Association for the Advancement of Science. Barth failed to turn up ('eager curiosity was baffled', as the newspapers put it), probably because he had undertaken to accept no such engagement for any society, since he was anxious to publish his journals as soon as possible.[124] But his reputation was not enhanced by the affair.

To make matters worse, by an unfortunate mischance a letter from Lord Clarendon to Barth, with enclosures from Vogel and Consul Herman, arrived opened. Barth was furious and denounced the Royal Geographical Society (in the person of Dr. Norton Shaw, its secretary) in trenchant terms for prying into his private correspondence. Even his own brother-in-law condemned his suspicion of Foreign Office persecution and a Royal Geographical Society conspiracy as unfounded. Later Barth relented[125] so far as to accept the distinguished award of

[124] R. Mansell Prothero, op. cit., p. 335, pleads that Barth 'intended to make no communication until these were completed.'
[125] 'Barth accepted the explanation that was given but did so grudgingly', comments R. Mansell Prothero, op. cit., p. 335.

the Royal Geographical Society's gold medal which was proposed at the Society's opening session and presented to him
in March 1856.

Meanwhile, on 13 October 1855, Barth paid a visit to his
native town, Hamburg, where he lived at 22 Hopfenmarkt.
He was accompanied by his Nigerian freed slaves, Abbega and
Durogu, whom he indulged in a grand holiday in Europe.
Barth had not yet made up his mind where to settle, although
the mounting unpleasantness between him and the Royal
Geographical Society tended to make him find England 'cold
and unfriendly'. He was unable to forgive England for treating
him so meanly and for, as he expressed it, 'reducing me to a
beggar abroad' when he had been to all intents and purposes
a representative of the British Government.

In Germany things promised better. With Humboldt and
Ritter he was invited to luncheon with the King at Sanssouci,
Potsdam, on 12 October, and a fortnight later letters patent
were granted, conferring upon him membership (third class)
of the Order of the Red Eagle. In a letter to Ritter dated
18 October, Barth mentioned that King Frederick William IV
had assured him of a subsidy of between £600 and £750 for
publication, and that the Ministry of Education had offered
him a professorship in geography for one semester at £225.
Ritter himself urged Barth's appointment to the Department
of Philosophy, where he knew the King considered Barth would
be a 'shining acquisition'.

Bunsen, however, had different plans for his protégé. He
had retired from his ambassadorship in 1854 and was now
living in Heidelberg. In an important series of correspondence[126]
he sought to persuade Barth to give up the idea of a chair at
Berlin and to return to England. He had hopes of an extra £300
for Barth from the British Government and a welcome increase
in the pension due to Overweg's sister. He offered his congratu-
lations on Barth's dignified reply to the Royal Geographical
Society ('your answer is worthy of a man and a German') and

---

[126] Schubert reproduces a facsimile of one of these key letters.

went on to caution Barth that, were he to become professor in Germany, he would alienate himself from the sympathy of the British Government and three-quarters of the British public, besides imposing on himself a heavier teaching programme that would not only bring in a miserable salary, but would also prevent him, by the amount of preparation for lectures required, from completing his manuscript for publication. Finally he urged Barth to ask himself whether his real interest was not in travelling, and whether as a professor he would be able to indulge such an interest.

## RESIDENCE IN ENGLAND

Barth yielded to Bunsen's arguments and by the end of November 1855, he was back in London, living at 39 Alpha Road, St. John's Wood. He was preoccupied with writing up his journals, but found time for a certain amount of social relaxation within a circle of friends that included Rear-Admiral Henry Smyth, Francis Galton, William Balfour Baikie, Desborough Cooley, Richard Burton, Sir Roderick Murchison, Colonel Sabine, and the Germans A. Bach and B. Seemann.[127] In December 1856, he met Livingstone, who later presented him with a signed copy of his *Missionary Travels and Researches in South Africa*, inscribed 'This work is offered as a token of kind regard, and high appreciation of his services in opening Africa; by his friend and fellow labourer.'[128] International honours flowed in: an honorary doctorate from Oxford, the title of honorary freeman of his own city Hamburg, an honorary Fellowship of the Royal Asiatic Society, the gold medals of the Paris and Hamburg Geographical Societies and the

[127] Dr. Seemann is, I believe, the addressee of a long letter of Barth's describing the principal trees of Central Africa.

[128] Barth later returned the compliment by editing, with special reference to Livingstone's travels, a review of East African exploration.

Patron's gold medal of the Royal Geographical Society,[129] the award of the prize by the Paris Geographical Society for the most important geographical discovery of the year, and the promise of investiture as a Companion of the Bath. The last-named was an exceptional royal honour, conferred, as the President of the Royal Geographical Society emphasized at the time,[130] upon neither Livingstone, Grant nor Speke, and one that in some measure contradicts the idea that England failed to recognize Barth's achievements properly.

Barth confided to his brother-in-law that he had reached that stage of life when he would like to marry: 'a wife, were I lucky enough to choose well, would be able to bring my life to its full development . . .'. At the same time his restless spirit was inevitably irked by the long hours of plodding and patient detail involved in preparing his book, for he naïvely felt that not until the first volume was through the press could he afford the time to search out friends with congenial interests. Such ambivalence is not unusual in scholar-travellers: as one of Barth's German biographers has put it, 'if he were sitting at a desk he longed to be out in the bush; when seated in the saddle he pined to be at his desk.'[131]

These were not happy years. On 3 November 1856, Barth's father, to whom he had been closely attached, died. The quarrel with the Royal Geographical Society had to some extent been made up, thanks to the unsparing efforts of Admiral Smyth and his friends, who succeeded in establishing a reconciliation sufficient to secure his election as a Fellow in March 1856, and to make possible the award of the Society's gold medal 'for your successful and extensive explorations in Central Africa, your

---

[129] E. W. Bovill, *Caravans of the Old Sahara*, 1933, p. 244, comments that 'to its lasting credit, the Royal Geographical Society accorded him [Barth] its highest award', though he is critical of the overall lack of appreciation shown to Barth. In view, however, of the award of the C.B. to Barth, Bovill is not quite accurate when he remarks that 'a kindly reception by Lords Palmerston and Clarendon was the only mark of favour shown him by the Government he had served so well.'

[130] *Journal of the Royal Geographical Society*, 1865, p. 135.

[131] Banse.

numerous excursions about Lake Chad, your discovery of the great River Benue, and for your hazardous and adventurous journey to and from Timbuktu'.[132]

Soon after this reconciliation, however, came an attack by the influential British and Foreign Anti-Slavery Society, which hurt him very deeply. The secretary of the Society censured him for having been involved in the slave trade in Africa, and for having brought back two slaves as servants. This infamous accusation was apparently based on the testimony of Corporal Church, whose behaviour on the African expedition Barth held in small esteem. Barth was so disturbed by the British public's misunderstanding of his motives towards his two freed slaves that he paid them off and arranged with the British Government that they should have a free journey back to Tripoli.

This misunderstanding over Abbega and Durogu caused yet another breach in Barth's friendships, this time with the missionary J. F. Schön. The story is too long to tell here,[133] but briefly Schön, acting in what he considered the best interests of all, took the two Nigerian youths off the ship at Southampton and looked after them for some time. He employed them in his writings on Hausa, and Barth's quarrel with him was further embittered when he publicly impugned Schön's scholarship.

His relations with the Foreign Office now began to deteriorate. Barth considered himself released from any contract with the Foreign Office, but Her Majesty's Government insisted on treating him as the leader of their African expedition for as long as Vogel remained in the field. Matters came to a head when Barth refused to allow the Foreign Office to see Vogel's private letters to him 'until their author officially requested this'. This incident brought into the open a latent hostility between Barth and Hammond of the Foreign Office, whom Barth described as ignorant and vindictive.

---

[132] *Journal of the Royal Geographical Society*, 1856, p. 168.

[133] It can be followed in 'Abbega and Durogu', A. H. M. Kirk-Greene, *West African Review*, September 1956. This paper is based on Schön's defence as expressed in the prefaces to his *Grammar of the Hausa Language*, 1862, and his *Dictionary of the Hausa Language*, 1876, and on Barth's case as presented in his introduction to his *Central African Vocabularies*, 1862–66.

In view of an unfavourable report in the press on Barth's conduct of the expedition, he determined to have an official denial published by the President of the Royal Geographical Society. Anxious that the British public should be aware of what the actual contractual relationship of Barth and Overweg with the British Government was—one of the roots of this continued hostility—Barth requested Lord Clarendon to publish the instructions to the expedition in the next annual report of the Royal Geographical Society. He drew up a strongly-worded rebuttal of the insinuations, which he forwarded to the Foreign Office for checking. 'As a report has got abroad', it read, 'that the expedition commencing under Richardson, Barth and Overweg and terminating with the researches of Vogel, have [sic] been a reckless expenditure of money, I deem it my duty to state that, having seen an account of the sums expended, I am of opinion [sic] . . . that financial expenditures have been conducted with greatest economy.' The Foreign Office replied simply on 19 June 1857: 'Lord Clarendon considers it will be better not to publish any statement on this subject. His Lordship knows nothing of the reports to which you allude, and this may safely be disregarded.'

The incident over the press report of the allegedly scandalously high cost of the Central African expedition led to a re-opening of Barth's quarrel with the Foreign Office. Their delay over his request only strengthened his suspicion, long felt, that not only had Richardson received secret instructions from the Foreign Office, but also that he had sent home confidential reports on the Germans.[134] A temporary reconciliation was effected when the Foreign Office invited Barth to put at their disposal his African experience and help them in planning the new Niger expedition. This was to be led by his old friend Baikie, in a vessel specially designed by Macgregor Laird, the *Dayspring*. Yet this move, too, ended in frustration and fury, for by a malicious twist of misfortune Barth was never officially

---

[134] The dissension (I doubt whether the word is too strong) between Richardson on the one hand and Barth and Overweg on the other invites further research.

1. Heinrich Barth

*Reproduced by permission of the Royal Geographical Society.*

yesterday at noon I had my sole companion and fellow
traveller into the grave and am now lonely and companion
less in these regions, where nobody does understand my doing,
the direction of my own expedition. But nevertheless I
am in good health and best spirits — as far as circumstances allow and shall not give "the last point I am"
not a man, who is afraid of death in such a cause, but
I shall be the more prudent and circumspective and it
will please God I trust to give me success and after that
safe return home redeemed by the sacrifice of two
lives out of three. But even if it should be my destiny
to add a name to those fallen in this cause, I trust that
the results of one expedition will be well deemed worth
three men's lives. My papers shall not be lost, I shall be
able. But I tell you, that I have full confidence in my
safe return and in my being able to lay the inward
of this expedition in an elaborate form before the public.

2. Letter from Barth, 26 September 1852

*Reproduced by permission of the Trustees of the British Museum.*

3. Barth's Grave, Berlin

informed of the public ceremony to mark the sailing of the
*Dayspring*. Naturally, he interpreted this as one more deliberate
slight.

Barth next became entangled in British foreign policy, which
he described in letters as 'a mask' and 'a sham'. The swing
in official sentiments towards North Africa since Barth's return
had meant that his invitation, on behalf of the British Government, to El Bakay in Timbuktu to send a trade mission to
England was now an embarrassment to the British Government.
The trade mission reached Tripoli in June 1857, but when it
asked whether it might proceed to Britain its members were
told that they would have to return to Timbuktu.[135] Meanwhile,
Lord Clarendon had somewhat hesitatingly agreed to Barth's
proposals to write to El Bakay and the Sultans of Sokoto and
Bornu, thanking them for their protection of the mission
and offering trade and friendly ties. There ensued a careless
mistranslation in Lord Clarendon's dispatch and an unfortunate
political misunderstanding, which culminated in the collapse of
diplomatic relations with Timbuktu and Bornu. Barth took this
as a personal affront and as a positive denial of his mission, an
attitude that was fortified by a private letter he received from
El Bakay through the Governor of Senegal in 1858, expressing
surprise at the brusque treatment he had received from the
British Government. He was, however, noble enough not to
connect his friend with this vacillation and weakness in high
places.[136]

The publication of the first three volumes of the Travels,
in 1857, did not arouse the enthusiasm Barth had expected.
Added to this disappointment were his unpleasant series of dis-
agreements with the Foreign Office, the British Government's

[135] Among the excuses made to this mission from Timbuktu, led by a nephew of
El Bakay, was that a British expedition was already on its way up the Niger to
make contact with the peoples on the upper river. F. Dubois, in his *Timbuctoo
the Mysterious*, 1897, pp. 338–344, considers that Barth inflated the importance
of El Bakay's influence and overplayed his recommendation to the British
Government.

[136] Honour was saved by the French generosity towards Barth's protector: see E. W.
Bovill, 'Henry Barth', *Journal of the African Society*, July 1926, p. 317.

rejection of his treaties,[137] the misunderstandings with the Royal Geographical Society, the attacks in the press on his leadership of the expedition, and the delayed award of the C.B. promised several years earlier—all this accumulated unhappiness caused him to regret his decision to settle in England. On 9 January 1858, he confessed to Bunsen that he could not stomach English politics.[138] Despite changes in personnel at the Foreign Office and the appointment of a friend of his, Francis Galton, as the new Secretary of the Royal Geographical Society, Barth was nevertheless determined to leave the country. As soon as volume V was off the press in the summer of 1858 he left for Germany, on 21 August.

Barth's feelings of resentment against England were well expressed in a long letter to Herman, the Consul-General at Tripoli, written on 24 December 1858.[138] Though he never completely lost his feeling of resentment, a later letter, addressed to his brother-in-law on 15 December 1860, showed some signs of a thaw.[138] And in January 1861, he was able to write an objective résumé of the quarrel with the Royal Geographical Society, to his friend Galton. By now Barth and the Foreign Office were once again engaged in official correspondence, and in May he received a personal invitation from Lord John Russell to return to England. Eventually, in 1862, he was awarded the C.B., an honour which had been promised to him in a letter from Lord Clarendon as far back as 28 September 1855, and had even been publicly announced in November 1858, but which had been held up by personal motives of animosity on the part of 'a clique of jealous officers'. In his last years Barth so far unbent as to write that he had at times enjoyed an interesting and fruitful intercourse with Englishmen.

---

[137] The treaties are to be found in *State Papers*, vol. 63, 1872–73, pp. 851 ff., and in *Treaties and Conventions*, L. Hertslet, 1894, vol. X (Africa), p. 702 (Treaty with Bornu), p. 704 (Treaties with Sokoto and Gwandu), and p. 707 ('Engagement of the Chief of Timbuctoo'). For a detailed study of the Bornu treaty and projected consulship, reference should be made to 'The British Consulate at Lake Chad', A. H. M. Kirk-Greene, *African Affairs*, October 1959.

[138] Schubert quotes many of these letters of Barth verbatim.

## FINAL RETURN TO GERMANY

In following Barth's feelings towards the British Government, I have stepped outside the chronological sequence of events. On his return to Germany at the end of 1858, he had his eye on the Hanseatic consulship in Constantinople, but he dropped this when he learned that the salary was not up to his needs. He spent the autumn of 1858 travelling, the first tour since his return from Africa, apart from his visit to Dublin in 1857 to address the British Association for the Advancement of Science on 'The Anomalous Period of the Rising of the Niger'.[139] During the course of his lecture he advocated the then unorthodox system of individual travelling in Africa. In September he attended the Congress of Philologists at Vienna; thence he returned via Bucharest to Constantinople, spending November and December in that region of Asia Minor. Returning to Germany early in 1859, Barth took a house at No. 6 Schellingstrasse, Berlin, and set about looking for a post.

None of the three men who sponsored his applications was to live long enough to see them through. Humboldt, who had planned to procure a consulship for Barth at Damascus, despite Barth's own preference for that of Siam, died on 6 May 1859.[140] Ritter, his old tutor, died on 28 September in the same year, and Bunsen, his first patron, exactly fourteen months later. On Ritter's death Barth was elected, at the second ballot, as President of the Berlin Geographical Society, over his opponent, Professor Dove, and together they organized the Karl Ritter Institute, in memory of the Society's founder.

Throughout these months Barth had been anxious about Vogel, whom he had last seen in Bornu in January 1855 and

---

[139] Surprisingly enough, there is no reference to this paper in Koner's otherwise apparently exhaustive bibliography of Barth's writings given at the conclusion of his memorial lecture to the Berlin Geographical Society in 1866. As only the title of the lecture is catalogued in the *Abstract of Miscellaneous Communications to the Sections* for the Dublin meeting of the British Association for the Advancement of Science, it is probable that Barth did not intend his paper for publication.

[140] It is interesting to note that in the centennial year of 1959 at least two long studies of Alexander von Humboldt were published in Berlin, a life by Herbert Scurla and a volume of his lectures edited by H. Beck on behalf of the Berlin Academy of Sciences.

from whom no dispatches had been received since May that year. In 1857, a report had been sent to the Foreign Office by the Consul-General at Tripoli, stating that Vogel had been murdered in Wadai. Worried by the subsequent silence, Barth drew up a plan for a relief expedition. Under the patronage of the Duke of Saxe-Coburg, a committee met on 15 July 1860, to approve this project, and the resulting Heuglin-Münzinger expedition left for Wadai in 1861. Perversely disregarding Barth's advice to start from Tripoli or Bengazi, they headed for Abyssinia; as this had nothing to do with recovering Vogel's papers, Barth promptly cut off their funds and ensured their recall in 1863.

This disciplinary action led to a renewed quarrel with Petermann, who had praised the expedition in his *Mittheilungen*. The breach had already occurred over other geographical matters and had led Barth to remark bitterly that Petermann had become so obsessed with his role in the African expedition that he was in danger of deluding himself that it was he and not Barth who had actually crossed the Sahara! Meanwhile, Barth had used his influence in England to ensure consular protection for another explorer, M. von Beurmann, to penetrate to Wadai and unravel the Vogel affair. Beurmann was murdered there in February 1863. What happened to Vogel is still unknown, and his papers have never been found.[141]

While directing these expeditions and keeping up a correspondence with most of the prominent explorers of that remarkable era of geographical exploration, and even considering a Polar expedition for himself in the new Prussian naval ships *Medusa* and *Adler*, Barth was still anxious to establish his position with the Prussian Government. It had been widely assumed that he would succeed Ritter to the professorship of geography at Berlin, an appointment recommended by Ritter himself, but to the chagrin of many no decision was announced by the Minister.

[141] Baikie was able to recover two of Vogel's books in Kano in 1862. Vogel's sister, Elise Polko, compiled a somewhat sentimental biography of her brother, based on his correspondence from Nigeria. Sir Richard Burton has an interesting footnote on Vogel's papers in his *Abeokuta and Cameroons Mountain*, 1863, Vol. 1, p. 10.

In 1862 Barth met with yet another setback when his friends, seeking to have him elected to full membership of the Royal Academy of Sciences, of which he had been a corresponding member for seven years, were defeated by personal intrigues. It is noticeable that Barth's obituary in *The Times*[142] commented upon this petty affront. Embittered by this experience, he decided to leave Berlin and to accept the chair offered him at Jena University.

Happily, on 13 May 1863, on the personal intervention of the new Minister of Culture, he was offered the appointment of professor-extraordinary at Berlin University at £225 per annum. Thus the academic year 1863–64 saw Barth once again lecturing at Berlin. This time there were up to sixty students in his class.

One of the principal merits of this appointment was that, unlike a full professorship, it allowed Barth ample opportunity to travel and to write. In 1858 he published his *Reise von Trapezunt durch die nördliche Hälfte Klein-Asiens nach Scutari im Herbst*. For the next few years he travelled regularly. 1861 took him to Spain, 1862 to the Balkan peninsula, 1863 to the Dolomites, 1864 to the Apennines, and 1865 to west Turkey. Truly, 'travel was Barth's element.'[143] In 1864 he published an account of his Asia Minor journeys, *Reise durch das Innere der Europaischen Turkei*, confining the accounts of his other travels to articles in German geographical magazines. He also published two important papers, *A General Historical View of the State of Human Society in Northern Central Africa* and *Neger und Negerstaaten*.

But the most significant work on which Barth was then engaged was his collection of Central African vocabularies. The *Journal of the Royal Geographical Society*, with a fine perception of the true methodology in African ethno-history that would win praise today, stressed how ' it is mainly from a comparison of dialects that we may hope to unravel some portion of the mutual relationships and the early history of the various races

---

142 *The Times* 2 December 1865. See also Schiffers, op. cit., p. 270, for a comment on the Academy's election.

143 Schubert.

which inhabit that large portion of the earth's surface.' The works, three volumes of which were published between 1862 and 1866, remained incomplete, and there is indeed a mystery about the fate of the remaining manuscripts. Twelve major vocabularies constitute Barth's own volumes, while a further twenty-four minor word-lists were discovered by the zealous P. A. Benton in 1910.[144]

### BARTH'S DEATH

Barth died on 26 November 1865, at the early age of 44, after only two days of illness. The attack was exacerbated by a dangerous error of diet that was not at once recognized by his doctors. He died in great pain. Disturbed by the rumour current in the Berlin press that it was a case of accidental poisoning—which was not in the circumstances impossible, as Barth had grown accustomed to treating himself in his long Saharan travels—his relatives asked for an autopsy. Professor Rudolf Virchow performed this operation and attributed death to a bursting of the stomach following an intestinal inflammation. In the process he found in Barth's thigh the bullet received during the Egyptian attack of June 1846.

Heinrich Barth was buried on the afternoon of 29 November, in the Jerusalem Cemetery, Berlin, and the funeral sermon was preached by the Reverend J. Mullensiefen. The grave was marked with a marble cross inscribed: *Der vielge-wanderte Erforscher Centralafrikas fand hier die Stätte der ewigen Ruhe.*[145] On 9 January 1866, the Berlin Geographical Society held a memorial session which was prefaced by the reading of international condolences and had as its highlight Professor Koner's great oration on Barth's life.

*The Times* noted Barth's death in its obituary columns, though it had failed to comment on his return from the Western Sudan in 1855. The *Journal of the Royal Geographical Society*, 1866, pointed out that he had been awarded the Society's highest

[144] For this detective epic, see the clues provided by the linguists Cust and Latham as well as the works of Nachtigal and Benton.

[145] Thanks to the courtesy of the Federal German Embassy in London, I have been able to obtain a photograph of Barth's grave. The tombstone is said to have been destroyed during the war, and the poplar tree alone marks the site.

honour for his original work in his travels in Nigeria, adding
that 'although he made no observations to fix with astronomical accuracy the latitude and longitude of places, the reckoning
of the distances he travelled over was so accurately and minutely
laid down, and his chronometer so studiously observed, that he
was enabled to add much to cartography, whilst his description
of the countries he traversed, and inhabitants he came in
contact with, was most telling and effective.' The President of
the Society, Sir Roderick Murchison, also paid tribute to
Barth's 'indomitable perseverance and skilful researches',
concluding that 'a more intelligent, indefatigable, trustworthy
and resolute traveller than Dr. Barth can rarely be found.' Petermann printed an obituary in his *Geographische Mittheilungen*.[146]
He paid tribute to 'a noble character and a sterling heart'
concealed behind a somewhat rough exterior; Barth paid little
attention to mere day-to-day formalities, and he was accordingly
misunderstood at times by those who did not penetrate the
façade.

Perhaps the finest tribute was Koner's memorial address to
the Geographical Society of Berlin.[147] From it I shall quote no
more than the thumbnail sketch of Barth and his two
companions on the Nigerian expedition:

On one side there was Richardson, exemplifying the strong
ecclesiastical orientation of England at that time, filled with the
humane thought of the abolition of the slave trade and of the
attainment of this goal by means of commercial treaties, but without
properly understanding that such a goal demanded a thorough
geographical and ethnographical investigation of those unknown
areas, a man without any higher intellectual impetus,[148] lacking

[146] 4 December 1865.

[147] While on the subject of obituary notices, mention should be made of the premature
obituary written by T. Gumprecht and published in *Die Zeitschrift für allgemeine
Erdkunde* 1855, pp. 53–89. The long silence from Barth, virtually imprisoned in
Timbuktu, coupled with a report from the British Consul at Tripoli that Barth
had indeed met his death, led both the German and English press to assume
that Barth had shared the fate of the other members of the Central African
Expedition. He was believed to have died at Menade, near Sokoto.

[148] R. Mansell Prothero, in his paper on 'Heinrich Barth and the Western Sudan',
*The Geographical Journal* CXXIV, September 1958, considers that Richardson
was something of a Philistine.

expertise and energy. Opposite him was Barth, with his cold, calm deliberation, his supra-honest mind that shunned any hint of intrigue, precise and restless in his use of time, a brave and manly character, unflinching before danger and undismayed by any failure or setback. And between the two of them was Overweg, a staunch young man, enthusiastic, a good friend of Barth's, but without any experience and failing to understand in his youthful mind the great task to whose solution he was called.

His shrewd brother-in-law noted that for much of his life Barth had cut himself off from society; absorbed in his work, 'his behaviour had taken on the serious, dignified, reserved, proud, almost arrogant quality of the behaviour of the Arab sons of the desert with whom he had lived so long.' Continually forced to be on guard against his environment and travelling companions, his innate distrust of mankind had grown to neurotic proportions, so that he suspected intrigue and calculated insults where none existed.

Barth was proud, priggish and prickly, but he was a brave man, a fine scholar, and an outstanding traveller.

## 2. CRITIQUE OF THE *TRAVELS AND DISCOVERIES*

Before examining the different editions of Barth's principal work, mention must be made of the very rare, beautiful, royal folio volume of August Petermann published in 1854, *An Account of the Progress of the Expedition to Central Africa by order of Her Majesty's Foreign Office under Messrs. Richardson, Barth, Overweg and Vogel in the years* 1850, 1851, 1852 *and* 1853. This contains, besides its thirteen sections of text and an appendix on astronomical observations, a magnificent frontispiece[1] with a map and four illustrations. The account derived from the Earl of Clarendon's generosity when he put at Petermann's disposal the dispatches and maps received from Barth at Kukawa in February 1853.

Barth's *Travels and Discoveries in North and Central Africa* were published in England by Messrs. Longmans Green. There were 2,250 copies of volumes I, II and III, which appeared in the summer of 1857, priced at three guineas; 1,000 copies of volumes IV and V followed in July, 1858.[2] This edition, comprising nearly 3,500 pages, is the standard English one. 'It will be seen,' ran the publisher's notice,[3] 'that Dr. Barth has connected the travels of Denham, Clapperton and the two Landers with those of Major Laing and Mungo Park . . . The regions traversed by Dr. Barth are in great part untrodden ground. Some of the geographical results of Dr. Barth's discoveries have been made known, but the narrative of his travels, discoveries and personal ventures in the vast regions of Central Africa is here for the first time placed before the public.' In 1890, Messrs.

---

[1] Reproduced as the frontispiece of this book.

[2] From information kindly supplied to the author by the publishers. They regretfully added that the loss of records during World War II has meant that the correspondence with Barth on the details of the publication of his *Travels and Discoveries* is no longer available.

[3] *Notes on Books*, May 1855–February 1860, Vol. 1.

Ward Lock brought out a useful edition, in two volumes, in their *Minerva Library of Famous Books*. The text is unabridged, and it lacks only the colour plates and the appendixes: had it been less of a bookseller's rarity, its compact size would have made it a ready companion[4] for many a traveller and resident in modern Nigeria.

In the United States, Harper and Brothers of New York published the complete edition (again without colour plates) in 1857–59, in three volumes, at $2.50 each. This edition was re-published in 1896 under the imprint of The Drallop Publishing Company of New York; their title page was simply incorporated into the former Harper edition.[5] Also extant is part of an edition published by D. Appleton at $12, which consists of the first three volumes in exactly the same form as the Longmans Green edition, but without the completing volumes.[6] In 1859, J. Bradley of Philadelphia brought out a one-volume abridgement, reputedly pirated. The blurb stated:

The author's reasons for issuing the work in this voluminous and expensive form are readily seen. His favorite object is the advancement of discovery in Africa; and wishing to render his work as useful as possible to all future travelers in the regions which he visited, he appears to have published the greater part of his entire journal for a period of more than five years. In it are noticed the incidents of travel from day to day and from week to week, with rather minute descriptions of monuments, mountains, rivers, deserts, rocks, trees seen on the route, as well as the important transactions of the expedition and the accounts of great cities and nations, their manners, customs, costumes, religion, government, finance, commerce, laws, etc. Now for the travelers who are to succeed Dr. Barth and for scientific enquirers, this minute journal is exactly what is wanted; such persons could well afford to pay for it. But with the general reading public it is quite the reverse. A general reader desires to know where Dr. Barth went, what new discoveries he made, what he

[4] For Barth's merits as a travelling-companion in Nigeria, see the final paragraphs of E. W. Bovill's appreciative essay, 'Heinrich Barth', *Journal of the African Society*, July 1926.

[5] The Hoover Library, California, has a copy of this curious edition.

[6] In a kind private letter to the author, the publishers (now Appleton-Century-Crofts Inc.) regretted the destruction of their files and records of the Barth contract in two serious fires.

saw, what dangers, difficulties, perils and adventures he went through, and what, on the whole, was accomplished by the expedition; but, on the other hand, ordinary readers are not willing for this purpose to pay $25 or $30 and wade through five octavo volumes of journal and itineraries, such as future travelers in Africa and scientific enquirers will most desire.

The French edition *Voyages et découvertes dans l'Afrique septentrionale et centrale pendant les années* 1849 *à* 1855 (undated: internal evidence suggests 1859 for Volume I; Volume IV has the imprint of 1861) is a sorry publication. A contemporary German geographer damned it as 'sketchy and unskilled'[7] and one of the later French critics rejected it as 'emasculated'.[8] Certainly the long list of acknowledged errata, the unnoticed excisions, the omission of the preface, and the errors in the text, all combine to make it an unworthy edition. In 1858–61 the Dutch edition was published, *Lotgevallen en ontdekkingen op eene reis in ket noorden en midden van Afrika,* and in 1859–60 a translation was made into Danish, *Reiser in Nord-og Mellem-Afrika.* Recently I came across a set of the *Travels and Discoveries* in High Dutch.

The German edition, *Reisen und Entdeckungen in Nord-und Central-Afrika in den Jahren* 1849 *bis* 1855, published simultaneously with the English one by Justus Perthes of Gotha, is for obvious reasons an important one. The prominent French Africanist Urvoy has declared that it is exactly the same as the English edition,[9] but a careful comparison of the two shows this statement to be incorrect. There are numerous differences in the text, here and there amounting to variations of major importance, in the arrangements of the appendixes, in the division of chapters, and in some titles of illustrations. Naturally, the dedication is to King Frederick William of Prussia instead of the Earl of Clarendon. The whole preface was substantially rephrased and repays attentive study. Reacting to criticism in the German press about the inordinate length of the five-volume

[7] Koner.    [8] Y. Urvoy.

[9] 'Essai de bibliographie des populations du Soudan Central', Y. Urvoy, *Bulletin du comité des Études historiques et scientifiques de l'A.O.F.,* XIX, 1936.

edition, Barth himself prepared a shorter version which was published, in two volumes, by Perthes in 1859–60.

The pride of the English and German editions justifiably lies in the sixty beautiful printed lithographs after J. M. Bernatz,[10] made from Barth's own sketches.[11] In his preface to the English edition, Barth pays tribute to this artist; but in the German edition he not only regrets that Bernatz could have added many a 'lively circumstance' had he had the text beside him as he worked, but also criticizes him for his Kano presentation,[12] 'in which the glowing, lively tone has been inadequately caught by the artist,' and goes so far, in a footnote that was omitted from other editions, to accuse Bernatz of undesirable artistic licence when copying his own sketches. The woodcuts are delightful, and it is revealing for the modern Nigerian to, say, compare the sketch of the Mandara Hills from Uba with the view today, or to retrace Barth's town-plans of Kano and Sokoto. The painstakingly drawn maps and informative line sketches are splendid, exemplifying the comment of a leading British geographer that Barth's 'capacity for meticulous observation depended on never missing an opportunity, however strange, of acquiring information'.[13]

## CONTEMPORARY REVIEWS

What was the public's reaction to the *Travels and Discoveries*? In 1856, a year before publication, the Royal Geographical Society had announced that they understood Barth's research and records were extensive enough to run to over five volumes, 'which, collected in such a country, must prove of the highest importance.' At the same time Petermann published in his geographical journal what is called in America a 'sneak-preview,' captioned *Plan und Inhalt des Reisewerkes*, along with a detailed summary of the book by Barth himself.[14] In the belief

[10] He was the artist of the 48 tinted litho plates reproduced in his folio volume *Scenes in Ethiopia*, 1851–52.

[11] E. W. Bovill comments in his *The Golden Trade of the Moors*, 1958, p. 44 (footnote), on how well Barth's sketches stand up to comparison with modern photographs.

[12] 19 February 1851.          [13] *People of the Veil*, F. R. Rodd, 1926, p. 91.

[14] *Mittheilungen*, 1855, p. 308.

that it is interesting and instructive to be aware of the contemporary reviews, research has been extended to some of the English and German literary journals of that period, from which the following extracts are taken.

The *Athenaeum*[15] declared that 'for extent and variety of subjects, the three volumes before us greatly surpass every other work on African travel with which it has been our fortune to meet. The books are got up in the most expensive style by the publishers, accompanied by an unexampled number of maps and adorned by beautiful plates and woodcuts.' While justly admiring the maps, the reviewer considered some of them as unnecessarily large, ' we may almost say too numerous for the book.' He went on to note that 'the work has evidently been carefully compiled, and due reverence paid to the more ancient as well as modern authors,' listing a formidable array of scholarship from Pliny and Leo Africanus down to Clapperton and Cooley. After summarizing the contents of each of three volumes the review concluded: 'it would be difficult before the issue of the last two volumes, including, as they will, Dr. Barth's visit to Timbuktu and return, to form a decided opinion of the addition to scientific geography which he appears to claim. As an indefatigable traveller, however, his merits are undoubted.'

The *Guardian*[16] commended the style: ' if the composition is his own, it deserves the praise of being remarkably good, simple and nervous English for a foreigner to write . . . the story is clearly told; such egotism as there is is neither offensive nor disagreeable; the general temper and spirit of the book are excellent.' It regretted ' the absence of reflection and generalization ' and condemned the format as being ' rather too much after the manner of a journal; sometimes, when the bulk of it is considered, with a disappointing dryness and internal brevity.'

The review in the *Spectator*,[17] published on the same day as that of the *Athenaeum*, but of considerably greater length, commented on Barth's plan of 'exhibiting his journal rather than the results of his journal.' It considered that the style might have been improved by condensing many of the 'trivial facts and

[15] 16 May 1857.    [16] 1 June 1857.    [17] 16 May 1857.

occurrences,' or even omitting them. 'So long a work on a subject with little bearing on the direct interests or sympathies of mankind, and whose sameness is great notwithstanding his variety of topics, is too much for any reader.' The reviewer suggested that the whole work should be cut to a third of its present length by starting the narrative with the separation of the travellers just north of Kano, since Richardson's journals had already covered the first period — 'we do not mean that curious delineations would not have been lost by this process, but there is a limit of length beyond which human power of continuous perusal with sustained attention does not pass.' The reviewer admired how 'there is not only freshness, but novelty in Dr. Barth's narrative' and emphasized that Barth looked about him 'with other eyes than those of our military and naval men.' Beyond all Barth's scholarly attributes,

he was a German, with a more cosmopolitan and tolerant mind than Britons always possess. This perhaps enabled him to adapt himself to unpleasant circumstances better than an Englishman, to form a higher estimate of Negro life and character, as well as to look leniently on social laxities.

He then goes on to describe Barth's continence towards 'the fair' [sic], made easier by his understanding of 'the customs of the country, whether the pagan or Mahometan, in such matters.' After praising the excellent description of the political turmoil of Central Africa at that time and the attractive character of its peoples, the reviewer concludes that 'notwithstanding its defects of plan ' this was the best account of Central Africa north of 9° yet written, just as ' he himself is the model of an explorer — patient, persevering, resolute and satisfied with little.'

Referring to the publication of the first three volumes in his annual address to the Royal Geographical Society in 1857, its President, Sir Roderick Murchison, reported that 'this meritorious explorer of vast regions has issued to the public three volumes, which, recording his earlier wanderings, are to be followed by two others, completing a work which will doubtless be considered the worthy termination of so many

years of patient research on the great privations.' While
reserving fuller judgment until the publication of the remaining
volumes, he praised the excellence of the maps and the richness
of the volumes which showed 'that Dr. Barth was so completely at home among the natives, with seven of whose
languages he was familiar, and made such very diligent inquiries,
that the information thus gathered is far more ample and
minute than that of his precursors.'

In Germany reviews largely followed the same lines, criticiz-
ing Barth for overburdening the text with unimportant triviali-
ties and, while acknowledging his accuracy and scholarship,
regretting his lack of an attractive style. One review compared Barth's work with the journal of Dr. Livingstone, which
appeared about the same time: 'while Barth conducted and
has presented his journey with more spirit and from a higher
standpoint as well as with a continuing usefulness, Livingstone's
book through its attractive presentation is reminiscent of
Herodotus.'

The literary critic of the *Augsburger Allgemeine Zeitung* was
more lavish in his enthusiasm:

Do not imagine the descriptions are composed merely for small
talk! The description has its effect purely through the greatness of
its task, through the steadfastness, perseverance and presence of
mind of the traveller, through the distance of his objectives and the
assiduity of his research. The book presupposes laborious studies and
is rich in perilously achieved scientific results, without the author
seeking to show off by alluding to what he performed or by a
display of erudition. Reliability is the stamp of every line; moreover
the language is simple, devoting itself all too often to greater brevity
in diary form, with ethnographic linguistic historical digressions, etc.[18]

This was a happy improvement on the review of his *Wanderungen*, whose style had been severely abused by the critics as
cumberous and involved —

a more perplexing specimen indeed, of some of the worst faults of
German prose has rarely fallen in our way. The task of constructing
periods entangled with strings of ill-joined parentheses, and bristling

*47551*                    [18] 12 May 1857.

with epithets often composed of entire sentences, is a serious addition to the labour of digesting the scientific matter of the volume.[19]

Curiously, Bunsen had always maintained to Barth that 'English prose is without a peer for clear, purposeful, concise statement of the facts of the case.'

When the remaining two volumes were published in 1858, criticism was voiced even more sharply. The *Guardian*[20] was less laudatory: 'their great length will be an obstacle not easily overcome in the way of their general popularity', it observed, at the same time admitting their indispensability to philologists and geographers. The volumes, it felt, were fatiguing: they were rather materials to be recast and popularized by those less learned, less industrious, but yet possessed of that 'invaluable gift of literary ability denied to Dr. Barth.'

The *Spectator's* reviewer wrote:

In the literary scheme of the volumes, necessity or design has effected some improvement. The progress of the story is not delayed by so many interrupting topics as in the former volumes . . . Our German doctor, however, omits no opportunity of introducing matters far better adapted to the pages of a special society's *Transactions*, or which should be relegated to an appendix, if they must appear in a popular work. The narrative itself is still extremely slow, arising from the same cause as induced the former volumes to drag heavily, namely a too full journalizing *en route*, without regard for the character of the thing described.[21]

He went on to recommend the use of large-scale maps with descriptive notes to record such geographical discoveries rather than the presentation of Dr. Barth. 'It is true that all the author's accounts are very real, still, even reality may approach tedium.' In conclusion, the reviewer felt that 'notwithstanding the bulk of Dr. Barth's book, he is not really to be considered an author or even a narrator, but as a traveller and discoverer . . . As a discoverer Dr. Barth is rather to be ranked as an elucidator of what was already discovered than the finder-out of the unknown.' Ending on the pessimistic note that he does not share Barth's hopes of commerce for these new regions, the reviewer wrote:

[19] *Athenaeum*, 2 March 1850.          [20] 3 October 1858.          [21] 7 August 1858.

4. View of Kano from Dala
From Barth's *Travels and Discoveries*.

5. The Shores of Lake Chad
From Barth's *Travels and Discoveries*.

6. The Dendal in Kukawa

From Denk', Travel and Disc...

we do not entertain so favourable an opinion of the practical results
to commerce and African civilization that are to spring from these
discoveries as Dr. Barth and many people. The capacity of a country
to produce, and the actual extent of its productions, are two very
different things.

The *Athenaeum* devoted a very long review[22] to the concluding
volumes of Barth's *Travels and Discoveries*, and was, as might be
expected from its attitude over the previous decade, favourably
disposed. 'Few books of travel,' the review starts, 'have we
closed with so keen an interest or so complete a confidence in
the narrator as these of Dr. Barth. Short of actual survey, they
leave the reader nothing to desire.' It praises Barth's delineation
of 'topics at present of high political and human concern, the
real state of Negroland', of its 'disposition to legitimate trade
and commerce', of its potential trade routes into the interior as
well as of its attractions to 'the lover of science or physical
history'. Much of the review is taken up with an outline of the
author's qualifications which placed him in the first rank of
scientific explorers, and a summary of the events of the expedition, interlarded with extensive verbatim quotations. Actual
literary assessment is confined to the last sentence of the 5,000
word review: 'of the merits of Dr. Barth as an indefatigable
explorer there can be little doubt; his work is full of minute
information, but it must be owned, after all, that five volumes
of 600 pages each do not seriously incline in a traveller's favour,
even philanthropic readers.'[23]

In his 1858 annual address to the Royal Geographical Society,
the President spoke of the two concluding volumes that were
about to be published. Noting that it would be 'perfectly
impossible for me to condense his [Dr. Barth's] results into a
few paragraphs,' Sir Roderick Murchison contented himself
with expressing his opinion that there was no method of
epitomizing Dr. Barth's labours so adequately as that of dis-
playing them upon large maps, 'variously shaded and tinted

[22] 7 August 1858.

[23] It should be noted that Barth compressed the events of the whole of the last year
of his travels into a mere hundred pages, vastly disproportionate to the ratio
of the four preceding years.

to show the races, nations, population, physical features of the country and so forth'. These, he hoped, would be published in the Society's *Journal*, ' and it must be to them rather than to any description of my own that I beg to refer all those readers who desire to learn the nature and extent of our gains in African geography due to the indefatigable industry of our medallist Dr. Barth.' In concluding, he declared that a geographer like Barth, 'whose line of inquiry is eminently historical and social', was remarkable for the patient accumulative industry of his countrymen the Germans, and that he had gathered 'a mass of matter which his voluminous publications appear insufficient to exhaust.'

### STYLE

This is not the place for a profound critical analysis of Barth's style. Enough has been said above to show what the contemporary criticisms were; in the interval since his death they have not noticeably changed. In this context, however, there are two points I should like to make, in the interest of scholarship and without the slightest denigratory intent.

First, we must not lose sight of the fact that, however fluent Barth undoubtedly was in English, his mother tongue was German. Some commentators have tended to assess Barth's English by the almost faultless style of his *Travels and Discoveries*, but a glance at his manuscript letters and original dispatches will show at once how a considerable amount of care and co-operation[24] must have been put into the revision of the journals before publication. This may well account for the stilted, meticulous style, careful to the point of boredom. Despite minor faults that here and there reveal themselves under a minute examination of the five volumes, no page in the printed text is marred by the misshapen phraseology and orthography of Barth's very human correspondence — the 'I have the honor of signing me yours most truely Dr. Barth', 'the letter is destined for pubblication', 'than has been bestowed to it till

[24] Dr. Cauvin was Barth's principal adviser on the English style of the London edition. It appears that Barth did not translate the two editions, but wrote them simultaneously.

at present', 'envelopped', 'castel', 'Allmighty', etc.[25] Here and
there in the printed text we come across the occasional off-key
phrase, disclosing a subliminal translation, such as 'deranged'[26]
to describe a thermometer that was out of order, or 'look after'[27]
instead of 'look for.' Yet, overall, Barth's passion for conscien-
tious exactitude is nowhere clearer than in his published
journals.[28]

The second point concerns humour. Barth is often accused of
being the stereotype Prussian without a sense of humour. In so
far as the journal is not bespattered with exclamation marks,
after the manner of some modern travelogues, this is mercifully
true; but the intended criticism is not wholly just. It would be
truer to say that although Barth seldom raises a laugh — the
very notion would probably have appalled him as an impro-
priety and irrelevancy in such an art form as the scholarly
record — he can frequently be amusing. One of his readiest
skills in this context is the typically English use of ironical under-
statement, which he uses frequently and effectively. Another
is his willingness to tell tales against himself. Yet a third is his
sensitive drawings of the men and women he encountered on
his travels.

Finally, in the matter of style, it is of interest to compare the
self-control and analytic objectivity of Barth (witness the
unpretentious opening of his five-volume travel-history, an
opportunity that could have lent itself to panache and fanfare,
or the unbelievably restrained account of what must have been
a moment of supreme rejoicing, the meeting with his fellow-
countryman Vogel after twenty-seven months alone in the
Western Sudan) with the subjectivity and uninhibited
ingenuousness of Richardson's diary or of the letters of Overweg
and Vogel.

[25] These examples are taken from Barth's unpublished MS letters in the British
Museum.
[26] Chapter IV, *Travels and Discoveries*, footnote to opening paragraph.
[27] Entry of 30 March 1850.
[28] Petermann pays tribute to Barth's tireless self-discipline where the writing-up of
his diaries was concerned, praising them as a model for every future traveller.

As I have written elsewhere, in a centenary memoir to mark the publication of his *Travels and Discoveries*:

For those of us who have trekked through the Barth country, the journal of that ' indefatigable African traveller ' remains a delightful companion, a source of priceless knowledge, and a humbling testament to his wondrous fortitude and resolution.[29]

[29] 'The Indefatigable African Traveller', A. H. M. Kirk-Greene, *West Africa*, 20 December 1958.

# 3. BARTH IN RETROSPECT

## CONTRIBUTIONS TO SCHOLARSHIP

For the sake of convenience we may look at Barth's notable contributions to the knowledge of the Western Sudan under three headings: Barth the geographer, Barth the historian, and Barth the linguist. It would be pointless to recapitulate all Barth's achievements in these fields as they stand out on each page of his journal. Here, then, I shall simply summarize his record under the first two heads, and discuss his linguistic scholarship in greater detail, since this is a remarkable talent of Barth's that is not at first apparent from his *Travels and Discoveries*.

The geographical results of Barth's unparalleled journey are truly impressive. He brought enlightenment to the knowledge of the Sahara, which had hitherto been regarded as little more than a flat wasteland. He discovered two highly developed empires, the existence of which had not been known before, Gwandu and Hamd-Allahi. He analysed the complex river systems of Adamawa and Baghirmi. Barth not only disproved the earlier theory that the River Benue flowed into Lake Chad, but he was also the first European to set eyes on the upper Benue[1] and to estimate accurately its probable course down to the confluence where Lokoja now stands. The Benue was first noticed by the Landers in 1830 and explored for no more than a hundred miles or so upstream by MacGregor Laird a few years later. Furthermore, he foresaw the vital role that this waterway would play in opening up the continent to trade: 'I am persuaded that in less than fifty years European boats will keep up a regular annual intercourse between the great basin

---

[1] The geographer R. Mansell Prothero, in his article 'Heinrich Barth and the Western Sudan', *The Geographical Journal*, CXXIV, September 1958, considers that Barth's ' single most important discovery was of the upper reaches of the River Benue.'

of the Tsad and the Bay of Biyafra,'[2] a thought again expressed
on his first beholding the Mother of Waters. He also rejected
the theory of previous geographers that the River Niger had
direct access to the Chad basin, and, expanding his discoveries
of this river, he added considerably to the store of geographical
knowledge in his observations of the Birnin Kebbi-Say-Gao-
Timbuktu region. He gave the first detailed account of the
Baghirmi, Musgu, Mora and Adamawa complex. His analysis
of Aïr and the Tuareg is still hard to fault.[3] Finally, besides
being the second European ever to set eyes on Lake Chad, he
was the first to penetrate as far as Yola.

Barth's meticulously drawn maps, detailed meteorological
registers and the exhaustive listing of routes given in the appendixes to the *Travels and Discoveries*, are the finest evidence of his
geographical exactitude.[4] Petermann, on receiving Barth's map
covering the whole of his travels up to his departure from Bornu
in 1852, wrote that he had 'no hesitation in pronouncing this
map as the most comprehensive and complete that has ever
resulted from the travels and researches of any single African
traveller.' This eminent geographer also offered, as an apologia
for the copious extracts in his periodicals from Barth's dispatches
and letters, the fact that Barth and Overweg 'must henceforth
take rank as among the first — if not as the first — of African
travellers, and whatever comes from them is important.'

As an historian, Barth is of no less value to us today. His
description of the contemporary history of the Western Sudan
is unrivalled,[5] and his exposition of the decline of the once great

[2] 5 January 1853. One thinks at once of Lenfant's remarkable venture in proving
the existence of an unbroken water route between the Benue and Chad: see
his *La Grande Route du Tchad*, 1905.

[3] F. R. Rodd, in an article in *The Geographical Journal*, 1923, p. 90, declared after
his visit to Aïr that there was little to add to Barth's description of seventy years
earlier. The Timbuktu controversy stemming from Dubois' attacks does not
concern us here.

[4] R. Mansell Prothero, loc. cit., points out that the accurate results of Barth's map-
making are all the more remarkable when it is recalled that he never made any
astronomical observations, relying on dead-reckoning.

[5] E. W. Bovill, in his 'Heinrich Barth', *Journal of the African Society*, July 1926,
claims that Barth's historical notes on the Western Sudan contain 'some of
the most valuable material for the modern student.'

Fulani Empire is masterly. Of vital importance to the historical reconstruction of what is now Nigeria is Barth's discovery of the *Diwan*, a chronicle comprising the whole history of Bornu down to the end of the Magumi dynasty. He was one of the first to explore the Sahara's hitherto unknown rock paintings. Barth's discovery of the *Tarikh es Sudan* in Gwandu marks a peak in the study of the history of this region, and the fact that he misattributed its authorship to Ahmed Baba, under circumstances of peculiar obscurity,[6] in no way invalidates either the find or the quality of Barth as an historian: as one French review has it, '*Barth a amorcé le problème, Dubois l'a résolu.*'[7] It must be remembered that Barth was allowed to see only fragments of this manuscript, for the full copy was not discovered for another forty years, when Dubois came across it in Jenne and was able to correlate it with yet another copy in Timbuktu. Furthermore, Barth suspected that the author, in his acknowledged citations from Ahmed Baba, was doing no more than observing the Arabic tradition of quoting himself.[8]

Barth's careful documentation of original sources in the Sudan has taken on an added value since so many of these documents are no longer to hand. Even today, a hundred years later, his résumé of the historical origins of the large emirates such as Sokoto, Kano, Bornu, Adamawa and Katsina, together with his passages on the history of the pagan peoples which had been all too often overlooked by others,[9] provides the background for every Nigerian historian and is an indispensable precursor of others of the same authoritative genre, such as Lady Lugard's *A Tropical Dependency*, E. W. Bovill's *Caravans of the Old Sahara*, and S. J. Hogben's *The Muhammadan Emirates*

[6] See E. W. Bovill, *Caravans of the Old Sahara*, 1933, p. 192. In reviewing the revised edition of this classic of Western Sudan history, *The Golden Trade of the Moors*, 1958, Dr. H. C. F. Smith points out in *Ibadan*, October 1958, p. 28, that Bovill is not correct in assuming that none of Ahmed Baba's works has survived, since a copy of his biographical dictionary is to be found in the Oriental Section of the British Museum. Ahmed Baba had a library of 1,600 books.

[7] *Mouvement Géographique*, 6 December 1896.

[8] There is an interesting article on this by A. O. Stafford, in the *Journal of Negro History*, 2/1917, pp. 139–146.

[9] The criticism is levelled by Leo Frobenius in his *The Voice of Africa*, 1913.

*of Nigeria.* Barth indeed, to quote a German critic,[10] 'created a new era in the history of African discovery and regeneration.' From internal evidence, it seems possible that Barth's collection of ethnographic and artistic specimens, gathered in Bornu and Kano, is still to be discovered in England.

The references in the diaries to his linguistic expertise are few. On the Saharan passage Barth completed 'an exact and full vocabulary of the Emgedesi language and could with more leisure indulge in a conversation with my friend the chief eunuch and confidential servant of the Sultan of Agades.' Before penetrating Adamawa, he set about studying Fulani, and at Humbutudi we find him taking language lessons: 'after I had finished taking angles, I sat down on this magnificent rocky throne, and several of the natives having followed me, I wrote from their dictation a full vocabulary of their language.' On his expedition with the Bornu army against Mandara, he describes how 'I applied myself strenuously to the study of the Kanuri language, which had discouraged me at first, owing to the difficulties of its grammatical structure'; and on his way to Timbuktu he writes of Songhay:

having entered a new country, where a language was spoken with which neither I nor any of my servants was acquainted, and not being able to give much time to its study, as I had to apply myself to the Fulfulde, the language of the conquering tribe, I was extremely anxious to take in my service a native of the country, or to liberate a Songhay slave; but I did not succeed at this time, and in consequence felt not so much at home in my intercourse with the inhabitants of the country to which I had next to pass as I had done formerly.

Barth's uncompleted *Sammlung und Bearbeitung Central-Afrikanischer Vokabularien* consists of three parts.[11] Part I, published in 1862, contains vocabularies in German, English, Kanuri, Teda, Hausa, Fulfulde, Songhai, Logone, Wandala, Bagrimma [sic] and Maba. Parts II and III, published in 1863

[10] A. Petermann.

[11] Overweg and Richardson also devoted some time to collecting vocabularies; the latter started a Hausa dictionary and declared: 'It is my intention to send home 50,000 African words for this expedition.'

and 1866, present a grammatical analysis of six of the languages and noun lists of nine of them. I shall analyse this work in some detail, partly because it has rarely been so examined, partly because of its revelation of Barth's brilliance as a linguist, and partly because it provides valuable supplementary information to the text of the *Travels and Discoveries*.

In the preface to his diaries, he wrote of his former African journey: 'I spent nearly my whole time with the Arabs, and familiarized myself with that state of human society where the camel is man's daily companion, and the culture of the date tree his chief occupation.' Beyond this learning of Arabic, he had no knowledge of the languages of Central Negroland — indeed, he pointed out that Providence led him to this new sphere of interest, as otherwise his interests and travels would have been concentrated on Asia and ' it is scarcely probable that I should ever have entered upon this African career'. Barth went on to say:

These tribes cannot but look upon the white stranger, who suddenly appears before them as if he were fallen from the sky, and regard him with the most profound suspicion, before they become convinced that this wonderful being has the same human feeling as themselves and similar, if not the same, principles of action, notwithstanding the total difference of his colour, his appearance, his manner of living, and his unintelligible and apparently absurd and foolish activity, especially if he has come to explore the country, lay down its physical features and describe its people.

Barth complained that the materials existing on the languages of the Western Sudan before his 1849 expedition were far from satisfactory, consisting of brief vocabularies collected by Seetzen, Burckhardt and Denham; Schön's Hausa vocabulary of 1843 was too incomplete to be more than a standby. Koelle had at that time only begun ' his diligent and accurate study ' of Kanuri, which would have helped him a lot, Barth admitted, though he dismissed the *Polyglotta* of this ' indefatigable and highly meritorious missionary ' as totally unreliable since the informants had largely forgotten their own idiom when engulfed in 'the linguistic Babel' of Sierra Leone.

When Barth started he had no more than an insight into the grammar of Berber and a good knowledge of Arabic. Aided by the liberated Negro slaves whom they attached to their caravan, he picked up Kanuri and Hausa. Since the mission intended to approach Bornu by a long south-westerly sweep through the Tuareg and Hausa states, Barth soon dropped Kanuri, 'although the country of Fezzan, where we made a longer stay, offered the greatest facility for acquiring that very language.' Instead, he set about learning the Kelowi dialect of Temasight and Hausa. On leaving Ghat, Hausa became the prevailing language and Barth began to specialize in it — 'moreover, the easy character and the rich development of the Hausa idiom caused it soon to be a favourite with me.' He commented on what is so obvious to us today, that the Hausa of the northern districts was very different from Schön's Hausa of the Lower Niger. Barth claimed that by the time he left Asben he was fluent enough in Hausa to converse with the sultan of Agades without an interpreter. He was able to polish his Hausa further with ' the communicative and cheerful old Hausa slave, Gadzere ' on his way through Katsina and Kano, and he reckoned that if he could have spent a further six months on Hausa he would have become 'fully master of the language with all its finest peculiarities.' The expedition had to push on eastwards and so Barth was obliged to turn his back on 'the territory of the Hausa language so rich in forms and so pleasant to the ear in which I had begun to feel quite at home' and once more to address himself to Kanuri.

Barth never employed an interpreter as such, but used his versatile servant Mohammed el Gatroni, who was of almost pure Teda blood; he had an indifferent knowledge of Arabic, but was reasonably well acquainted with Kanuri. Kukawa was not, Barth found, the best place to pick up Kanuri, as at that time it was ' justly to be called the seat of a second-hand copy of Arab civilization', and the influx of going and coming pilgrims led Barth to forsake Kanuri and take advantage of this opportunity of obtaining new geographical material from these travellers. In any case, his aim, 'cherished with great zeal and

never left out of sight', was Adamawa, where only Fulfulde
would be of use to him. Barth now set about learning Fulani
through Hausa and Kanuri. On his expulsion from Yola he
gave it up, with no regrets 'as the dialect spoken in Adamawa
contained a great many instances of idiotism [sic] and bar-
barism' — one wonders how far this opinion was influenced by
his expulsion. Returning to Bornu he worked hard on his
Kanuri with the help of Kacella Billama, Haj Idris and
Shettima Makaremma, the last named a capable but exacting
teacher. On his 'wearisome and unfortunate expedition to
Kanem', Barth started a Teda glossary, a language that he
believed to be intimately connected with Kanuri. By the time
of the Musgu expedition Barth had so perfected his Kanuri that
he was able to offer a reward to his teacher, Haj Idris, for every
error corrected or new word added to his vocabulary! During
the course of the same expedition he compiled a Wandala
(Mandara) vocabulary.

Throughout 1852 Barth's media were Kanuri and Arabic.
In Baghirmi he worked on a vocabulary, admitting that he
found Denham's Wandala and Baghirmi lists useful, in contrast
to that of Koelle who had employed as his informant the *only*
Baghirmi boy in Sierra Leone! Whilst at Masena, Barth, using
Arabic as a medium, wrote his vocabulary of the Maba
language, and on the same journey, this time using Kanuri as
the go-between, he compiled a vocabulary of Logone from 'as
chief authorities a very cheerful old couple who contradicted
and corrected each other.' He maintained that he never
spoke Kanuri as well as Hausa, though 'I dare say I spoke it
with a tolerable degree of accuracy and fluency.'

In Timbuktu he applied himself to Songhai and Fulani, but
he was unable to acquire any degree of fluency in these
languages since he failed to find 'some clever individual of the
Songhai tribe' to attach to his household as servant-teacher.
In addition, he found that the language was dying out in
Timbuktu and had become no more than a degraded dialect. In
Katsina he studied the western dialect of Fulfulde, but regret-
tably had to drop this as the Fulani of Masena were so hostile to

him. He was delighted to return to the Hausa-speaking area and on his journey to Timbuktu and back he used Hausa exclusively, he also used this language all the time with his servants.

## MODERN ASSESSMENT OF BARTH

What opinion of Barth is held by modern scholars? As I have pointed out earlier, Barth has been regrettably neglected by recent and contemporary scholars, but here and there the occasional appreciation can be found. Lord Rennell of Rodd, himself an outstanding Saharan explorer, praising Barth's knowledge of the Tuareg and Aïr, noted thirty years ago that 'it is even more tragic to realize how few have heard of the German, Dr. Heinrich Barth, than whom it may be said there never has been a more courageous or meticulously accurate explorer', and he sought to rescue Barth's name from 'unmerited oblivion in these days of sensational and superficial books of travel.'[12] Another sympathetic interpreter is E. W. Bovill, who has paid tribute to Barth in an excellent article[13] as well as in his *Caravans of the Old Sahara* and its revised version, *The Golden Trade of the Moors.* He wrote how Barth was 'inspired by an insatiable craving for knowledge rather than by that spirit of adventure which usually spurs the explorer to even greater endeavours,' and concluded that Barth's work 'remains to this day one of the principal authorities on the Western Sudan, and its historical notes some of the most valuable material to the modern student.' Yet it was left, Bovill points out, to later generations to appreciate that it was Barth 'who finally lifted from Northwestern Africa the veil which earlier and more famous explorers had only penetrated.' Barth's *Travels and Discoveries* were assiduously read by Sir George Goldie during his 'Garden of Allah'[14] years in the Egyptian Sudan, and his most recent biographer has declared them an essential study for any serious student of West African history. 'The British Government,' Dr. Flint goes on, 'could not have summoned a

[12] *People of the Veil*, F. R. Rodd, 1926, p. 22.
[13] 'Henry Barth', E. W. Bovill, *Journal of the African Society*, July 1926, pp. 311–320.
[14] Dorothy Wellesley, *Sir George Goldie, Founder of Nigeria*, 1934, p. 94.

better emissary to preach the morals of Europe to Africa, and reveal the secrets of Africa to Europe. His greatest virtue, greater than his courage in wandering through so-called savage lands without military protection, greater than his instinctive flair for diplomacy in the intricate politics of African courts, greater even than his industry, was his curiosity.'[15] Thomas Hodgkin considers that Barth has a strong claim to recognition as Northern Nigeria's greatest historian, a scholar who constructed the frame of reference within which all subsequent historical work has been done. Above all, 'Barth had the temper and training which led him to ask historical questions of a kind no European has asked before. He never described the contemporary situation of the various African communities through which he travelled without attempting to relate it to the past; so that his work, unlike almost all preceding European studies, is a work of exploration in a double sense — in time as well as space'.[16] The anonymous contributor of the very brief article on Barth in the *Encyclopaedia Britannica* states that 'for accuracy, interest, variety and extent of information, Barth's *Travels* has few rivals among works of the kind. It is a book that will always rank as a standard authority on the regions in question.'

Two Saharan enthusiasts, Heinrich Schiffers and René Lecler, have also sought to bring to Barth some of the credit he so deserved. Schiffer's attractively-presented anthology included in its biographical notes a summary of Schubert's life of Barth, while an earlier volume recounted Barth's African journey in a somewhat colloquial style.[17] Lecler headed one of the chapters of his historical account of the Sahara 'The Master's Touch', though he is perhaps a little more romantic than true scholars would approve (Overweg did *not* die in Barth's arms; Barth would probably have disliked being called 'The Modern Marco Polo of Africa'[18]; nor can we be certain

---

[15] J. E. Flint, *Sir George Goldie and the Making of Nigeria*, 1960, pp. 18–19.
[16] Thomas Hodgkin, *Nigerian Perspectives: An Historical Anthology*, 1960, pp. 15–16.
[17] H. Schiffers, *Im Banne der Sahara*, 1950, and *Die Grosse Reise*, 1954.
[18] René Lecler, *World Without Mercy*, 1954, p. 95.

that Barth had the typical Prussian fair hair and blue eyes.) But
the admiration is there:

Above all, Barth was a type of explorer never yet seen in the
Sahara: he had the master's touch in everything he did. He was
exact, thorough, reliable, completely confident of his mission. He
was a no-nonsense man. Not for him the dreams and fancies of
romantics like Caillié or the unyielding righteousness of Laing: he
would be right as long as he could, but when being right threatened
the outcome of his journey, circumstances would find him adaptable.
He was proud but just. He had, compared to his predecessors, one
supreme skill: he was able diplomatically to resist the extortions of
the Sahara's eternal buccaneers, and yet he knew how to give when
necessary.

'In terms of exploration,' Lecler concluded, 'no single man
ever equalled Heinrich Barth's magnificent journey . . . Yet the
world soon forgot him . . . He had asked for nothing but to be
judged by his work, and half a century later when white men
began to know most parts of the Great Desert, they had to
concede that Barth had been right in everything he had
reported.'

The French critics A. Jacobs and Yves Urvoy have briefly
praised Barth and we find further appreciation of his discoveries
in the works of Monteil, Dubois, and especially Hourst, who
opens his book with a tribute to Barth, ' the greatest traveller
of modern times, our illustrious predecessor in the Niger.' As
regards modern German critics, Banse has maintained that
even if Barth had made no African journey he would have been
recognized as a famous geographer, for he is of the opinion that
certain other European geographers pirated Barth's ideas
without acknowledging their source. Burg, quoting Alexander
von Humboldt's praise that Barth opened a new area of the
world to us, remarked that 'it died away and is forgotten like
Barth himself.'

R. M. Prothero, lecturer in geography at Liverpool University, and one of the few connoisseurs of Barth's life and works,
delivered a notable centennial lecture to the Royal Geographical
Society in November 1957, in which for virtually the first time

in English[19] a serious analysis of Barth's life and works, together with a discerning tribute, was made — a tribute that was echoed in the comments of Lord Rennell of Rodd, E. W. Bovill and Professor Robert Steel in the discussion after the lecture. Basil Davidson has acclaimed Barth as 'surely the most intelligent of all the nineteenth century travellers in Africa',[20] who wrote of the Western Sudan 'with a mastery and brilliance that none has yet repeated.' Elsewhere,[21] he adds: 'Precise and intelligent, Barth was never content with general observations: he had the good reporter's love of fact. He always went to the heart of the matter.'

### REASONS FOR THE NEGLECT OF BARTH

Why has Barth been neglected in spite of this praise? Why are his works ignored and his life unknown? Why, indeed, as one modern scholar has put it, is it 'tempting to suggest that Barth dead was of greater significance as news than Barth alive, and that if he had perished in Africa, as had so many of his predecessors and contemporaries, he might have commanded a much greater share of public attention'?[22]

This neglect is due, I suggest, to a number of causes. As we have seen, many people of importance in England in the 1850's had a tendency to dislike or disapprove of Barth; there was also a considerable amount of anti-German feeling in the press, both during the Saharan expedition and after his return from Africa. Again, the exceptional delay in granting Barth his C.B., years after the award had been publicly announced, caused a significant waning in public interest — it is arguable that a similar reaction of oblivion and apathy might well have set in had Colonel Hunt and Dr. Fuchs received their well-merited awards of knighthood in, say, 1960, instead of on the immediate achievement of their geographical triumphs. Another consideration is the general lack of interest in West African affairs in

---

[19] The only comparable occasion is Bovill's paper in the *Journal of the African Society*, op. cit.

[20] *Old Africa Rediscovered*, Basil Davidson, 1959, p. 22.

[21] ibid., p. 93.

[22] 'Heinrich Barth and the Western Sudan', R. Mansell Prothero, *The Geographical Journal*, Vol. CXXIV, September 1958, p. 336.

England at that time, shifting in favour of Livingstone and the south and culminating in the famous resolution of withdrawal presented by the 1865 Committee. West Africa did not return to favour until the Berlin Conference a generation later.

Apart from contemporary factors, literary considerations must be taken into account. The inordinate length of Barth's *Travels and Discoveries* is a primary obstacle. His arid style, lacking the adventure-spirit of his compatriot Rohlfs or the subjectivity of Stanley, was weighed down with erudition, and did not commend itself to a wide public, as did Livingstone's exciting account of his journeys. Subsequent generations, curious perhaps to learn something about this remarkable traveller, have found no biography or substantial critical analysis in English to guide them in their interests.

## CONCLUSION

To conclude this biographical analysis of a man 'who is probably one of the greatest geographical explorers that this country or Europe has ever had', as Lord Rennell of Rodd recently described Barth,[23] I should like to suggest two other reasons why, just tribute and fascinating scholarship apart, Barth is so important today.

As Professor Dike has said, 'seemingly abstract considerations such as those of culture and history are as important as more material ones in building a nation . . . they are at the root of the question of self-government.'[24] It was Barth who first revealed and sympathetically interpreted the existence of highly civilized and effectively structured administrative kingdoms in the Western Sudan, both Muslim and pagan, upon which the prosperity of post–1900 Northern Nigeria has been founded. This historical approach is well summarized in his own preface:

The great and momentous struggle between Islamism and paganism is here continually going on . . . we find Mohammedan

[23] *The Geographical Journal*, Vol. CXXIV, September 1958, p. 339.
[24] 'African History and Self-Government', K. Onwuka Dike, *West Africa*, 28 February 1953.

learning engrafted on the ignorance and simplicity of the black races, and the gaudy magnificence and strict ceremonials of large empires side by side with the barbarous simplicity of naked and half-naked tribes. We here trace a historical thread which guides us through this labyrinth of tribes and overthrown kingdoms; and lively interest is awakened by reflecting on their possible progress and restoration, through the intercourse with more civilized parts of the world.

Furthermore, Barth was one of the first scholars to develop the thesis of many modern Africanists, namely that West African history is not so utterly barren of pre–1800 written documents (though many were destroyed by the Fulani *jihad*) as has been too often assumed.

There is no memorial to Barth in Nigeria. Perhaps, as his leading biographer[25] put it, 'in his deeds he set up for himself an indestructible memorial.' I followed in Barth's footsteps from the northern tip of the Mandara Mountains south through the Marghi country to Yola, but found few reminders of his journeys there, or in my researches in Bornu. The 'English house' at Kukawa is impossible to delineate among the corn stubble; Haj Bashir's family is almost extinct; Rabeh destroyed the presents given to the Sheikh of Bornu by Barth; Kuka and Wurno are but proud memories of the past.

Perhaps — and this is not only currently the most easily realizable wish, but is also the recognition that Barth himself would have liked best of all — this anthology will extend the circle of Barth's admirers, and encourage more people to turn to the full five volumes that contain the record and superb description of his travels among some of those prominent West African civilizations that provide the foundation for Nigeria.

[25] Schubert.

## 4. A NOTE ON PRINCIPAL SOURCE MATERIALS

The question of the various editions of Barth's *Travels and Discoveries in North and Central Africa* is adequately discussed on pages 45–56 of the Introduction.

For the biographical details that form the base of this Introductory Essay, I have drawn heavily on German sources. The principal biography of Barth is that written by his brother-in-law, Gustav von Schubert, *Heinrich Barth: der Bahnbrecher der deutschen Afrikaforschung*, 1897; it has yet to be surpassed for information. Another valuable source is Professor Koner's memorial lecture to the Berlin Geographical Society in January 1866. Augustus Petermann's writings are also of prime importance: they include his *Account of the Progress of the Expedition to Central Africa by Order of Her Majesty's Foreign Office under Messrs. Richardson, Barth, Overweg and Vogel in the Years 1850, 1851, 1852 and 1853*, 1854, and his frequent contributions to his own *Geographische Mittheilungen* and the *Athenaeum* during and immediately after the period of the expedition. Useful, too, are E. Banse's two informative essays in *Grosse Forschungsreise*, 1933, and *Unsere Grossen Afrikaner*, 1942. T. Gumprecht published a selection of letters in *Barth und Overwegs Untersuchungsreise nach dem Tschadsee und in das innere Afrika* in 1852. *Die Zeitschrift für allgemeine Erdkunde* during the 1850s carried a number of relevant articles. The biographical data in Heinrich Schiffers, *Die Grosse Reise*, 1954, and P. Burg, *Forscher, Kaufherrn und Soldaten*, 1936, are only a digest of Schubert's book.

In this German connexion, I wish to express my gratitude to my brother C. W. E. Kirk-Greene, Assistant Master in Modern Languages at Eastbourne College, for his substantial help in unravelling some of the more complex syntax of nineteenth-century German prose.

The biographical material in English on Barth is distressingly scarce. It has been pointed out that in the catalogue of the

Royal Geographical Society library there is only one reference to a paper published in England on Barth. With a handful of notable exceptions, the material consists of nothing more than a severely limited basic record in the manner of an encyclopaedia-entry, or simply of narration and summary of Barth's African journey. The outstanding exceptions are characterized by a scholarly and sympathetic approach: E. W. Bovill in his article 'Henry Barth', *Journal of the African Society*, July 1926 and again in his *Caravans of the Old Sahara*, 1933, and its revised form, *The Golden Trade of the Moors*, 1958; F. R. Rodd, *People of the Veil*, 1926; and two commemorative essays, 'Heinrich Barth and the Western Sudan', delivered to the Royal Geographical Society by R. Mansell Prothero and published in *The Geographical Journal*, September 1958, and 'Barth: A Centenary Memoir', A. H. M. Kirk-Greene, *West Africa*, 20 and 27 December 1958.

Apart from analyses of the expedition by V. A. Malte-Brun in the late 1850s and by A. Jacobs in the *Revue des Deux Mondes* of the same period, the French sources consulted consist of incidental references in the African writings of Dubois, Monteil, Tilho, and, above all, Hourst.

Besides extending my research to contemporary newspapers and journals, especially the *Journal of the Royal Geographical Society* and the *Athenaeum*, I have consulted Barth's other published works as well as the diaries, and some of the correspondence of James Richardson, Adolf Overweg and Edward Vogel. I have also examined the Barth MSS in the British Museum, (Add. MSS 32117 E, pp. 15–63) and made a preliminary survey of some of the dispatches and unpublished papers of the Central African Expedition in the Public Record Office (in particular F.O. 101/23, 26, 30, 34, 36, 45, and F.O. 93). In collaboration with Mr. R. Mansell Prothero, lecturer in geography at the University of Liverpool and one-time research fellow of the West African Institute for Social and Economic Research, I am planning to extend this research into the papers of the British Consulate at Tripoli and publish a monograph on Barth. To the best of our belief, the only other scholar to have drawn on these records, apart from Dr. A. A. Boahen

(Lecturer in History at the University of Ghana), is P. A. Benton, who fifty years ago reproduced some of the Foreign Office minutes and correspondence in his *Notes on Some Languages of the Western Sudan*, 1912, and his translation of Schultze's *Das Sultanat von Bornu*, 1913; both books now rank in the steadily growing list of rare Africana.

## 5. A CALENDAR OF BARTH'S NIGERIAN JOURNEY

### 1849

| | |
|---|---|
| *October* 5 | invited to join the Central African expedition. |
| *December* 12 | sailed from Marseilles with Overweg. |
| 11 | landed in North Africa, at Philippeville. |
| 15–30 | Tunis. |

### 1850

| | |
|---|---|
| *January* 18 | reached Tripoli. |
| *February* | exploration of the Ghurian mountains. |
| *March* 2 | arrival of Richardson. |
| 24 | trial camp outside Tripoli. |
| *April* 2 | start of the expedition proper. |
| *May* 6–*June* 13 | Murzuk. |
| *July* 18–26 | Ghat. |
| *August* 20–27 | pillage in caravan. |
| *September* 4 | Tintellust. |
| *October* 4–30 | Agades. |
| *November* 5– | |
| *December* 12 | Tinteggana. |

### 1851

| | |
|---|---|
| *January* 10 | Richardson left Barth and Overweg. |
| 13 | Parting of Barth and Overweg. |
| 21–30 | Katsina. |
| *February* 2– | |
| *March* 9 | Kano. |
| *March* 13 | Gumel. |
| 24 | received news of Richardson's death (March 4). |
| *April* 2–23 | Kukawa. |
| 24 | Ngornu and Lake Chad. |
| *May* 7 | Overweg reached Kukawa. |
| 29 | departure for Adamawa. |

*June* 11   Mubi.

18   reached the River Benue.

20–24   Yola.

*July* 22   returned to Kukawa.

*September* 11–

*November* 14   expedition to Kanem with Overweg.

*November* 25   left Kukawa on the Mandara expedition.

*December* 1   Dikwa.

23   entered the Musgu country.

## 1852

*February* 1   returned to Kukawa.

*March* 4   left for exploration of Bagirmi.

*May*   imprisoned in Masena by the Sultan of Bagirmi.

*August* 10   returned to Kukawa.

*September* 27   death of Overweg.

*November* 25   departure from Kukawa on Timbuktu expedition.

*December* 16   Muniyo.

25   Zinder.

## 1853

*February* 2–

*March* 21   Katsina.

*April* 3   Wurno.

20–24   Sokoto.

*May* 8   departure from Wurno.

*June* 6   left Gwandu.

20   reached the River Niger.

*September* 7   arrived in Timbuktu.

## 1854

*May* 17   left Timbuktu.

*June* 19   Gao.

*August* 2   recrossed the River Niger.

17   Gwandu.

26   Sokoto.

*August* 30–
  *October* 5   ill in Wurno with dysentery.
*October* 17–
*November* 21   Kano.
*December* 1   meeting with Vogel.
        11   regained Kukawa.
        29   Vogel joined Barth in Kukawa.


## 1855

*January* 20   Vogel left Kukawa for Bauchi.
*Febraury* 20   abortive attempt to leave Bornu.
    *May* 4   final departure from Kukawa.
        20   left Bornu frontier, at Barruwa.
   *June* 11   Bilma.
   *July* 14   Murzuk.
*August* 28   reached Tripoli.
*September*   returned to England.
  *October*   returned to Germany.

## CHAPTER 1
# THE JOURNEY OUT (1849–1850)

'Mr. Richardson was waiting in Paris for despatches,' Barth opens his narrative, 'when Mr. Overweg and I reached Tunis . . . on 15th December, 1849.' There Barth engaged a servant, Mohammed Belal, the son of a freed slave from Gobir; Overweg waited till Tripoli, where he took on Ibrahim, a liberated Bagirmi boy who had travelled extensively in Mandara and who, besides speaking Kanuri, had a good knowledge of the Mindif-Mora area. Subsequently Ibrahim refused to work with Mohammed Belal, 'who was a very clever but unscrupulous and haughty fellow, and bore the character of a libertine', and, urged on by his wives' demand for a divorce if he intended to leave them in Tripoli, he withdrew his services.

New Year's Eve 1849 was spent in a camp a day's march out of Tunis.

I shall never forget this, the last night of the year 1849, which opened to us a new era with many ordeals, and by our endurance of which we were to render ourselves worthy of success. There were, besides ourselves, our servants, and our two muleteers, four horsemen of the Bey, and three natives from Jirbi. When midnight came my fellow traveller and I saluted the new year with enthusiasm, and with a cordial shake of the hand wished each other joy. Our Mohammedan companions were greatly pleased when they were informed of the reason of our congratulating each other, and wished us all possible success for the new year. We had also reason to be pleased with them; for by their not inharmonious songs they relieved the fatigue of a long, sleepless, and excessively cold night.

They embarked at Sfax on 5 January for a tedious journey across the bay, regarded by Barth as 'on the whole a very fair trial in the beginning of an undertaking the success of which was mainly dependent upon patience and resolute endurance'. At Tripoli, which they reached on 18 January, they were surprised to find that Richardson had not yet arrived from Malta, but they were welcomed by Mr. Crowe, the Consul-General, and Mr. Reade,[1] the vice-consul. Later they met another vice-consul, one of the celebrated consular family of Warringtons:

Mr. F. Warrington is perhaps the most amiable possible specimen of an Arabianized European. To this gentleman, whose zeal in the objects of the expedition was beyond all praise, I must be allowed to pay my tribute as a friend. By the charm of friendship he certainly contributed his share to my success.

While awaiting the arrival of their leader with the boat, scientific instruments, tents and arms, Barth and Overweg, with character-istic energy, decided to make a preliminary expedition into the mountains round Tripoli. This section of Barth's diary is particularly rich in sketches.

At last, on 24 March, 'seated in solemn state upon our camels', the mission set forth in earnest. They pitched their tents a few miles out in the desert,

in order that we might be duly seasoned for our long journey. I would advise every traveller who would calculate upon all means of ensuring success to adopt a similar course. A few days' stay in his tent will familiarise him with the little store which is henceforward to form his principal, if not his only resource, and will enable him to bear the heat of the sun with ease.

Mr. Warrington prepared a farewell dinner-party, 'an immense bowl of kuskus, seasoned in the most savoury manner; and our whole party indulged in the remembrance of this delicate dish as a luxury beyond reach'.

They parted from Mr. Warrington on 4 April. The trans-Saharan stage of their great expedition had now begun.

With the background thus set, I shall in this chapter sketch in but the barest outline the trials of the passage through the Hamada el Homra,[2] 'the fearful burning plain', and across the Sahara proper, taking up in the subsequent chapters the detailed movements of the mission from the time of its entry, in January 1851, into that part of the Western Sudan that is now Nigeria. This is not to infer

[1] At the time of writing (autumn 1959), three original letters from Barth to Reade have just come on the market. They were written on 4 September 1855 (Malta); 19 October 1861 (Berlin); and 6 November 1861 (Berlin). I have not come across any previous reference to the existence of these MS letters.

[2] Alan Houghton Brodrick calls it 'a petrified sea rippled with murderous lines of stones': *Mirage of Africa*, 1953, p. 38.

that the Saharan episodes are of no account; on the contrary, they
are of intense interest, both intrinsically and as a background to the
history of the expedition. But limitations of space make such a
summary necessary here.

The journey was slow—the camels settled down to a rate of half a
mile in twelve minutes—and Barth was continuously breaking away
from the caravan to climb a rocky outcrop, to visit an old Roman
monument, or to make a careful sketch and measurement of the
abundant North African ruins. Typical entries of this period are:
'While our people were busily employed pitching the tents, I went
at once to examine a monument which, for the last hour of our
march, had stood as a landmark ahead of us'; and 'I could not
withstand the temptation of ascending, in the afternoon, a projecting
eminence'. But the Sahara does not yield lightly to conquest: after
a climb at the end of the desert crossing Barth confessed that 'I was
quite exhausted when I reached the tent, but a cup of strong coffee
soon restored me. However, I never afterwards on my whole
journey felt strong enough to ascend a mountain of moderate
elevation.'

Overweg, too, was seldom idle, since, apart from his own geological interests, the distinction between a doctor of philosophy and
a doctor of medicine was too fine a nuance for the peoples of the
desert.

His practice was rather of a remarkable kind, for he used
generally to treat his patients, not according to the character
of their sickness, but according to the days of the week on
which they came. Thus he had one day of calomel, another of
Dover's powder, one of Epsom salts, one of magnesia, one of
tartar emetic, the two remaining days being devoted to some
other medicines; and it of course sometimes happened that the
man who suffered from diarrhoea got Epsom salts, and he who
required an opening medicine was blessed with a dose of
Dover's powder. Of course, my friend made numerous exceptions to his calendary method of treating disease, whenever
time and circumstances allowed him to study more fully the
state of a patient.

The mission was obliged to spend a month in Murzuk, waiting
for the chiefs of Ghat who were to take the expedition under their
protection—an arrangement whose practicability Barth doubted,
justifiably, as events turned out. Leaving Murzuk on 13 June, they

marched west to Ghat, a region that Barth believed to have been originally inhabited by the Gobir people. They entered the town on 18 July, but not before Barth had very nearly perished in the desert:

This was a *dies ater* for me. Overweg and I had determined to start early in the morning for the remarkable mountain; but we had not been able to obtain from the Tawárek a guide to conduct us from thence to the next well, whither the caravan was to proceed by the direct road. Hatíta and Utaeti having again resisted all our solicitations for a guide, I at length, determined as I was to visit the mountain at any cost, started off in the confidence of being able to make out the well in the direction indicated to me. By ill-luck, our provision of zummíta (a cool and refreshing paste on which we were accustomed to breakfast) was exhausted the day before, so that I was obliged to take with me dry biscuit and dates, the worst possible food in the desert when water is scarce.

But as yet I needed no stimulus, and vigorously pushed my way through the sand-hills, which afforded no very pleasant passage. At last I began to feel fatigued from walking over the sharp-pointed pebbles, as the distance proved to be greater than I had originally imagined; and I did not seem to have got much nearer to the foot of the Enchanted Mountain. In fact it proved that the crest of the mount formed a sort of horseshoe, so that its middle part, for which I had been steering all the time, in order to gain a depression which seemed to afford an easy ascent, was by far the remotest. I therefore changed my course and turned more eastward, but only met with more annoyance, for, ascending the slope which I hoped would soon convey me to the summit, I suddenly came to the steep precipice of a deep ravine, which separated me from the crest.

Being already fatigued, the disappointment, of course, depressed my spirits, and I had to summon all my resolution and energy in order to descend into the ravine and climb the other side. It was now past ten o'clock; the sun began to put forth its full power, and there was not the slightest shade around me. In a state of the utmost exhaustion I at length reached the narrow pinnacled crest, which was only a few feet broad, and exhibited neither inscriptions nor sculptures. I had a fine prospect towards the S.W. and N.E.; but I looked around in vain for any traces of our caravan. Though exposed to the full rays of the sun, I lay down on my high barbacan to seek repose; but my dry biscuit or a date was quite unpalatable, and being anxious about my little provision of water, I could only sip an insufficient draught from my small water-skin.

As the day advanced I got anxious lest our little band, thinking that I was already in advance, might continue their march in the afternoon, and, in spite of my weakness, determined to try to reach the encampment. I therefore descended the ravine, in order to follow its course, which, according to Hatíta's indications, would lead me in the direction of the well. It was very hot; and being thirsty, I swallowed at once the little water that remained. This was about noon; and I soon found that the draught of mere water, taken upon an empty stomach, had not at all restored my strength.

At length I reached the bottom of the valley. Hatíta had always talked as if they were to encamp at no great distance from the mountain; yet, as far as I could strain my view, no living being was to be seen. At length I became puzzled as to my direction, and, hurrying on as fast as my failing strength would allow, I ascended a mound crowned with an ethel-bush, and fired my pistols; but I waited in vain for an answer: a strong east wind was blowing dead against me. Reflecting a moment on my situation, I then crossed the small sand-hills, and ascending another mound, fired again. Convinced that there could be nobody in this direction, at least at a moderate distance, I bethought myself that our party might be still behind, and, very unluckily, I kept more directly eastward.

The valley was here very richly overgrown with sebót; and to my great delight I saw at a distance some small huts attached to branches of the ethel-tree, covered on the top with sebót, and open in front. With joy in my heart I hastened on towards them, but found them empty; and not a living being was to be seen, nor was there a drop of water to be got.

My strength being now exhausted, I sat down on the naked

plain, with a full view before me of the whole breadth of the wadi, and with some confidence expected the caravan. I even thought, for a moment, that I beheld a string of camels passing in the distance. But it was an illusion; and when the sun was about to set, not being able to muster strength enough to walk a few paces without sitting down, I had only to choose for my night's quarters between the deserted huts and an ethel-tree which I saw at a little distance. I chose the latter, as being on a more elevated spot, and therefore scrambled to the tree, which was of a respectable old age, with thick tall branches, but almost leafless. It was my intention to light a fire, which promised almost certain deliverance; but I could not muster sufficient strength to gather a little wood. I was broken down and in a feverish state.

Having lain down for an hour or two, after it became quite dark I arose from the ground, and, looking around me, descried to my great joy a large fire S.W. down the valley, and, hoping that it might be that of my companions, I fired a pistol, as the only means of communicating with them, and listened as the sound rolled along, feeling sure that it would reach their ears; but no answer was returned. All remained silent. Still I saw the flame rising towards the sky, and telling where deliverance was to be found, without my being able to avail myself of the signal. Having waited long in vain, I fired a second time — yet no answer. I lay down in resignation, committing my life to the care of the Merciful One; but it was in vain that I tried to sleep, and, restless and in a high fever, I tossed about on the ground, looking with anxiety and fear for the dawn of the next day.

At length the long night wore away, and dawn was drawing nigh. All was repose and silence; and I was sure I could not choose a better time for trying to inform my friends, by signal, of my whereabouts. I therefore collected all my strength, loaded my pistol with a heavy charge, and fired — once — twice. I thought the sound ought to awaken the dead from their tombs, so powerfully did it reverberate from the opposite range and roll along the wadi; yet no answer. I was at a loss to account for the great distance apparently separating me from my companions, who seemed not to have heard my firing.

The sun that I had half longed for, half looked forward to with terror, at last rose. My condition, as the heat went on increasing, became more dreadful; and I crawled around, changing every moment my position, in order to enjoy the little shade afforded by the leafless branches of the tree. About noon there was of course scarcely a spot of shade left — only enough for my head — and I suffered greatly from the pangs of thirst, although I sucked a little of my blood till I became senseless, and fell into a sort of delirium, from which I only recovered when the sun went down behind the mountains. I then regained some consciousness, and crawled out of the shade of the tree, throwing a melancholy glance over the plain, when suddenly I heard the cry of a camel. It was the most delightful music I ever heard in my life; and raising myself a little from the ground, I saw a mounted Tarki passing at some distance from me, and looking eagerly around. He had found my footsteps in the sandy ground, and losing them again on the pebbles, was anxiously seeking traces of the direction I had taken. I opened my parched mouth, and crying, as loud as my faint strength allowed, 'áman, áman' (water, water), I was rejoiced to get for answer 'íwah! íwah!' and in a few moments he sat at my side, washing and sprinkling my head, while I broke out involuntarily into an uninterrupted strain of 'el hamdu lilláhi! el hamdu lilláhi!'

Having thus first refreshed me, and then allowed me a draught which, however, I was not able to enjoy, my throat being so dry, and my fever still continuing, my deliverer, whose name was Musa, placed me upon his camel, mounted himself in front of me, and brought me to the tents. They were a good way off. The joy of meeting again, after I had been already despaired of, was great; and I had to express my sincere thanks to my companions, who had given themselves so much trouble to find me. But I could speak but little at first, and could scarcely eat anything for the next three days, after which I gradually recovered my strength. It is, indeed, very remarkable how quickly the strength of a European is broken in these climes, if for a single day he be prevented from taking his usual food.

By mid-August the expedition had reached 'the Marárraba, the "half-way" between Ghát and Aïr, a place regarded with a kind of religious awe by the natives, who in passing place each a stone upon the mighty granite blocks which mark the spot'. A few days later one of the caravan made an assault on Barth, trying to throw him to the ground and testing whether he could still reach the pistols that he wore in his belt. This was followed by a grave threat to the lives of all three of them by their Tuareg escort:

The whole affair had a very solemn appearance from the beginning; and it was apparent that this time there were really other motives in view besides that of robbing us. Some of our companions evidently thought that here, at such a distance from our homes and our brethren in faith, we might yield to a more serious attack upon our religion, and so far were sincerely interested in the success of the proceeding; but whether they had any accurate idea of the fate that awaited us, whether we should retain our property and be allowed to proceed, I cannot say. But it is probable that the fanatics thought little of our future destiny; and it is absurd to imagine that, if we had changed our religion as we would a suit of clothes, we should have thereby escaped absolute ruin.

Our own people were so firmly convinced that, as we stoutly refused to change our religion, though only for a day or two, we should immediately suffer death, that our servant Mohammed, as well as Mukni, requested us most urgently to testify, in writing, that they were innocent of our blood. Mr. Richardson himself was far from being sure that the sheikhs did not mean exactly what they said. Our servants, and the chiefs of the caravan, had left us with the plain declaration that nothing less than certain death awaited us; and we were sitting silently in the tent, with the inspiring consciousness of going to our fate in a manner worthy alike of our religion and of the nation in whose name we were travelling among these barbarous tribes, when Mr. Richardson interrupted the silence which prevailed,

with these words:—'Let us talk a little. We must die; what is
the use of sitting so mute?' For some minutes death seemed
really to hover over our heads; but the awful moment passed by.
We had been discussing Mr. Richardson's last propositions for
an attempt to escape with our lives, when, as a forerunner of
the official messenger, the benevolent and kind-hearted Slimán
rushed into our tent, and with the most sincere sympathy
stammered out the few words, ' You are not to die'.

Leaving Richardson and Overweg at Tintellust, Barth coura-
geously set out on his

long-wished for excursion to A'gades. For although at that time
I was not aware of the whole extent of interest attaching to that
place, it had nevertheless been to me a point of the strongest
attraction. For what can be more interesting than a considerable town, said to have been once as large as Tunis, situated in
the midst of lawless tribes, on the border of the desert and of
the fertile tracts of an almost unknown continent established
there from ancient times, and protected as a place of rendez-
vous and commerce between nations of the most different
character, and having the most various wants. It is by mere
accident that this town has not attracted as much interest in
Europe as her sister town, Timbúktu.

Unperturbed by a disastrous attempt at riding a bullock, Barth
reached Agades without further mishap and accomplished a
brilliant piece of geographical discovery. His detailed and observant
description of Agades is a masterpiece, suggestive of the fine descriptive writing that may be anticipated in the rest of his diary.

The caravan continued at the end of October.

'I felt as if I had enjoyed a glimpse of a totally different world,
a new region of life, many relations of which were as yet obscure
to me'. Barth's excitement was infectious: 'in the enthusiasm
awakened by the thought of going southward, I with all my heart
joined in the exclamation sé fataúchi sé Kanó, "no rest before Kanó!"'

There was another delay at Tinteggana, where they had to wait
for the Bilma salt-caravan in whose company it was thought prudent
to travel on to Kano; but 'at length the day broke when we were
to move on and get nearer the longed-for object of our journey'.

The going now became harder. Christmas Eve was cheerless,
New Year's Eve brought little comfort: 'all our enjoyment of the
last evening of the year centred in an extra dish of two ostrich-eggs.'
But the Hamada was behind them and 'the land of promise' lay
ahead. Now they glimpsed the first cornfields of Damergum, the
first Nigerian-type hut, 'that peculiar style of architecture which,
with some more or less important varieties, extends through the
whole of Central Africa', the first corn-bins and the first ant-hill,
all signs of a different region of the Sudan.

This was certainly an important stage in our journey. For
although we had before seen a few small patches of garden-
fields, where corn was produced (as in Selúfiet, A'uderas, and
other favoured places), yet they were on so small a scale as to
be incapable of sustaining even a small fraction of the population; but here we had at length reached those fertile regions of
Central Africa, which are not only able to sustain their own
population, but even to export to foreign countries. My heart
gladdened at this sight, and I felt thankful to Providence that
our endeavours had been so far crowned with success; for here
a more promising field for our labours was opened, which might
become of the utmost importance in the future history of
mankind.

It was past four o'clock in the afternoon when we encamped
upon an open stubble-field, and we were greatly cheered at
observing here the first specimen of industry in a good sense,
—for of industry in a bad sense the Tagáma had already given
us some proof. As soon as we were dismounted, two muscular
blacks, girded with leather aprons round their loins, came
bounding forward, and in an instant cleared the whole open
space around us, while in a few minutes several people, male
and female, followed, offering a variety of things for sale, such
as millet, beans (of two sorts), and those cakes called dodówa,
which were duly appreciated by the late Captain Clapperton
for the excellent soup made of them. Of their preparation I
shall speak when we meet the first tree of that species, the
dorówa — the name of the cake and that of the tree being
distinguished by the change of a consonant. The cakes obtained
here, however, as I afterwards learned, were of a most inferior

and spurious character—of that kind called 'dodówa-n-bósso' in Háusa, and in some districts 'yákwa'. We felt here the benefit of civilization in a most palpable way, by getting most excellent chicken-broth for our supper. Our servants, indeed, were cooking the whole night.

On 10 January 1851, at Tagelel, they decided to proceed singly, 'on account of the low state of our finances, in order to try what each of us might be able to accomplish single-handed and without ostentation, till new supplies should arrive from home'. Barth, not without 'some sinister foreboding', said good-bye to Richardson, arranging to meet him in Kukawa on the first of April. Three days later he bade farewell to Overweg, who was to travel via Gobir and Maradi.

'I now went on alone, but felt not at all depressed by solitude, as I had been accustomed from my youth to wander about by myself among strange people.' Dinner that first night alone was disappointing, but on the next day 'I might have fancied myself a prince; for I had a splendid supper, consisting of a fowl or two, while a solitary maimólo cheered me with a performance on his simple three-stringed instrument, which, however monotonous, was still expressive of much feeling, and accompanied with a song in my praise.'

Barth could at last afford to indulge in the relaxation of contentment and pleasurable anticipation: he had reached Hausaland.

## CHAPTER 2

# KATSINA (1851)

## ENTRY INTO KATSINA

*January* 21. We started, with general enthusiasm, at an early
hour; and the people of our troop seeing the fires of the other
divisions of the salt-caravan in front of us still burning, jeered at
their laziness, till at length, on approaching within a short distance of the fires, we found that the other people had set out
long before, leaving their fires burning. A poor woman, carrying
a load on her head, and leading a pair of goats, had attached
herself to our party in Gazáwa; and though she had lost her
goats in the bustle of the previous afternoon, she continued her
journey cheerfully and with resignation.

After five hours' march the whole caravan was suddenly
brought to a stand for some time, the cause of which was a ditch
of considerable magnitude, dug right across the path, and
leaving only a narrow passage, the beginning of a small path
which wound along through thick thorny underwood. This,
together with the ditch, formed a sort of outer defence for the
cultivated fields and the pasture-grounds of Kátsena, against
any sudden inroad. Having passed another projecting mass of
granite rock, we passed two small villages on our left, called
Túlla and Takumáku, from whence the inhabitants came out
to salute us. We encamped at length in a large stubble-field,
beyond some kitchen-gardens, where pumpkins (dúmma) were
planted, two miles N.E. from the town of Kátsena. While
we were pitching my tent, which was the only one in the whole
encampment, the sultan or governor of Kátsena came out with
a numerous retinue of horsemen, all well dressed and mounted;

and having learnt from Elaíji that I was a Christian traveller
belonging to a mission (a fact, however, which he knew long
before), he sent me soon afterwards a ram and two large
calabashes or dúmmas filled with honey — an honour which
was rather disagreeable to me than otherwise, as it placed me
under the necessity of making the governor a considerable
present in return. I had no article of value with me; and I began
to feel some unpleasant foreboding of future difficulties.

*January* 22. The governor, who spends a great deal of his time
in a country-house which he has recently built outside the town,
about noon held a sort of review of several hundred horsemen,
whose horses, in general, were in excellent condition. They
were armed with a straight sword hanging on the left, a long
heavy spear for thrusting, and a shield, either of the same
description as that of the Tawárek, of oblong shape, made of
the hide of the large antelope (*Leucoryx*), or else of bullock's
or elephant's hide, and forming an immense circular disk of
about five feet in diameter; some of them wore also the dagger
at the left arm, while I counted not more than four or five
muskets. Their dress was picturesque, and not too flowing for
warlike purposes, the large shirt, or shirts (for they generally
wear two), being fastened round the breast with an Egyptian
shawl with a red border; and even those who were dressed in
a bernús had it wound round their breast. Most of them wore
black ' ráwani ', or shawls, round their faces, a custom which
the Féllani of Háusa have adopted from the Tawárek merely on
account of its looking warlike; for they have no superstitious
reason for covering the mouth. The harness of the horses was all
of Háusa manufacture, the saddles very different from those of
the Tawárek (which seem to be identical with the old Arab
saddles). The stirrups formed a very peculiar kind of medium
between the large unwieldy stirrups of the modern Arab and
the small ones of Tawárek and Europeans, the sole of the
stirrup being long, but turned down at both ends, while it is so
narrow that the rider can only thrust the naked foot into it.

A troop of eight mounted royal musicians ('masukídda-n-
serkí'), who had been playing the whole day before the several

divisions of the ' aïri ', came likewise to my tent in the course
of the afternoon, and gratified my ears with a performance on
their various instruments. There was the drum, or 'ganga',
very much like our own instrument of that kind, and of about
the same size as the common regimental drum; the long wind
instrument, or 'pampámme'; a shorter one, a sort of flute, or
' elgaita '; a sort of double tambourine, or 'kalángo'; a simple
tympanum, or 'kóso'; a sort of double Egyptian darabúka,
called 'jójo', and a small horn, or 'kafó'. The most common
among them is the 'jójo', which in Háusa is the chief instrument made use of in an expedition, and, if accompanied by the
voice, is not disagreeable. With these various instruments the
well-mounted horsemen made a pretty good noise; but it was
neither harmonious nor characteristic — to all this pompous
imitative music I prefer a few strains with natural feeling by a
solitary maimólo. I was obliged to reward my entertainers with
a large quantity of cloves, as I had scarcely anything else left.

I was rather astonished to hear that the A'sbenáwa do not
pay passage-money to the governor according to the number
of their camels, but that every freeman among them makes him
a present of one kántu of salt. For every beast of burden, be it
pack-ox or donkey, five hundred kurdí are generally paid.

## AUDIENCE WITH THE EMIR OF KATSINA

*January* 23. Having assorted such a present as I could afford, I
protested once more to Elaíji that, my other luggage having
gone on in advance to Kanó, I had but very little to offer the
governor.

I went about noon with my protector and a great number of
A'sbenáwa to offer the governor my compliments and my
present. Sitting down under a tree at a considerable distance
from the spot where he himself was seated, we waited a little,
till we should be called into his presence, when his brother, who
held the office of ghaladíma, came to us — a man of immense
corpulency, resembling a eunuch. Indeed nothing but the cut
of his face, his aquiline nose, and rather light colour, and the

little goatlike beard which ornamented his chin, could expose
him to the suspicion of being a Púllo or Ba-Féllanchi.

Mohammed Béllo Yeríma, the eldest son of the former well-
known governor Mállem Ghomáro was seated under a wide-
spreading and luxuriant tamarind-tree, dressed simply in a
large white shirt with a black ráwani round his face. The
A'sbenáwa, who formed a large semicircle around him, were
dressed most gaudily. Stepping into the opening of the semicircle, I saluted the governor, telling him that as I and my
companions had lost, on the border of A'sben, almost all the
valuable property we had brought with us, and as the few
things left to me had gone on to Kanó, he ought to excuse me
for being unable at the present moment to offer him a present
worthy of his high position, that it was my desire to go on
without delay to Kanó, in order to settle my affairs, and to
proceed to Bórnu, where we expected to receive fresh supplies,
after which one of our party certainly would go to Sókoto, in
order to pay our respects to the Emír el Múmenín. The
governor answered my address with much apparent kindness,
telling me that I was now in his 'imána', or under his protection, and that he had no other purpose but to do what would
be conducive to my advantage. He then asked the news of my
companions, though he knew all about them, and did not
appear to take the least offence at Mr. Overweg's going to
Marádi, although the people and the ruler of that place were
his most inveterate enemies. But things must not be looked
upon here as they would be in Europe; for here people are
accustomed to see strangers from the north pay visits to all sorts
of princes, whatever may be their policy. However, while he
spoke in rather friendly terms to me, and while my presents
were received thankfully by the servants, he declared to the
people who were sitting near him, that as the ruler of Bórnu had
laid hold of one of my companions, and that of Marádi of the
other, he should be a fool if he were to let me pass out of his
hands. I therefore took leave of him with no very light heart.

My present consisted of two fine red caps, a piece of printed
calico which I had bought in Múrzuk for four Spanish dollars,

but which was of a pattern not much liked in Sudán, an English razor and scissors, one pound of cloves, another of frankincense, a piece of fine soap, and a packet of English needles. Though it certainly was not a very brilliant present, yet, considering that I did not want anything from him, it was quite enough; but the fact was, that he wanted something more from me, and therefore it was not sufficient.

## DETAINED IN KATSINA

The Emir of Katsina prevented Barth from leaving with the Kano-bound caravan and ordered him to move from his tent outside the walls into the heart of the city proper.

*January* 24. The immense mass of the wall, measuring in its lower part not less than thirty feet, and its wide circumference, made a deep impression upon me. The town (if town it may be called) presented a most cheerful rural scene, with its detached light cottages, and its stubble-fields shaded with a variety of fine trees; but I suspect that this ground was not entirely covered with dwellings even during the most glorious period of Kátsena. We travelled a mile and a half before we reached the 'zínsere', a small dwelling used by the governor as a place of audience — on account, as it seems, of a splendid wide-spreading fig-tree growing close to it, and forming a thick shady canopy sufficient for a large number of people.

I, however, was conducted to the other side of the building, where a quadrangular chamber projects from the half-decayed wall, and had there to wait a long time, till the governor came into town from his new country-seat. Having at last arrived, he called me, and, thanking me for remaining with him, he promised that I should be well treated as his guest, and that without delay a house should be placed at my disposal. He was a man of middle age, and had much in his manners and features which made him resemble an actor; and such he really is, and was still more so in his younger days.

Taking leave of him for the present, I followed Bel-Ghét

to my quarters; but we had still a good march to make, first through detached dwellings of clay, then leaving the immense palace of the governor on our left, and entering what may be strictly called the town, with connected dwellings. Here I was lodged in a small house opposite the spacious dwelling of Bel-Ghét; and though on first entering I found it almost insupportable, I soon succeeded in making myself tolerably comfortable in a clean room neatly arranged. It seemed to have once formed the snug seat for a well-furnished harím; at least the dark passages leading to the interior could not be penetrated by a stranger's eye. We had scarcely taken possession of our quarters, when the governor sent me a ram and two oxloads of corn — one of 'dáwa' and the other of 'géro'. But instead of feeling satisfied with this abundant provision, we were quite horrified at it, as I with my three people might have subsisted a whole year on the corn sent us; and we began to have uneasy forebodings of a long detention. Indeed we suspected, and were confirmed in our suspicion by the statements of several people, that it was the governor's real intention to forward me directly to Sókoto.

## FAREWELL TO THE EMIR

After a week of royal demands and presents, Barth's release from detention was negotiated and he was bidden to the palace to take his leave.

*January* 29. Béllo received me in his private apartment, and detained me for full two hours while I gave him complete information about the use of the medicines. He wanted, besides, two things from me, which I could not favour him with—things of very different character, and the most desired by all the princes of Negroland. One of these was a 'mágani-n-algúwa' (a medicine to increase his conjugal vigour); the other, some rockets, as a 'mágani-n-yáki' (a medicine of war), in order to frighten his enemies.

Not being able to comply with these two modest wishes of his, I had great difficulty in convincing him of my good will; and

he remained incredulous to my protestations that we had
intentionally not taken such things as rockets with us, as we
were afraid that if we gave such a thing to one prince, his
neighbour might become fiercely hostile to us. But he remarked
that he would keep such a gift a secret. I was very glad he
did not say a word more about the pistols; but in order to give
me a proof that he knew how to value fine things, he showed me
the scissors and razor which I had given him the other day, for
which he had got a sheath made, and wore them constantly at
his left side. He then told me he would make me a present of an
'abi-n-háwa' (something to mount upon), intimating already
by this expression that it would not be a first-rate horse, as I
had not complied with his heart's desire, but that it would be
furnished with saddle and harness, and that besides he would
send me a large 'hákkori-n-gíwa' (an elephant's tooth) to
Kanó. This latter offer I declined, saying that, though my
means were very small at present, I did not like to turn merchant. He reminded me then of my promise to return; and we
parted the best of friends. Notwithstanding the injustice of
every kind which he daily commits, he has some sentiment of
honour; and feeling rather ashamed for having given me so
much trouble for nothing, as he was aware that it would
become known to all his fellow-governors, and probably even
to his liege lord, the Emír el Mumenín, he was anxious to
vindicate his reputation. It was from the same motive that he
begged me most urgently not to tell anybody that I had made
him the presents here, adding, that he would afterwards say
that he had received them from me from Kanó.

## HISTORY OF KATSINA

The town, if only half of its immense area were ever tolerably
well inhabited, must certainly have had a population of at least
a hundred thousand souls; for its circuit is between thirteen
and fourteen English miles. At present, when the inhabited
quarter is reduced to the north-western part, and when even
this is mostly deserted there are scarcely seven or eight thousand

people living in it. In former times it was the residence of a
prince, who, though he seems never to have attained to any
remarkable degree of power, and was indeed almost always in
some degree dependent on, or a vassal of, the king of Bórnu,
nevertheless was one of the most wealthy and conspicuous rulers
of Negroland. Every prince at his accession to the throne had
to forward a sort of tribute or present to Birni Ghasréggomo,
the capital of the Bórnu empire, consisting of one hundred
slaves, as a token of his obedience; but this being done, it does
not appear that his sovereign rights were in any way interfered
with. In fact, Kátsena, during the seventeenth and eighteenth

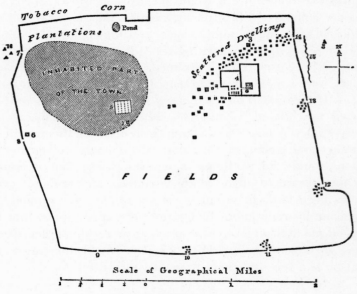

FIG. 2.   The City of Katsina

| | |
|---|---|
| 1. House where I was lodged during my first stay in Kátsena in 1851. | 9. Kofa-n-Koya. |
| 2. House belonging to the quarter Dóka where I was lodged in 1853. | 10. Kofa-n-Gazúbi. |
| | 11. Kofa-n-Káura. |
| 3. The Zénsere. | 12. Kofa-n-Marúsa. |
| 4. Palace of the governor. | 13. Kofa-n-Dúrdu. |
| 5. Market-place. | 14. Kofa-n-Samrí. |
| 6. Old mosque. | 15. A brook formed by a spring. |
| 7. Kofa-n-Gúga. | 16. Former place of encampment of salt caravan. |
| 8. Kofa-n-Yendúkki. | |

centuries of our era, seems to have been the chief city of this part of Negroland, as well in commercial and political importance as in other respects; for here that state of civilisation which had been called forth by contact with the Arabs seems to have reached its highest degree, and as the Háusa language here attained the greatest richness of form and the most refined pronunciation, so also the manners of Kátsena were distinguished by superior politeness from those of the other towns of Háusa.

But this state of things was wholly changed, when, in the very beginning of the present century, in the year 1222 of the Hejra, or 1807 of our era, the Fúlbe, called Féllani by the Háusa, and Felláta by the Bórnu people, raised to the highest pitch of fanaticism by the preaching of the Reformer or Jihádi 'Othmán dan Fódiye, and formed into the religious and political association of the Jemmáá, or, as they pronounce it, Jemmára, succeeded in possessing themselves of this town. However, while Kanó fell ingloriously, and almost without resistance, into the hands of Slimán (the Háusa king El Wáli having escaped to Zária), the struggle for Kátsena was protracted and sanguinary. Indeed Mállem Ghomáro had carried on unrelenting war against the town for seven years, before he at length reduced it by famine; and the distress in the town is said to have been so great that a dead 'ángulú' or vulture (impure food which nobody would touch in time of peace) sold for five hundred kurdí, and a kadángeré or lizard for fifty. But the struggle did not cease here; for the 'Hábe' succeeded once more in expelling the conquerors from the town, without, however, being able to maintain their position, when Mállem Ghomáro returned with a fresh army. Five princes of Kátsena, one after the other, fell in this struggle for religious and national independence; and the Púllo general was not quite secure of his conquest till after the total destruction of the town of Dánkama, when Mágajin Háddedu was slain only four months after his predecessor Mahamúdu had succumbed in Sabóngarí. Even then the new Háusa prince Benóni, who still bore the title of 'serkí-n-Kátsena', did not lay down his arms, but maintained the contest till he likewise was conquered and slain in Túntuma.

From this time the town declined rapidly, and all the principal foreign merchants migrated to Kanó, where they were beyond the reach of this constant struggle; and even the Asbenáwa transferred their salt-market to the latter place, which now became the emporium of this part of Negroland, while Kátsena retained but secondary importance as the seat of a governor. This is indeed to be lamented, as the situation of the town is excellent, and, both on account of its position to the various routes and of its greater salubrity, is far preferable to Kanó. However, as matters stand, unless either the Fúlbe succeed in crushing entirely the independent provinces to the north and north-west (which, in the present weak state of the empire of Sókoto, is far from probable), or till the Goberáwa and Mariadáwa, whose king still bears the title of serkí-n-Kátsena, reconquer this town, it will continue to decline and become more desolate every year. In fact Mohammed Béllo, the present governor, had conceived the design of giving up this immense town altogether, and of founding a new residence of smaller compass in its neighbourhood; but his liege lord, Alíyu, the Emír el Múmenín, would not allow him to do so.

The only inhabited part of the town at present is the north-west quarter, although any one who should omit to take into account the population scattered over the other parts, principally round about the residence of the governor, and the people settled in the hamlets near the gates, would make a great mistake. Here it may be added, that most of the importance which Kátsena has still preserved, in a commercial aspect, is due to its position with respect to Núpe, with which it keeps up a tolerably-lively intercourse, the route from it to that industrious but most unfortunate country being practicable even for camels, while the road from Kanó can only be travelled with horses and asses. Almost all the more considerable native merchants in Kátsena are Wangaráwa (Eastern Mandingoes).

The province of Kátsena was formerly far more extensive than it is at present, but it has been curtailed, in order not to leave its governor too much inducement to make himself independent. Besides, many parts of it, being much exposed to the continual incursions of the independent Háusáwa, have greatly suffered, so that probably the population of the whole province does not now exceed three hundred thousand souls, of whom only about one half seem to pay tribute. Every head of a family has to pay here two thousand five hundred kurdí-n-kassa, or ground-rent, and the whole of the kurdí-n-kassa of the province is estimated by those best acquainted with the affairs of the country at from twenty to thirty millions; a tax of five hundred kurdí is levied also on every slave. The military force of the province consists of two thousand horsemen, and about eight thousand men on foot, most of them archers. Altogether the province of Kátsena is one of the finest parts of Negroland, and being situated just at the water-parting between the basin of the Tsád and that of the Kwára, at a general elevation of from 1200 to 1500 feet, it enjoys the advantage of being at once well watered and well drained, the chains of hills which diversify its surface sending down numerous rapid streams, so that it is less insalubrious than other regions of this continent.

## DEPARTURE FROM KATSINA

*January* 30. I was extremely glad when, after a long delay — for we had been obliged to wait more than an hour for the poor nag presented to me by the governor, — we reached the south-eastern gate of the town, the 'kófa-n-Káura'. It was as if I had just escaped from a prison, and I drew my breath deeply as I inhaled the fresh air outside the wall. I should have carried with me a very unfavourable impression of Kátsena, if it had not been my destiny to visit this place again under more favourable circumstances; and I should have obtained a very false idea of the character of the Fúlbe, if, from the little experience which I had acquired in this place, I had formed a definitive judgment of them.

A little before four o'clock in the afternoon we encamped

close to a village called Shibdáwa, the celebrated town of
Dáura being distant two days' march.

*January* 31.[1] It was a most beautiful morning; and I indulged
in the feeling of unbounded liberty, and in the tranquil enjoyment of the beautiful aspect of God's creation. The country
through which we passed on leaving Shibdáwa, formed one of
the finest landscapes I ever saw in my life. The ground was
pleasantly undulating, covered with a profusion of herbage not
yet entirely dried up by the sun's power; the trees, belonging to
a great variety of species, were not thrown together into an
impenetrable thicket of the forest, but formed into beautiful
groups, exhibiting all the advantage of light and shade. There
was the kaña, with its rich dark-tinged foliage; the kadeña, or
butter-tree, which I here saw for the first time, exhibiting the
freshest and most beautiful green; then the marké, more airy,
and sending out its branches in more irregular shape, with light
groups of foliage; young tamarind-trees rounding off their
thick crown of foliage till it resembled an artificial canopy
spread out for the traveller to repose in its shade, besides the
gámji, the shéria, the sokútso, the turáwa, and many other
species of trees unknown to me; while above them all, tall and
slender górebas unfolded their fan-crowns, just as if to protect
the eye of the delighted wanderer from the rays of the morning
sun, and to allow him to gaze undisturbed on the enchanting
scenery around. Near the village Káshi even the gónda-tree or
*Carica Papaya*, which is so rarely seen in these quarters, enlivened
the scenery. The densely-luxuriant groves seemed to be the
abode only of the feathered tribe, birds of numberless variety
playing and warbling about in the full enjoyment of their
liberty, while the ' serdi ', a large bird with beautiful plumage
of a light-blue colour, especially attracted my attention. Now
and then a herd of cattle was seen dispersed over the rich

[1] This passage is a fine example of the observant interest that Barth took even when
simply riding from village to village. One can almost breathe, with him, the
inspiring freshness of the bush after a spell confined in town. Interestingly
enough, there is a strikingly similar botanical description of trekking in the same
Kano area, given by Lugard in a letter to his wife dated 20 January 1905 and
quoted in Margery Perham, *Lugard*, 1960, II, 218–19.

pasturage-grounds, all of white colour, and the bulls provided with a large fat hump or ' tózo ' hanging down on one side. But in this delightful spectacle objects of destruction also were not wanting, the poisonous plant 'túmnia' starting forth everywhere.

Cotton and karásia fields interrupted the parklike scenery; and near Kámri, a small place surrounded with a low clay wall, we were delighted with the view of a green patch of low ground laid out into beds, and, with the help of a number of drawbeams, 'khattatír', or 'lámbuna', producing wheat and onions. This ground too is only worked with the gélma and the fertáña or small hoe.

*February* 1. After a march of about two miles and a half, over clayey ground greatly broken up by the rains, we reached the N.W. corner of the considerable town Kusáda, and continued along its western wall, where a group of very tall and majestic rimis (*Bombax* or *Eriodendron Guineense*), though at present leafless, formed a most conspicuous object. It is very singular and highly characteristic, that this tree (the bentang-tree of Mungo Park) generally grows near the principal gate of the large towns in Háusa, while otherwise it is not frequent, at least not the large full-grown specimens; and it is not improbable that the natives purposely planted them in those places as a kind of waymark— or perhaps it may be a remnant of their pagan customs, this tree being deemed holy by several pagan tribes. It is almost incredible at what an immense distance these stupendous trees, the tallest of the vegetable kingdom, may be seen.

Kusáda is a town of importance, and is very little less than Gazáwa, though not so thickly inhabited; the wall of the town is in tolerably good repair, and the interior is rich in trees, making it look very cheerful and comfortable. Most of the huts consist of clay walls, with a thatched roof, which is certainly the mode of architecture best adapted to the climate and the whole nature of the country.

When leaving the south side of this town we were joined by a troop of women very heavily-laden, each carrying upon the head from six to ten enormous calabashes filled with various articles:

but they did not prove to be agreeable company; for not being able to walk steadily for any length of time with their loads, they stopped every few minutes, and then went on at a running pace, till they were obliged again to halt, so that they came frequently into collision either with my camel or with the bullock. It is really incredible what loads the native women of Negroland can carry on their heads, but I think no other tribe is equal in this respect to the Tápua or Nyffáwa.

The industry of the natives was also well represented; for soon after we had met a troop of men carrying home loads of indigo-plants, in order to prepare them in their simple way, we passed over extensive tobacco-fields, which had very nearly reached maturity. Rich aromatic bushes were growing everywhere in the fields, affording most nourishing food for bees, for which purpose hives, formed of thick hollow logs, were fastened to the branches of the colossal kúka-trees.

## CHAPTER 3

# KANO (1851)

## ENTRY INTO KANO

*February* 2. Early the next morning we started with an enthusiastic impulse, in order to reach before night the celebrated emporium of Central Negroland. Kanó, indeed, is a name which excites enthusiasm in every traveller in these regions, from whatever quarter he may come, but principally if he arrives from the north. We thus started in the twilight, passing in the bush some herds of cattle remaining out in the pasture-grounds, and meeting several troops of travellers, which made us fancy the capital to be nearer than it really was. We listened to the tales of our comely and cheerful companion, the 'babá-n-báwa' of Tágelel, who detailed to us the wonders of this African London, Birmingham, and Manchester — the vastness of the town, the palace and retinue of the governor, the immense multitudes assembled every day in its market-place, the splendour and richness of the merchandise exposed there for sale, the various delicacies of the table, the beauty and gracefulness of its ladies. At times my fiery Tunisian mulatto shouted out from mere anticipation of the pleasures which awaited him.

Keeping steadily along, we reached, after about five miles, the very considerable town of Béchi, the well-kept high clay walls of which started forth suddenly from a most luxuriant mass of vegetation, where we saw again the beautifully-feathered serdi fluttering about from branch to branch.

The town is very remarkable, as exhibiting the peculiar circumstances of the social state in this country; for it belongs partly to the Tawárek tribe of the Itísan, whose búgaje or serfs — properly half-castes, born of free mothers, but slaves from the father's side — live here, cultivating for their lords the fields around the town. Thus we see Tawárek everywhere, not only as occasional merchants, but even as settlers and proprietors. The town has but one gate; and a great many of the houses are of the kind described above. Beyond the town the country becomes less cultivated, and is mostly covered with the wild gónda-bush, which bears a most delicious fruit, richly deserving to be called the cream-apple. I suspected it for some time to be identical with the custard-apple; but I afterwards assured myself that it is not. I call the attention of every African traveller to this fruit; which affords the greatest relief after a long day's journey.

We accordingly pressed on with our varied little caravan, consisting of a very lean black horse, covered with coarse wool-like hair, worth four dollars, or perhaps less; a mare, scarcely worth more in its present condition; a camel, my faithful Bú-Séfi, evidently the most respectable four-footed member of the troop, carrying a very awkward load, representing my whole travelling household, with writing-table and bedding-boards; a sumpter-ox, heavily laden; then the four human bipeds to match, viz. one half-barbarized European, one half-civilised Góberáwi Tunisian mulatto, a young lean Tébu lad, and my stout, sturdy, and grave overseer from Tágelel. As we then entered some fields of sesamum, or ' nóme ' (quite a new sight for me in this country, but which was soon to become of very common occurrence), Gajére descried in the distance between the trees the top of the hill Dalá, and we all strained our eyes to get a first glimpse of this hill, which is the real landmark of Kanó.

A little while afterwards we saw the first single date-palm, a tree also most characteristic of Kanó; and now, the country becoming clear, we obtained a full sight of both the hills, Dalá and Kógo-n-dútsi, which rise from the flat level of the plain; but nothing was as yet visible of the town, and we had but faint hopes of reaching it before sunset. However, we went on, though a little disheartened, as we had some foreboding that we should incur the displeasure of the governor; and passing through the gate, in front of which part of the aïri were encamped, without stopping, as if we were natives of the country, went on across the open fields. It took us forty minutes to reach the house of Báwu from the gate, though this lies near the very outskirts of Dalá, the northernmost quarter of the town.

It was quite dark, and we had some trouble in taking possession of the quarters assigned to us by our host.

Kanó had been sounding in my ears now for more than a year; it had been one of the great objects of our journey as the central point of commerce, as a great storehouse of information, and as the point whence more distant regions might be most successfully attempted. At length, after nearly a year's exertions, I had reached it.

Kanó for us was a station of importance not only from a scientific, but also from an economical point of view. Instead of being provided with ready cash, we had received in Múrzuk, on account of the British government, merchandise which, we had been assured, would not only be safer than money, but would also prove more advantageous for us. In consequence of the heavy extortions to which we were subjected on the road to Aïr, and of our long delay in that country, we had been deprived of the small articles which we carried for barter, so that we were entirely thrown upon the merchandise which we had forwarded in advance from Tintéggana; and I for my part, on my arrival in Kanó, had to liquidate a debt of not less than 112,300 kurdí: viz. 55,000 for the carriage of this very merchandise from Tintéggana to Kanó; 8300 as my share of the presents or passage-money given on the road; 18,000 to Gajére, as hire for the mare and bullock; and 31,000 to a man of the name of Háj el Dáwaki, on account of Abú-Bakr el Wákhshi, for the articles bought from him in Kátsena, in order to satisfy the governor of that place. Besides, I was aware that I had to make a considerable present to the governor of Kanó; and I was most desirous to discharge Mohammed e' Túnsi, whom I had discovered to be utterly useless in these countries, and who, besides his insupportable insolence, might bring me into trouble by his inconsiderate and frivolous conduct.

These were material calls upon my encumbered property. On my mind, too, there were claims of a not less serious character; for, from my very outset from Europe, I had steadily fixed my eyes upon that Eastern branch of the Kwára, or so called Niger, which Laird, Allen and Oldfield had navigated for the distance of some eighty miles, and which the former (although he himself did not penetrate further than Fánda) had, with reasons decisive in my eyes, and which could not be overthrown in my opinion by Captain William Allen's ingenious but fanciful hypothesis, concluded to have no communication whatever with Lake Tsád, but to proceed from another and very different quarter.

I had therefore cherished the hope, that I should be capable of penetrating from Kanó in the direction of 'Adamáwa, a country wherein I was sure that the question respecting the course of the river would be decided; but obviously such an undertaking could not be engaged in without pecuniary means, and all therefore depended on my success in selling advantageously the merchandise with which I was provided.

For all these reasons, nothing could be more disagreeable and disheartening to me, though I was not quite unprepared for it, than the information which I received the very evening of my arrival in Kanó, that the price of merchandise such as I had was very low.

## AUDIENCE WITH THE EMIR OF KANO

*February* 18. Being lodged in dark, uncomfortable and cheerless quarters, which I was forbidden to leave before the governor had seen me, destitute of a single farthing in cash, while I was daily called upon and pestered by my numerous creditors, and laughed at on account of my poverty by an insolent servant, my readers may fancy that my situation in the great far-famed entrepôt of Central Africa, the name of which had excited my imagination for so long a time, was far from agreeable. Partly

from anxiety, partly from want of exercise, in the course of a
few days I had a very severe attack of fever, which reduced me
to a state of great weakness. Fortunately, however, I mustered
sufficient strength to avail myself of a summons which called
me at length into the presence of the governor, on the 18th of
February; and by sacrificing what few things remained to me,
I paved the road for my further proceedings, while the degree of
exertion which was necessary to undergo the fatigue of the visit
carried me over my weakness, and restored me gradually to
health. The distances in Kanó, though less than those of
London, are very great; and the ceremonies to be gone through
are scarcely less tedious than those at any European court.

Clothing myself as warmly as possible in my Tunisian dress,
and wearing over it a white tobe and a white bernús, I mounted
my poor black nag.

Passing through the market-place, which had only begun to
collect its crowds, and crossing the narrow neck of land which
divides the characteristic pool 'Jákara', we entered the quarters
of the ruling race, the Fúlbe or Féllani, where conical huts of
thatchwork, and the gónda-tree, are prevalent, and where most
beautiful and lively pictures of nature meet the eye on all sides.
Thus we proceeded, first to the house of the gadó (the Lord of
the Treasury), who had already called several times at my
house, and acted as the mediator between me and the governor.

His house was a most interesting specimen of the domestic
arrangements of the Fúlbe, who, however civilized they may
have become, do not disown their original character as
'berroróji', or nomadic cattle-breeders. His courtyard, though
in the middle of the town, looked like a farm-yard, and could
not be conscientiously commended for its cleanliness. Having
with difficulty found a small spot to sit down upon without
much danger of soiling our clothes, we had to wait patiently till
his Excellency had examined and approved of the presents.
Having manifested his satisfaction with them by appropriating
to himself a very handsome large gilt cup, which with great risk
I had carried safely through the desert, he accompanied us on
horseback to the 'fáda', 'lamórde', or palace, which forms a

real labyrinth of courtyards, provided with spacious round huts of audience, built of clay, with a door on each side, and connected together by narrow intricate passages. Hundreds of lazy, arrogant courtiers, freemen and slaves, were lounging and idling here, killing time with trivial and saucy jokes.

We were first conducted to the audience-hall of the ghaladíma, who, while living in a separate palace, visits the 'fáda' almost every day, in order to act in his important and influential office as vizier; for he is far more intelligent, and also somewhat more energetic, than his lazy and indolent brother 'Othmán, who allows this excessively wealthy and most beautiful province, 'the garden of Central Africa', to be ransacked with impunity by the predatory incursions of the serkí Ibrám of Zínder, and other petty chiefs. Both are sons of Dábo and Shékara — the latter one of the celebrated ladies of Háusa, a native of Dáura, who is still living, and has three other children, viz. a son (Makhmúd) and two daughters, one of them named Fátima Záhar, and the other Sáretu. The governor was then eight and thirty, the ghaladíma seven and thirty years of age. They were both stout and handsome men, the governor rather too stout and clumsy. Their apartments were so excessively dark that, coming from a sunny place, it was some time before I could distinguish anybody. The governor's hall was very handsome, and even stately for this country, and was the more imposing as the rafters supporting the very elevated ceiling were concealed, two lofty arches of clay, very neatly polished and ornamented, appearing to support the whole. At the bottom of the apartment were two spacious and highly decorated niches, in one of which the governor was reposing on a 'gadó', spread with a carpet. His dress was not that of a simple Púllo, but consisted of all the mixed finery of Háusa and Barbary; he allowed his face to be seen, the white shawl hanging down far below his mouth over his breast.

The ghaladíma made some intelligent observations, while the governor only observed that, though I had suffered so severely from extortion, yet I seemed to have still ample presents for him. Nor was he far wrong; for the black 'kába' (a sort of bernús, with silk and gold lace, which I gave him) was a very handsome garment, and here worth sixty thousand kurdí: besides, he got a red cap, a white shawl with red border, a piece of white muslin, rose oil, one pound of cloves, and another of jáwi or benzoin, razor, scissors, an English clasp-knife, and a large mirror of German silver. The ghaladíma got the same presents, except that, instead of the kabá, I gave him a piece of French striped silk worth fifty thousand kurdí.

## THE CITY OF KANO

*February–March.* Having now at length made my peace with the governor, and seeing that exercise of body and recreation of mind were the best medicines I could resort to, I mounted on horseback the next day again, and, guided by a lad well acquainted with the topography of the town, rode for several hours round all the inhabited quarters, enjoying at my leisure, from the saddle, the manifold scenes of public and private life, of comfort and happiness, of luxury and misery, of activity and laziness, of industry and indolence, which were exhibited in the streets, the market-places, and in the interior of the courtyards. It was the most animated picture of a little world in itself, so different in external form from all that is seen in European towns, yet so similar in its internal principles.

Here a row of shops filled with articles of native and foreign produce, with buyers and sellers in every variety of figure, complexion, and dress, yet all intent upon their little gain, endeavouring to cheat each other; there a large shed, like a hurdle, full of half-naked, half-starved slaves torn from their native homes, from their wives or husbands, from their children or parents, arranged in rows like cattle, and staring desperately upon the buyers, anxiously watching into whose hands it should be their destiny to fall. In another part were to be seen all the necessaries of life, the wealthy buying the most palatable things for his table, the poor stopping and looking greedily upon a handful of grain; here a rich governor dressed in silk and gaudy clothes, mounted upon a spirited and richly capar-isoned horse, and followed by a host of idle, insolent slaves;

there a poor blind man groping his way through the multitude, and fearing at every step to be trodden down; here a yard neatly fenced with mats of reed, and provided with all the comforts which the country affords — a clean, snug-looking cottage, the clay walls nicely polished, a shutter of reeds placed

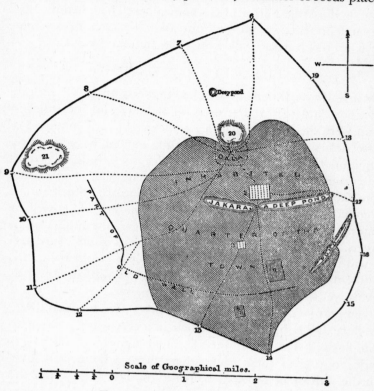

FIG. 3.   The City of Kano

1. My own quarters in Dalá. During my second stay in Kanó, I also resided in Dalá, at a short distance from my old quarters.
2. Great market-place.
3. Small market-place.
4. Palace of Governor.
5. Palace of Ghaladíma.
6. Kofa Mazúger.
7. Kofa-n-'Adama.
8. Kofa-n-Gúdan.
9. Kofa-n-Kansákkali.
10. Kofa-n-Limún, or Káboga.
11. Kofa-n-Dakanye, or Dukánie.
12. Kofa-n-Dakaina.
13. Kofa-n-Naïsa.
14. Kofa-n-Kúra
15. Kofa-n-Nasaráwa.
16. Kofa-n-Máta.
17. Kofa-n-Wambay.
18. Kofa-n-Magardi.
19. Kofa-n-Rúa (at present shut.)
20. Mount Dalá.
21. Mount Kógo-n-dútsi.

against the low, well-rounded door, and forbidding intrusion on the privacy of life, a cool shed for the daily household work, — a fine spreading alléluba-tree, affording a pleasant shade during the hottest hours of the day, or a beautiful gónda or papaya unfolding its large feather-like leaves above a slender, smooth, and undivided stem, or the tall date-tree, waving over the whole scene; the matron in a clean black cotton gown wound round her waist, her hair neatly dressed in 'chókoli' or bejáji, busy preparing the meal for her absent husband, or spinning cotton, and at the same time urging the female slaves to pound the corn; the children naked and merry, playing about in the sand at the 'urgi-n-dáwaki' or the 'da-n-chácha', or chasing a straggling stubborn goat; earthenware pots and wooden bowls, all cleanly washed, standing in order. Further on a dashing Cyprian, homeless, comfortless, and childless, but affecting merriment or forcing a wanton laugh, gaudily ornamented with numerous strings of beads around her neck, her hair fancifully dressed and bound with a diadem, her gown of various colours loosely fastened under her luxuriant breast, and trailing behind in the sand; near her a diseased wretch covered with ulcers, or with elephantiasis.

Now a busy 'máriná', an open terrace of clay, with a number of dyeing-pots, and people busily employed in various processes of their handicraft: here a man stirring the juice, and mixing with the indigo some colouring wood in order to give it the desired tint; there another, drawing a shirt from the dye-pot, or hanging it up on a rope fastened to the trees; there two men beating a well-dyed shirt, singing the while, and keeping good time; further on, a blacksmith busy with his rude tools in making a dagger which will surprise, by the sharpness of its blade, those who feel disposed to laugh at the workman's instruments, a formidable barbed spear, or the more estimable and useful instruments of husbandry; in another place, men and women making use of an ill-frequented thoroughfare, as a 'kaudi tseggenábe', to hang up, along the fences, their cotton thread for weaving; close by, a group of indolent loiterers lying in the sun and idling away their hours.

Here a caravan from Gónja arriving with the desired kola-
nut, chewed by all who have 'ten kurdí' to spare from their
necessary wants, or a caravan laden with natron, starting for
Núpe, or a troop of A'sbenáwa going off with their salt for the
neighbouring towns, or some Arabs leading their camels,
heavily laden with the luxuries of the north and east (the
'káya-n-ghábbes') to the quarter of the Ghadamsíye; there, a
troop of gaudy, warlike-looking horsemen galloping towards
the palace of the governor to bring him the news of a new
inroad of Serkí Ibrám. Everywhere human life in its varied
forms, the most cheerful and the most gloomy, seemed closely
mixed together; every variety of national form and complexion
— the olive-coloured Arab, the dark Kanúri, with his wide
nostrils, the small-featured, light, and slender Ba-Féllanchi, the
broad-faced Ba-Wángara (Mandingo), the stout, large-boned,
and masculine-looking Núpe female, the well-proportioned and
comely Ba-Háushe woman.

I was much worried during my stay in Kanó by a son of the
governor of Zária, who, suffering dreadfully from stricture or
some other obstruction, had come expressly to Kanó in the hope
of being relieved by me; and it was impossible for me to convince him that I had neither the knowledge nor the instruments
necessary for effecting the cure of his disease. It would, no
doubt, have been of great service if I had been able to cure him, as
he was the son of one of the most powerful princes of Negroland;
but as it was, I could only afford him a little temporary relief.
My intercourse with this man was indeed most painful to me,
as I felt conscious of entire inability to help him, while he
conjured me, by all that was dear to me, not to give him up and
abandon him. He died shortly afterwards. More agreeable to
me was a visit from the eldest son of the governor of Kanó, who,
accompanied by two horsemen, came to call upon me one day,
and not finding me at home, traced me whither I had gone, and
having met me, followed silently till I had re-entered my
quarters. He was a handsome, modest, and intelligent youth of
about eighteen years of age, and was delighted with the
performance of my musical-box. I gave him an English

clasp-knife, and we parted the best of friends, greatly pleased with each other.

## HISTORY OF KANO

I became so seriously ill on the 8th, that I looked forward with apprehension to my departure, which was fixed for the following day. But before leaving this important place, I will make a few general observations with regard to its history and its present state.

The town of Kanó, considered as the capital of a province, must be of somewhat older date than Kátsena, if we are to rely on Leo's accuracy, though from other more reliable sources (which I shall bring to light in the chapter on the history of Bórnu) it is evident that even in the second half of the 16th century there could have been here only the fortress of Dalá, which, at that period, withstood the attacks of the Bórnu king. I think we are justified in supposing that, in this respect, Leo (when, after an interval of many years, he wrote the account of the countries of Negroland which he had visited) confounded Kanó with Kátsena. The strength of the Kanáwa, that is to say, the inhabitants of the province of Kanó, at the time of the Bórnu king Edrís Alawóma, is quite apparent from the report of his imám; but from that time forth the country seems to have been tributary to Bórnu; and the population of the town of Kanó is said, with good reason, to have consisted from the beginning mostly of Kanúri or Bórnu elements. However, the established allegiance or subjection of this province to Bórnu was evidently rather precarious, and could be maintained only with a strong hand; for there was a powerful neighbour, the king of Korórofa or Júku, ready to avail himself of every opportunity of extending his own power and dominion over that territory. We know also that one king of that country, whose name, however, I could not obtain, on the entry of a new governor into office in Kanó, made an expedition into that country, and installed his own representative in the place of that of Bórnu, and though the eastern provinces of Korórofa itself (I mean the district in-habited by the Koána or Kwána) became afterwards tributary to Bórnu, yet the main province (or Júku Proper) with the capital Wukári, seems to have always remained strong and independent, till now, at length, it seems destined to be gradually swallowed up by the Fúlbe, if the English do not interfere. But to return to our subject. As long as Kátsena continued independent and flourishing, the town of Kanó appears never to have been an important commercial place; and it was not till after Kátsena had been occupied by the Fúlbe, and, owing to its exposed position on the northern frontier of Háusa, had become a very unsafe central point for commercial transactions, that Kanó became the great commercial entrepôt of Central Negroland. Before this time, that is to say, before the year 1807, I have strong reason to suppose that scarcely any great Arab merchant ever visited Kanó.

As to the period when the Kanáwa in general became Mohammedans, we may fairly assume it to have been several years later than the time when Máji, the prince of Kátsena, embraced Islám, or about the 17th century, though it is evident that the larger portion of the population all over Háusa, especially that of the country towns and villages, remained addicted to paganism till the fanatic zeal of their conquerors the Fúlbe forced them to profess Islám, at least publicly. Nevertheless even at the present day there is a great deal of paganism cherished, and rites really pagan performed, in the province of Kanó as well as in that of Kátsena,— a subject on which I shall say something more on another occasion.

With regard to the growth of the town, we have express testimony that Dalá was the most ancient quarter. The steep rocky hill, about 120 feet high, naturally afforded a secure retreat to the ancient inhabitants in case of sudden attack; but it is most probable that there was another or several separate villages within the wide expanse now encompassed by the wall, which rather exceeds than falls short of fifteen English miles, and it seems inconceivable why the other hill 'Kógo-n-dútsi' (which is inclosed within the circumference of the walls) though it is not quite so well fortified by nature, should not have afforded a strong site for another hamlet. We have, indeed, no means of describing the way in which the town gradually increased to its present size; this much, however, is evident, that the inhabited quarters never filled up the immense space comprised within the walls, though it is curious to observe that there are evident traces of a more ancient wall on the south side, which, as will be seen from the plan, did not describe so wide a circumference, particularly towards the south-west, where the great projecting angle seems to have been added in later times, for merely strategical purposes. The reason why the fortifications were carried to so much greater extent than the population of the town rendered necessary, was evidently to make the place capable of sustaining a long siege (sufficient ground being inclosed within the walls to produce the necessary supply of corn for the inhabitants), and also to receive the population of the open and unprotected villages in the neighbourhood. The inhabited quarter occupies at present only the south-eastern part of the town between Mount Dalá and the wall, which on this side is closely approached by the dwellings.

On the northern margin of the Jákara is the market-place, forming a large quadrangle, mostly consisting of sheds built in regular rows like streets; but the westernmost part of it forms the slaughtering-place, where numbers of cattle are daily butchered, causing an immense quantity of offal and filth to accumulate, for which there is no other outlet than the all-swallowing Jákara. It is the accumulation of this filth in the most frequented parts of the town which makes it so unhealthy. On the north-east side of the sheds is the camel-market, where also pack-oxen are sold. The shed where the slaves are sold is at the north-west corner; and thence, along the principal street, which traverses the market, is the station of the people who sell firewood. The market is generally immensely crowded during the heat of the day, and offers a most interesting scene.

The wall, just as it has been described by Captain Clapperton, is still kept in the best repair, and is an imposing piece of workmanship.

All over the town, clay houses and huts, with thatched conical roofs, are mixed together; but generally in the southern quarter the latter prevail. The clay houses, as far as I have seen them in Dalá, where of course Arab influence predominates, are built in a most uncomfortable style, with no other purpose than that of obtaining the greatest possible privacy for domestic life, without any attempt to provide for the influx of fresh air and light, although I must admit that a few houses are built in somewhat better taste; but invariably the courtyard is extremely small, and in this respect the houses of Kanó are very inferior to those of A'gades and Timbúktu, which are built almost on the same principle as the dwellings of the ancient Greeks and Romans.

## KANO'S COMMERCIAL EMINENCE

In estimating the population of the town at 30,000, I am certainly not above the truth. Captain Clapperton estimated it at from 30,000 to 40,000. The population, as might be expected in a place of great commercial resort, is of a rather mixed nature; but the chief elements in it are Kanúri or Bórnu people, Háusáwa, Fúlbe or Féllani, and Nyffáwa or Núpe; a good many Arabs also reside there, who by their commerce and their handicraft contribute a great deal to the importance of the place. The influx of foreigners and temporary residents is occasionally very great, so that the whole number of residents during the most busy time of the year (that is to say from January to April) may often amount to 60,000. The number of domestic slaves, of course, is very considerable; but I think it hardly equals, certainly does not exceed, that of the free men, for, while the wealthy have many slaves, the poorer class, which is far more numerous, have few or none. It would be very interesting to arrive at an exact estimate of the numbers of the conquering nation, in order to see the proportion in which they stand to the conquered. As for the town itself, their whole number, of every sex and age, does not, in my opinion, exceed 4000; but with regard to the whole country I can give no opinion.

The principal commerce of Kanó consists in native produce, namely, the cotton cloth woven and dyed here or in the neighbouring towns, in the form of tobes or rígona (*sing.* ríga); túrkedí, or the oblong piece of dress of dark-blue colour worn by the women; the zénne or plaid of various colours; and the ráwani bakí, or black lithám.

The great advantage of Kanó is, that commerce and manufactures go hand in hand, and that almost every family has its share in them. There is really something grand in this kind of industry, which spreads to the north as far as Múrzuk, Ghát, and even Tripoli; to the west, not only to Timbúktu, but in some degree even as far as the shores of the Atlantic, the very inhabitants of Arguin dressing in the cloth woven and dyed in Kanó; to the east, all over Bórnu, although there it comes in contact with the native industry of the country; and to the south it maintains a rivalry with the native industry of the I'gbira and I'gbo, while towards the south-east it invades the whole of 'Adamáwa, and is only limited by the nakedness of the pagan *sans-culottes*, who do not wear clothing.

As for the supply sent to Timbúktu, this is a fact entirely overlooked in Europe, where people speak continually of the fine cotton cloth produced in that town, while in truth all the apparel of a decent character in Timbúktu is brought either from Kanó or from Sansándi; and how urgently this article is there demanded is amply shown by the immense circuit which the merchandise makes to avoid the great dangers of the direct road from Kanó to Timbúktu travelled by me, the merchandise of Kanó being first carried up to Ghát and even Ghadámes, and thence taking its way to Timbúktu by Tawát.

I make the lowest estimate in rating this export to Timbúktu alone at three hundred camel-loads annually, worth 60,000,000 kurdí in Kanó — an amount which entirely remains in the country, and redounds to the benefit of the whole population, both cotton and indigo being produced and prepared in the country. In taking a general view of the subject, I think myself justified in estimating the whole produce of this manufacture, as far as it is sold abroad, at the very least at about 300,000,000; and how great this national wealth is, will be understood by my readers when they know that, with from fifty to sixty thousand kurdí, or from four to five pounds sterling a year, a whole family may live in that country with ease, including every expense, even that of their clothing: and we must remember that the province is one of the most fertile spots on the earth, and is able to produce not only the supply of corn necessary for its population, but can also export, and that it possesses, besides, the finest pasture-grounds. In fact, if we consider that this industry is not carried on here, as in Europe, in immense establishments, degrading man to the meanest condition of life, but that it gives employment and support to families without compelling them to sacrifice their domestic habits, we must presume that Kanó ought to be one of the happiest countries in the world; and so it is as long as its governor, too often lazy and indolent, is able to defend its inhabitants from the cupidity of their neighbours, which of course is constantly stimulated by the very wealth of this country.

Besides the cloth produced and dyed in Kanó and in the neighbouring villages, there is a considerable commerce carried on here with the cloth manufactured in Nýffi or Núpe, which, however, extends only to the first and the third of the articles above mentioned, viz. the 'ríga', or shirt worn by men, and the 'zénne', or plaid; for the Nyffáwa are unable to produce either túrkedí or ráwaní — at least for export, while they seem, with the exception of the wealthier classes, to supply their own wants themselves. The tobes brought from Nýffi are either large black ones, or of mixed silk and cotton.

The chief articles of native industry, besides cloth, which have a wide market, are principally sandals. The sandals are made with great neatness, and, like the cloth, are exported to an immense distance; but being a cheap article (the very best, which are called 'táka-sárakí', fetching only 200 kurdí), they bear of course no comparison in importance with the former. I estimate this branch at ten millions. It is very curious that the shoes made here by Arab shoemakers, of Sudan leather, and called 'bélghá', are exported in great quantities to North Africa. The 'nesísa', or twisted leather strap, is a celebrated article of Kanó manufacture, and ' jebíras ', richly ornamented, are made by Arab workmen.

The other leather-work I will not mention here, as it does not form a great article of commerce; but tanned hides ('kulá-bu') and red sheepskins, dyed with a juice extracted from the stalks of the holcus, are not unimportant, being sent in great quantities even as far as Tripoli. I value the amount of export at about five millions.

Besides these manufactures, the chief article of African produce in the Kanó market is the 'gúro', or kola-nut; but while on the one hand it forms an important article of transit, and brings considerable profit, on the other large sums are expended by the natives upon this luxury, which has become to them as necessary as tea or coffee to us. On another occasion I shall enumerate the different kinds of this nut, and the seasons when it is collected. The import of this nut into Kanó, comprising certainly more than five hundred ass-loads every year, the load of each, if safely brought to the market — for it is a very delicate article, and very liable to spoil — being sold for about 200,000 kurdí, will amount to an average of from eighty to one hundred millions. Of this sum, I think we shall be correct in asserting about half to be paid for by the natives of the province, while the other half will be profit.

But we must bear in mind that the greater part of the persons employed in this trade are Kanáwa, and that therefore they and their families subsist upon this branch of trade.

A very important branch of the native commerce in Kanó is certainly the slave-trade; but it is extremely difficult to say how many of these unfortunate creatures are exported, as a greater number are carried away by small caravans to Bórnu and Núpe than on the direct road to Ghát and Fezzán. Altogether, I do not think that the number of slaves annually exported from Kanó exceeds 5,000; but of course a considerable number are sold into domestic slavery either to the inhabitants of the province itself, or to those of the adjoining districts. The value of this trade, of which only a small percentage falls to the profit of the Kanáwa, besides the tax which is levied in the market, may altogether amount to from a hundred and fifty to two hundred millions of kurdí per annum.

Another important branch of the commerce of Kanó is the transit of natron from Bórnu to Núpe or Nýffi, which here always passes into other hands, and in so doing leaves a considerable profit in the place. The merchandise is very cheap; but the quantity is great, and it employs a great many persons, as I shall have ample occasion to illustrate in the course of my proceedings. Twenty thousand loads, at the very least, between pack-oxen, sumpter-horses, and asses, of natron must annually pass through the market of Kanó; which, at 500 kurdí per load, merely for passage-money, would give 10,000,000 kurdí.

I here also mention the salt-trade, which is entirely an import one, the salt being almost all consumed in the province. Of the three thousand camel-loads of salt which I have above computed as comprising the aïri with which I reached Kátsena, we may suppose one-third to be sold in the province of Kanó; and therefore that hereby a value of from fifty to eighty millions annually is drained from the country. But we must not forget that the money which is paid for this requisite (and not only for that consumed in Kanó, but also in other provinces) is entirely laid out by the sellers in buying the produce of Kanó; viz., cloth and corn. Here, therefore, is an absolute balance — a real exchange of necessaries and wants.

As for ivory, at present it does not form a very important branch of the commerce of Kanó; and I scarcely believe that more than one hundred kantárs pass through this place. The lowest price of the kantár is in general thirty dollars, or 75,000 kurdí; but it often rises to forty dollars, or 100,000 kurdí, and even more, though I have seen it bought with ready money for twenty-five dollars.

The principal European goods brought to the market of Kanó are bleached and unbleached calicoes, and cotton prints from Manchester; French silks and sugar; red cloth from Saxony and other parts of Europe; beads from Venice and Trieste; a very coarse kind of silk from Trieste; common paper with the sign of three moons, looking-glasses, needles, and small ware, from Nuremberg; sword blades from Solingen;

razors from Styria. It is very remarkable that so little English merchandise is seen in this great emporium of Negro-land, which lies so near to the two branches of 'the Great River' of Western Africa, calico and muslins (or tanjips, as they are called by the merchants) being almost the only English articles. Calico certainly is not the thing most wanted in a country where home-made cloth is produced at so cheap a rate, and of so excellent a quality; indeed the unbleached calico has a very poor chance in Kanó, while the bleached calico and the cambric attract the wealthier people on account of their nobler appearance. In Timbúktu on the contrary, where the native cloth is dearer, unbleached calico is in request; and it would be so in an extraordinary degree, if it were dyed dark blue. It is very interesting to observe that a small propor-tion of the calico imported into Kanó is again exported, after having been dyed, returning even the long way to Ghadámes. I estimate the whole amount of Manchester goods imported into Kanó at about forty millions; but it may be somewhat more. The sale of tanjips is very considerable; and the import of this article into Kanó certainly equals in value that of the former.

The very coarse silk, or rather refuse, which is dyed in Tripoli, is imported to a very considerable amount, this forming the principal merchandise of most of the caravans of the Ghadámsíye merchants, and about one third of their whole commerce, amounting certainly to not less than from three to four hundred camel-loads annually, worth in Kanó each about 200,000 kurdí; this would give a value of about seventy millions imported. But according to some well-informed people, even as many as one thousand loads of this article pass annually through Ghadámes; so that, if we take into consideration that the supply of the northerly markets (as Tasáwa, Zínder) may well be compensated by what is brought by way of Múrzuk, the value of the import of this article into Kanó may be much more. A great deal of this silk, I have no doubt by far the greatest part, remains in the country, being used for ornamen-ting the tobes, sandals, shoes, and other things.

Woollen cloth of the most ordinary quality, chiefly red, but about one third of the whole amount of green colour, was formerly imported to a great extent; but it has gone out of fashion, and I think a better quality, like that with which the market of Timbúktu is supplied by way of Mogador or Swaira, would succeed. I estimate this branch at present at only fifteen millions.

Beads, in very great variety, form an important article of import; but the price has become so low of late years that there has been very little profit, and the supply has been kept back to raise the prices. The import of this article certainly amounts to more than fifty millions of kurdí, of which sum the value of twenty may remain in the country.

Of sugar, I think about one hundred camel-loads are imported every year, each containing eighty small loaves, of two and a half pounds each, which are sold in general at 1500 kurdí; so that the import of this article would amount to about twelve millions. It is very remarkable that in all Central Negroland the large English sugarloaf is scarcely ever seen, while it is the only one seen in Timbúktu. However, I was greatly surprised when, on my return from that place in 1854, 'Alíyu, the Emír el Mumenín of Sókoto, presented to me an English loaf of sugar; and I heard that he had received several of them as presents from a merchant of Tawát. The small loaf has certainly a great advantage in such a country, where money is scarce; and I found in 1854 that its weight had even been reduced to two pounds.

Common paper, called on the coast 'tre lune', from the mark of three moons which it bears, is imported in great quantity, being used for wrapping up the country cloth; but it is a bulky, heavy article, and in larger quantities is sold at a very cheap rate. The whole amount of this import may be about five millions of kurdí.

Needles, with the emblem of the pig, and small looking-glasses called 'lemmá', in boxes, form important but very cheap articles, and I think their amount together will not much exceed the value of eight millions. Generally, the needles in large quantities are sold for one 'urí' or shell each, but often even cheaper; and I was obliged to sell a thousand for six hundred kurdí. Also, fine needles for silk-work are in request, but only in small quantity, while large darning-needles are not at all wanted here, where the cotton cloth is fine, but are the most profitable thing in Eastern Negroland, from Bagírmi inclusive to Abyssinia.

Sword-blades, which are set here, are imported in considerable quantity; as not only the Kél-owí and the neighbouring Tárki tribes, but also the Háusáwa, Fúlbe, Nyffáwa, and Kanúri or Bórnu people, are supplied from this market. Fifty thousand may be the general annual amount of this article, which produces (the blade being reckoned at one thousand kurdí) fifty millions. Almost all of them that I saw, not only here, but even among the Tawárek near Timbúktu, were from Solingen. Only a small proportion of the import remains in the country; but the setting of the blades, which are again exported, secures a great profit to the natives.

Very few fire-arms, as far as I became aware, are imported into this market, although common muskets have begun to be imported by way of Nýffi at extraordinarily cheap prices by the Americans. Pistols and blunderbusses are privately sold by the merchants to princes or great men.

The common razors, made in Styria, with black wooden handles, bad as they are, are very much liked by the inhabitants, who know how to sharpen them most beautifully, and strengthen the wretched handle with a guard of copper. I had a tolerable supply of English razors, and found that those bought for sixpence at home would sell profitably, but that nobody would give, for a good razor, though ever so excellent, more than one thousand kurdí; however, the better sort are very fit for presents to men of importance, who know well their value. In any case the handles ought to be strong, and not likely to break. This commodity does certainly not much exceed two or three millions.

French silks, called 'hattáya', were formerly in great request, but at present seem to be a little out of vogue; and most of what is imported here is exported again by second-hand buyers to Yóruba and Gónja. The amount of this import into the Kanó market, I think, does not exceed twenty millions.

An important branch of import is formed by articles of Arab dress, chiefly bernúses, caftans, sedríyas, trowsers, red caps, red sashes, shawls. It is difficult to state, even approximately, the value of these articles; but it cannot certainly be much less than fifty millions altogether. The sort of dress most in request comes from Tunis, but a good deal also from Egypt; and from the latter country come all the white shawls with red borders, called 'subéta' in Arabic, 'aliyáfu' in Háusa, and very much liked by the negroes as well as by the Tawárek. The import of this article alone exceeds the value of ten millions. The common articles of dress, of coarser workmanship, are made in Tripoli. Red caps of very coarse description are now imported from Leghorn, and find a sale, but are not liked by the free people.

Frankincense and spices — principally jáwi, benzoin, the resin obtained from a species of styrax, 'símbil' or *Valeriana Celtica*, and cloves — form a not inconsiderable article of import, perhaps amounting to fifteen millions. However, I exclude from this sum the value of the rose-oil which is annually imported in considerable quantity, and, being a dear article, forms also an important one; but very little of it comes into the general trade, almost all of it being disposed of privately to the princes and great men, or given to them in presents. I am inclined to estimate the value of this article imported at about forty millions. Tin and many other smaller articles may together be estimated at ten millions.

In the trade of Kanó there is another very interesting article, which tends to unite very distant regions of Africa; this is copper — 'ja-n-kárfi'. A good deal of old copper — say fifty loads, together with about twenty loads of zinc — is imported from Tripoli; but a considerable supply of this useful and handsome metal is also imported every year by the Jellába of Nímro in Wadáy, who bring it from the celebrated coppermine, 'el hófra', situate to the south of Dar-Fúr, of which I shall have occasion to speak in the following volume. I estimate the whole import of this metal at about from fifteen to twenty millions; but it is to be remarked that, so far from being to the disadvantage of the Kanáwa, it proves a new material of industry, while only the smaller part remains in the country.

With regard to the precious metals, a small supply of silver is imported by the merchants, but rather exceptionally, most of the latter being but agents or commissioners engaged to effect the sale of the merchandise forwarded from Tripoli and Fezzán. The silver likewise supplies a branch of industry, the silversmiths, who are generally identical with the blacksmiths, being very clever in making rings and anklets. In Kanó scarcely any tradesman will object to receive a dollar in payment. With regard to iron, which forms a very considerable branch of industry in the place, I will only say that it is far inferior to that of Wándala or Mándara and Bubanjídda, which I shall mention in the course of my proceedings. Spears, daggers, hoes, and stirrups are the articles most extensively produced in iron.

As for gold, though a general standard, of the mithkál at four thousand kurdí, is usually maintained, in Timbúktu its price greatly varies, from three thousand five hundred up to four thousand five hundred kurdí; but this unreasonable fluctuation is but nominal, gold being scarcely ever bought in Timbúktu for ready money, but for túrkedís, when a túrkédi bought in Kanó for eighteen hundred, or at the utmost two thousand, fetches there a mithkál. One hundred mithkáls of gold may easily be bought in Kanó at any time. Even the common currency of the Kanó market, the 'urí' (*pl.* kurdí) or shell (*Cypræa moneta*), 2,500 of which are equal to the Spanish or Austrian dollar, forms an important article of import and commerce.

## GOVERNMENT OF KANO PROVINCE

The province of Kanó, which comprises a very fertile district of considerable extent, contains, according to my computation, more than two hundred thousand free people, besides at least an equal number of slaves; so that the whole population of the province amounts to more than half a million;

though it may greatly exceed this number. The governor is able to raise an army of seven thousand horse, and more than twenty thousand men on foot. In the most flourishing state of the country, the governor of Kanó is said to have been able to bring into the field as many as ten thousand horse.

The tribute which he levies is very large, considering the state of the country, amounting altogether to about one hundred millions of kurdí, besides the presents received from merchants. The most considerable item of his revenue consists in the 'kurdí-n-kása' (what it called in Kanúri 'lárderám'), or the ground-rent. It is said to amount to ninety millions, and is levied, both here and in the province of Kátsena, not from the ground under cultivation, but every head of a family has to pay two thousand five hundred kurdí, or just a Spanish dollar; in the province of Zégzeg, on the contrary, the kurdí-n-kása is a tax of five hundred kurdí levied on every fertáña or hoe, and a single hoe will cultivate a piece of ground capable of producing from one hundred to two hundred 'démmi' or sheaves of grain (sorghum and pennisetum), each of which contains two kél, while fifty kél are reckoned sufficient for a man's sustenance during a whole year. Besides the kurdí-n-kása, the governor levies an annual tax called 'kurdí-n-korófi', of seven hundred kurdí on every dyeing-pot or korófi, of which there are more than two thousand in the town alone; a 'fítto' of five hundred kurdí on every slave sold in the market; an annual tax, 'kurdí-n-debíno' of six hundred kurdí on every palm-tree, and a small tax called 'kurdí-n-ráfi' on the vegetables sold in the market, such as dánkali or sweet potatoes, gwáza or yams, rísga, rógo, &c. This latter tax is very singular, as the meat, or the cattle brought into the town, as far as I know, does not pay any tax at all. Clapperton was mistaken in stating that all the date-trees in the town belong to the governor, which is not more true than that all the sheds in the market belong to him.

The authority of the governor is not absolute, even without considering the appeal which lies to his liege lord in Sókoto or Wúrno, if the subjects' complaints can be made to reach so far; a sort of ministerial council is formed; to act in conjunction with the governor, which in important cases he cannot well avoid consulting. At the head of this council stands the ghaladíma, whose office originated, as we shall see, in the empire of Bórnu, and who very often exercises, as is the case in Kanó, the highest influence, surpassing that of the governor himself; then follows the 'serkí-n-dáwakay' (the master of the horse), an important charge in barbarous countries, where victory depends almost always on the cavalry; then the 'bánda-n-Kanó' (a sort of commander-in-chief); then the 'alkáli' or chief justice, the 'chiróma-n-Kanó' (the eldest son of the governor, or some one assuming this title), who exercises the chief power in the southern part of the province; the 'serkí-n-báy' (properly, the chief of the slaves), who has the inspection of the northern districts of the province as far as Kazáure; then the 'gadó' or lord of the treasury, and finally the 'serkí-n-sháno' (the master of the oxen, or rather the quartermaster-general), who has all the military stores under his care; for the ox, or rather the bull, is the ordinary beast of burden in Negroland. It is characteristic that, when the governor is absent paying his homage to his liege lord, it is not the ghaladíma, but the gadó and the serkí-n-sháno who are his lieutenants or substitutes.

With regard to the government in general, I think, in this province, where there is so much lively intercourse, and where publicity is given very soon to every incident, it is not oppressive, though the behaviour of the ruling class is certainly haughty, and there is, no doubt, a great deal of injustice inflicted in small matters. The etiquette of the court, which is far more strict than in Sókoto, must prevent any poor man from entering the presence of the governor. The Fúlbe marry the handsome daughters of the subjugated tribe, but would not condescend to give their own daughters to the men of that tribe as wives. As far as I saw, their original type has been well preserved as yet, though, by obtaining possession of wealth and comfort, their war-like character has been greatly impaired, and the Féllani-n-Kanó have become notorious for their cowardice throughout the whole of Negroland.

## CHAPTER 4

# THE HAUSA-BORNU BORDERLAND (1851)

### DEPARTURE FROM KANO

*March* 9. The traveller who would leave a place where he has made a long residence, often finds that his departure involves him in a great deal of trouble, and is by no means an easy affair. Moreover my situation when, after much delay, I was about to leave Kanó was peculiarly embarrassing. There was no caravan; the road was infested by robbers; and I had only one servant upon whom I could rely, or who was really attached to me, while I had been so unwell the preceding day as to be unable to rise from my couch. However, I was full of confidence; and with the same delight with which a bird springs forth from its cage, I hastened to escape from these narrow, dirty mud-walls into the boundless creation.

### ON THE MARCH

*March* 10. The quiet course of domestic slavery has very little to offend the mind of the traveller; the slave is generally well treated, is not over worked, and is very often considered as a member of the family. Scenes caused by the running away of a slave in consequence of bad and severe treatment occur every day with the Arabs, who generally sell their slaves, even those whom they have had some time, as soon as occasion offers; but with the natives they are very rare. However, I was surprised at observing so few home-born slaves in Negroland — with the exception of the Tawárek, who seem to take great pains to rear slaves — and I have come to the conclusion, that marriage among domestic slaves is very little encouraged by the natives; indeed I think myself justified in supposing that a slave is very rarely allowed to marry. This is an important circumstance in considering domestic slavery in Central Africa; for if these domestic slaves do not of themselves maintain their numbers, then the deficiency arising from ordinary mortality must constantly be kept up by a new supply, which can only be obtained by kidnapping or, more generally, by predatory incursions, and it is this necessity which makes even domestic slavery appear so baneful and pernicious. The motive for making these observations in this place was the sight of a band of slaves, whom we met this morning, led on in two files, and fastened one to the other by a strong rope round the neck.

Animated scenes succeeded each other:— now a well, where the whole population of a village or zángo were busy in supplying their wants for the day; then another, where a herd of cattle was just being watered; a beautiful tamarind-tree spreading a shady canopy over a busy group of talkative women selling victuals, ghussub-water, and sourmilk, or 'cotton.' About ten o'clock detached dúm-palms began to impart to the landscape a peculiar character, as we approached the considerable but open place Gabezáwa, which at present exhibited the busy and animated scene of a well-frequented market. In this country the market days of the towns succeed each other by turns, so that all the inhabitants of a considerable district can take advantage every day of the traffic in the peculiar article in which each of these places excels.

For part of the way Barth travelled in the company of 'the most noble Arab merchant I have ever seen in Negroland', and together they shared the trekking and camp life.

*March* 12. Here we sat tranquilly down near the market-place, in the shade of some beautiful tamarind-trees, and indulged in the luxuries which my gentleman-like companion could afford. I was astonished, as well as ashamed at the comfort which my African friend displayed, ordering one of the female attendants of his sirríya to bring into his presence a basket which seemed to be under the special protection of the latter, and drawing forth from it a variety of well-baked pastry, which he spread on a napkin before us, while another of the attendants was boiling the coffee.

## THE TOWN OF GUMEL

*March* 13. Not waiting for the new horseman whom I was to receive here early in the morning, I went on in advance with my companion, in order to reach Gúmmel before the heat of the day; and we soon met in the forest a string of twelve camels, all laden with kurdí or shells, and belonging to the rich Arab merchant Bú-héma, who resides in Múniyo, and carried on a considerable commerce between Kanó and Kúkawa. I will here mention, that in general 100,000 kurdí are regarded as a camel-load; fine animals, however, like these will carry as much as a hundred and fifty thousand, that is, just sixty dollars or twelve pounds' worth. It is easy to be understood that, where the standard coin is of so unwieldy a nature, the commerce of the country cannot be of great value.

About two miles before we reached the frontier-town of the Bórnu empire in this direction, we were joined by the horseman of the governor of Gérki; and we here took leave of Háusa with its fine and beautiful country, and its cheerful and industrious population. It is remarkable what a difference there is between the character of the ba-Háushe and the Kanúri — the former lively, spirited, and cheerful, the latter melancholic, dejected and brutal; and the same difference is visible in their physiognomies — the former having in general very pleasant and regular features, and more graceful forms, while the Kanúri, with his broad face, his wide nostrils, and his large bones, makes a far less agreeable impression, especially the women, who are very plain and certainly among the ugliest in all Negroland, notwithstanding their coquetry, in which they do not yield at all to the Háusa women.

We reached the considerable town of Gúmmel just when the sun began to shine with great power; and at the gate we separated, the sheríf taking his way directly towards his quarters in the southern part of the town, while I was obliged to go first to the house of the governor, the famous Dan-Tanóma (the son of Tanóma, his own name being entirely unknown to the people); but on account of his great age, neither on this nor on a later occasion did I get a sight of him. Indeed he was soon to leave this world, and by his death to plunge not only the town wherein he resided, but the whole neighbouring country, into a destructive civil war between his two sons.

However, on my first visit Gúmmel was still a flourishing place, and well inhabited, and I had to pass through an intricate labyrinth of narrow streets enclosed between fences of mats and reeds surrounding huts and courtyards, before I reached the dwellings of the few Arabs who live here; and after looking about for some time I obtained quarters near the house of Sálem Maidúkia (the Rothschild of Gúmmel), where my Morocco friend was lodged. But my lodgings required building in the first instance, as they consisted of nothing but a courtyard, the fence of which was in a state of utter decay, and a hut entirely fallen in, so that there was not the least shelter from the sun, whereas I had to wait here two days at least for my new friend, whose company I was not inclined to forego, without very strong reasons, on my journey to Kúkawa.

However building is not so difficult in Negroland as it is in Europe; and a most comfortable dwelling, though rather light, and liable to catch fire, may be erected in a few hours; even a roof is very sufficiently made, at least such as is here wanted during the dry season, with those thick mats, made of reed, called 'síggedi' in Bórnu. But most fortunately Sálem had a conical roof just ready, which would have afforded satisfactory shelter even from the heaviest rain. I therefore sent immediately my whole remaining supply of kurdí to the market to buy those mats and sticks; and getting four men practised in this sort of workmanship, I immediately set to work, and, long before my camels arrived, had a well-fenced private courtyard, and a splendid cool shade, while my tent served as a store for my luggage, and as a bedroom for myself.

Having, therefore, made myself comfortable, I was quite

prepared to indulge in the luxurious luncheon sent me by the maidúkia, consisting of a well-cooked paste of Negro millet with sourmilk, after which I received visits from the few Arabs residing here, and was pleased to find one among them who had been Clapperton's servant, and was well acquainted with the whole proceedings of the first expedition.

*March* 14. The next morning I went with 'Abd el Khafíf to pay our compliments to old Dan-Tanóma. His residence, surrounded by high clay walls, and including, besides numbers of huts for his household and numerous wives, some spacious halls of clay, was of considerable extent; and the courtyard, shaded by a wide-spreading, luxuriant tamarind tree, was a very noble area. While we sat there awaiting the governor's pleasure, I had a fair insight into the concerns of this little court, all the well-fed, idle parasites coming in one after the other, and rivalling each other in trivial jokes. The Háusa language is the language of the court; and the offices are similar to those which I mentioned above with regard to Kanó. Having waited a long time in vain, the weak old man sending an excuse, as he could not grant us an interview, we returned to our quarters.

To-day being Friday was market-day; and in order to see the market in its greatest activity I mounted at noon on horseback, and went out. In all these parts of Negroland, the customs of which are in every respect so different from those of Yóruba and the neighbouring countries, the market (in Kúkawa and Maseña, as well as in Kanó, Sókoto, and even Timbúktu) is always most frequented and most busy in the hottest hours of the day, notwithstanding the great fatigue which all the people, and particularly the strangers, have to undergo.

The market of Gúmmel is held outside the town, between the two gates on the west side, but nearer to the 'chínna-n-yalá' (the northern gate), which is remarkable on account of its well-fortified condition.

Though I had heard a good deal about Gúmmel, I was nevertheless surprised at the size and the activity of the market, although that held on Saturday is said to be still more important.

Gúmmel is the chief market for the very extensive trade in natron, which, as I have mentioned above, is carried on between Kúkawa and Múniyo on one side, and Núpe or Nýffi on the other; for this trade passes from one hand into another, and the Bórnu people very rarely carry this merchandise further than Gúmmel. Large masses of natron, certainly amounting to at least one thousand loads of both qualities mentioned above, were offered here for sale — the full bullock's load of the better quality for five thousand, an ass's load of the inferior sort for five hundred kurdí. There were also about three hundred stalls or sheds, but not arranged in regular rows, where a great variety of objects were offered for sale, — all sorts of clothing, tools, earthenware pots, all kinds of victuals, cattle, sheep, donkeys, horses — in short, everything of home or foreign produce which is in request among the natives.

Greatly delighted with my visit to the market, though not a little affected by the exposure to the sun during the hot hours, I returned to my quarters; for though a practised traveller will bear very well the most scorching power of the sun, if he sets out in the morning, and by degrees becomes inured to greater and greater heat, he may suffer fatally from exposing himself for a long time to the mid-day sun, after having spent the morning in the shade. Later in the afternoon, the governor sent, as a gift to me and 'Abd el Khafíf, through his principal courtiers (such as the ghaladíma, the chiróma, and others, who were accompanied by a long train of followers), a young bullock, they being instructed at the same time to receive in return the present, or 'salám', as it is generally called, which we had prepared for him. I gave them a subéta and a small flask with rose oil, which is an article in great request with the fashionable world in Háusa and Bórnu. In the evening, we received also corn for our horses.

## HISTORY OF HADEJIA

*March* 18. Scarcely had we left Benzári behind us when my ears were struck by the distant sound of drums and singing, and I learnt on inquiry that it was Bokhári, or, as the Bórnu people call him, Bowári, the deposed governor of Khadéja, and the brother of A'hmedu, the present ruler of that town. Bokhári's name was then new, not only to me, but even to the natives of the neighbouring provinces. He had been governor of Khadéja, but being a clever and restless man he, or rather his jealous brother, had excited the suspicion of his liege lord 'Alíyu, the ruler of Sókoto, who had deposed him and given the government to his brother A'hmedu, whereupon Bokhári had nothing else to do but to throw himself upon the hospitality and protection of the Bórnu people, who received him with open arms, the governor of Máshena, with the sanction of his liege lord the sheikh of Bórnu, assigning to him a neighbouring place, Yerímarí, for his residence. This is an incident of very frequent occurrence in these loosely connected empires; but it is particularly so with the Fúlbe, among whom one brother often cherishes the most inveterate hatred against another. Exactly the same thing we have seen already in Kátsena. Bokhári having remained some time quietly in this place, strengthening his party and assisted underhand with arms and men by the vizier of Bórnu, had just now set out to try his fortune against his brother, and was beating the drums in order to collect as many people as possible.

Predatory incursions are nothing new in these quarters, where several provinces and entirely distinct empires have a common frontier; but this, as the event proved, was rather a memorable campaign for the whole of this part of Negroland, and was to become 'the beginning of sorrows' for all the country around. For Bokhári having taken the strong town of Khadéja, and killed his brother, was not only able to defend himself in his new position, vanquishing all the armies sent against him, and amongst them the whole military force of the empire of Sókoto, which was led on by the vizier in person, 'Abdu the son of Gedádo, Clapperton's old friend, but spread terror and devastation to the very gates of Kanó. Indeed, on my second journey through these regions, I shall have the sad duty of describing the state of misery into which districts, which on my former visit I had found flourishing and populous, had been reduced by this warlike chieftain, who, instead of founding a strong kingdom and showing himself a great prince, chose rather, like most of his countrymen, to base his power on the destruction and devastation of the country around him, and to make himself a slave-dealer on a grand scale. Tens of thousands of unfortunate people, pagans as well as Mohammedans, unprotected in their well-being by their lazy and effeminate rulers, have from the hands of Bokhári passed into those of the slave-dealer, and have been carried away from their native home into distant regions.

Kept in alarm by the drumming, and making some not very tranquillizing reflections on the weakness of our little band, which consisted of three men and a boy, in the turbulent state of the country through which we were passing, we continued silently on, while the character of the landscape had nothing peculiarly adapted to cheer the mind.

## THE MANGA DISTRICT

*March* 18. Having then passed through a monotonous tract of country covered with tall reed-grass and with the *Asclepias*, we reached the town of Yélkazá at half-past nine o'clock in the morning. Here the governor of the province of Máshena, who generally has his residence in the town of the same name, was staying at present, apparently on account of the expedition of Bokhári, which he was assisting underhand; and I accordingly had to pay him my compliments, as my horseman, who was a servant of Dan Tanóma, could not well conduct me any further.

We therefore entered the town by the north gate, and found people very busy repairing the fortification, consisting of two walls and three ditches of considerable depth, two of which ran outside round the outer wall, while the third was inclosed between the two walls.

Having presented ourselves at the residence of the governor, which was situated in the middle of the town, and consisted altogether of reed-work, we obtained good quarters, with a spacious and cool shed, which was the only thing we wanted; for being anxious not to lose any more time, I had resolved to start again in the afternoon. In order, therefore, to obtain a guide as soon as possible, I went to pay my compliments to the governor, whose name was Mohammed. After a little delay, he came out of the interior of his reed house into the audience-hall, which likewise consisted entirely of reed-work, but was spacious and airy; there he sat down upon a sort of divan, similar to the ánkaréb used in Egypt, and made of the branches of the tukkurúwa, which had been brought in expressly for the purpose. My interview, however, was short, for neither was he himself a lively or inquisitive man, nor was my Tébu servant, whom, as I myself was not yet able to speak Kanúri with tolerable fluency, I was obliged to employ as interpreter, at all distinguished either by eloquence or by frankness, though in other respects he was an excellent lad.

I obtained, however, all that I wanted, the governor assigning me immediately a man who should accompany me to Ghaladíma 'Omár, the governor of Búndi, and I was glad that he did not grumble at my present, which consisted only of a small phial of rose oil and a quarter of a pound of cloves. The best and most usual present for the governors on this road, who are justly entitled to some gift, as no tolls are to be paid, is a subéta, or white shawl with red or yellow border, such as are brought from Egypt, which may be accompanied with some spices. The old man also sent me, after a little while, when I had returned to my quarters, a dish which at least was not richer than my present, consisting in a very unpalatable paste of Negro corn, with a nasty sauce of míya, or molukhíya. Háusa with its delicacies was behind us; and I was unable to procure, either for hospitality's sake or for money, a dish of 'fura', which I had become very fond of.

*March* 19. My fine lancer, with whose manly bearing I had been very much pleased yesterday, appeared to have thought that, instead of exposing himself alone, by accompanying me further through a disturbed and infested district, he would do better to retrace his steps in the company of these people; for the next morning he was gone, and no trace of him was to be found. Perhaps he was anxious to join the expedition against Khadéja, where the soldier might make his fortune, while with me he could only expect to gain a few hundred shells; but whatever was his reason for decamping, he left me in a state of great perplexity, as I was in a hurry to go on as fast as possible; and in a country where there are no highroads, but where even tracks so important as that from Kanó to Kúkawa are nothing but small paths leading from one village or from one town to another, I could not well dispense with a guide. As regards security, I could only rely upon Providence and my own courage.

Having in vain searched for my man, I loaded the camels, and mounting my horse, proceeded to the residence of the governor, who is the vassel of the ruler of Máshena. He, having been informed by his servants, soon came forth, a tall imposing figure, and seeing that my complaint was just, his liege lord having expressly assigned me the horseman in order to conduct me to Búndi, he assured me that he would find another guide for me; but as it would take some time, he ordered one of his servants to lead me out of the town to a place where the camels meanwhile might graze a little. Seeing that he was a just and intelligent man, I thanked him for his kindness, and followed his servant, who conducted us a few hundred yards from the town, where there was most excellent pasturage for the camels.

While we were waiting here for the guide, my companion, who was a sociable sort of man, helped me to pass the time most agreeably with his instructive talk. I had observed a very curious object at the governor's house, — a leathern parcel of considerable dimensions, tied up with great care and hung on a long pole, and I had fancied that it contained the body of a criminal exposed there to every man's sight as a warning example of severe punishment; but to my great astonishment I now learned that it was a powerful talisman suspended in order to protect the town against the Felláta, as the Bórnu people call the Fúlbe, whose inroads were greatly feared. He likewise informed me that four years ago there was a desperate struggle for Taganáma, when that town very narrowly escaped falling into the hands of those fanatical invaders. He praised his master, whose name as I now learned was I'sa. The cheerful aspect of the town seemed fully to confirm his praises, and I expressed my hope that his watchfulness and energy might be a better safeguard to the inhabitants than that monstrous talisman, the dimensions of which were really frightful.

I was greatly pleased also to observe here the very first signs of preparing the ground for the approaching season, the slaves being busy clearing the soil with a sort of strong rake provided, with four long wooden teeth, called 'kámga'; but this is very rarely done, and the preparatory labours of agriculture must differ more or less in different districts according to the peculiar nature of the ground.

At length we saw the guides coming towards us. Instead of a horseman there were two archers on foot, short muscular men, clad only with a leathern apron round their loins, and for arms bearing, besides bow and arrows, the peculiar little Mánga battle-axe, which they carry on their shoulders, while a good sized leathern pocket for carrying provisions, and several diminutive garra bottles hung down by their sides. In short, they were real Mánga warriors, though they certainly did not inspire us with all the confidence which we should have wished to repose in a guide.

## CHAPTER 5

# BORNU (1851)

## THE MARCHES OF WESTERN BORNU

*March* 21. Having then passed a thick forest[1] of underwood, and some cultivated ground, half an hour before noon we reached Búndi, the residence of the ghaladíma 'Omár, fortified in the same way as A'lamáy, and went up directly to the house of the governor, which consists entirely of reed-work. However, the mats ('lágará') which surround the whole establishment are of very great height, at least fifteen feet, and of considerable thickness, made of the peculiar reed called 'súgu', and being sustained by long poles, and kept in a good state of repair, do not look ill. Besides, they are in general strengthened still further on the outside by a fence of thorny bushes.

The ghaladíma, or governor of the Gháladí, which (as we shall see in the historical account of the Bórnu empire) comprised all the western provinces of Bórnu from the komádugu Wáube (the so-called Yéou) to the shores of the Kwára, having his residence in Bírni Ngurú, near Mármar, in former times was an officer (or rather an almost independent feudal vassal) of immense power; at present, however, he has sunk to great insignificance, and in real power is much inferior to his neighbours the governors of Múniyo, Zínder, and even that of Máshena. But the present ghaladíma 'Omár is an intriguing man; and it would have been imprudent to pass on without

---

[1] Barth skirted what he calls 'the Great Forest of Bornu' during his journey to Kuka and again on the way from Kuka to Katsina. This may sound an anachronism in the context of stereotype Bornu, but D. J. Stenning has shown, in his *Savannah Nomads*, 1959, *passim*, that what we today recognize as the Damaturu and Fune districts at that time sheltered the pastoral Wodaabe.

paying him the compliment of a visit; and I was justified in hoping that I might reach as soon as possible the presence of his liege lord the sheikh of Bórnu.

Not being able to see him directly, I was obliged to sacrifice half a day, and to make up my mind to spend the night here. I therefore asked for quarters, and was lodged in a spacious but dirty courtyard, where I could procure but a very insufficient shade with my little English bell-tent of thin canvass. Having passed two uncomfortable hours without any refreshment, I was called in the afternoon into the presence of the governor, and being obliged to leave my servant behind to take care of my luggage while 'Abd-Alla was pasturing the camels, I went alone, and found the great man in a spacious room or hall formed entirely of matwork, where he was lying upon an elevated platform or divan spread with a carpet. He was a short, well-fed, dark-coloured man, of about sixty years of age, his large, broad face looking forth from the hood of a blue cloth bernús, with a neutral expression indicating neither stupidity nor cleverness; his courtiers were grouped around him on the ground. Having saluted him and made the usual polite inquiries, I expressed my ardent desire to reach Kúkawa as soon as possible, as the day which I had fixed with my elder brother (Mr. Richardson) for a meeting in that place was drawing nigh; and I begged him, therefore, to grant me a guide who might conduct me there by the most direct road, of which I myself was ignorant, much time having been already lost in groping my way from one place to another. I then delivered my little present, consisting of an English razor and clasp-knife, a large mirror of German silver, a parcel of English darning-needles, half a pound of cloves, and a piece of scented soap. Having looked at these things with satisfaction, he asked me if I had not anything marvellous with me; and I consented to return to my quarters and fetch my musical box, with the performance of which the ghaladíma was highly pleased, but greatly desired to see some other curious things, such as pocket-pistols, whereupon I told him that I had nothing else calculated to gratify his curiosity. I was much fatigued, and on returning to my tent was not at all pleased to be still troubled by the governor's servant, who came to ask, in the name of his master, for calico, sugar, rose oil, and sundry other articles.

Búndi is a place of tolerable size, but with little industry; and the province of which it is the capital is going to ruin more and more, on account of the laziness and negligence of its governor, — a statement which will be amply proved by the account of my journey through the same district in 1854. The town probably contains eight or nine thousand inhabitants, who belong to the Mánga nation, which seems to be the chief element of the Kanúri, and preserves many very remarkable customs. The special name of the clan of this tribe which dwells hereabouts is Kárda. There is no market here of any importance; but the inhabitants seem to be tolerably at their ease, and there was music and racing, or 'kadáske', in the evening, accompanied by the joyous shrill voices, the 'wulúli', of the women. We, however, seemed to be forgotten; and it was nine o'clock at night, long after we had supped, when we received a dish for ourselves, and corn for the horse. It is rather remarkable that these western provinces of Bórnu were never conquered by the Fúlbe or Felláta, though lying so much nearer to those countries of which they have definitively taken possession than that part of Bórnu situated between the old capital and the great lagoon. The consequence is, that a certain degree of independence is allowed to them, and that they do not pay any tithes to the sheikh.

*March* 23. I had now entered Bórnu proper, the nucleus of that great Central African empire in its second stage, after Kánem had been given up. It is bordered towards the east by the great sea-like komádugu the Tsád or Tsáde, and towards the west and north-west by the little komádugu which by the members of the last expedition had been called Yéou, from the town of that name, or rather Yó, near which they first made its acquaintance on their way from Fezzán. I had now left behind me those loosely-attached principalities which still preserve some sort of independence, and henceforth had only to do with Bórnu officers.

## DEATH OF RICHARDSON

*March* 24. Next morning, when we resumed our march, the fan-palm for some time continued to be the prevailing tree; but some kukas also, or *Adansonia digitata*, and other more leafy trees began to appear, and after a while a thick underwood sprang up. Then followed a few scattered, I might say forlorn, date-trees, which looked like strangers in the country, transplanted into this region by some accident. The sky was clear; and I was leaning carelessly upon my little nag, musing on the original homes of all the plants which now adorn different countries, when I saw advancing towards us a strange-looking person of very fair complexion, richly dressed and armed, and accompanied by three men on horseback, likewise armed with musket and pistols. Seeing that he was a person of consequence, I rode quickly up to him and saluted him, when he, measuring me with his eyes, halted and asked me whether I was the Christian who was expected to arrive from Kanó; and on my answering him in the affirmative, he told me distinctly that my fellow-traveller Yakúb (Mr. Richardson) had died before reaching Kúkawa, and that all his property had been seized. Looking him full in the face, I told him that this, if true, was serious news; and then he related some particulars, which left but little doubt as to the truth of his statement. This sad intelligence deeply affected me, as it involved not only the life of an individual, but the whole fate of the mission.

*March* 25. We might have passed a very comfortable evening with the natives, who took great interest in me, had it not been for my faithful old companion the Bu-séfi, the best (or rather the only good one) of my three camels, which, when it was growing dark, and 'Abd-Alla went to bring the animals back from their pasture, could not be found. The careless boy had neglected to fasten the camel's legs; and being very hungry, it had gone in search of better herbage. This was a very disagreeable accident for me, as I was in the greatest hurry; and my two young lads, who were well aware of it, went for several hours, accompanied by the inhabitants of the place, in every direction, through the whole tract where the camels had been grazing, lighting the ground with torches but all in vain.

Wearied and exhausted, they returned about midnight and lay down to sleep, the music and dance also, which the cheerful natives had kept up, dying away at the same time. About an hour later, being too much excited from anxiety to obtain sleep, I went out once more to see if all was right, when I saw my favourite coming slowly along towards the tent; and on reaching it he laid down by the side of his two inferior companions. There was no moonlight; the night was very dark; evidently only the brightness of the well-known white tent guided the 'stupid' animal. But this was no great proof of stupidity; and I am rather afraid that Europeans often make camels stupid by their own foolish treatment of them, whereas I was wont to treat this noble animal, which had carried myself or the heaviest of my things all the way from Tripoli, as a sensible companion, giving it in the beginning the peel of the oranges I was eating, of which it was particularly fond, or a few of my dates (for which it did not fail to turn round its beautiful neck), or granting it a little extra feed of Negro millet, which it ate like a horse. Rejoiced at seeing my favourite, the absence of which had created such anxiety, returning of its own accord to my tent, and lying down near it, I aroused my servant from his sleep to tell him the joyful news. I wanted to reward it with some corn, but it had taken such good care of itself, that it refused its favourite food.

I was much grieved in consequence of being obliged to part with my old companion; but camels from the coast will not stand the effects of a rainy season in Negroland. I hoped it would safely return to its native country; but the Arab who bought it from me, went first to Kanó when the rainy season was already setting in, and the poor animal died not far from the place where Mr. Richardson had succumbed. Its fidelity will ever remain in my memory as one of the pleasantest recollections of my journey.

*March* 27. We were quietly pitching our tent on the east side of the village, and I was about to make myself comfortable, when I was not a little affected by learning that the girls, who had been bringing little presents to the festival, and who were just returning in procession to their homes, belonged to Ngurútuwa, the very place where the Christian (Mr. Richardson) had died. I then determined to accompany them, though it was late, in order to have at least a short glimpse of the 'white man's grave,' and to see whether it was taken care of. If I had known, before we unloaded the camels, how near we were to the place, I should have gone there at once to spend the night.

Ngurútuwa, once a large and celebrated place, but at present somewhat in decay, lies in a wide and extensive plain, with very few trees, about two miles N.E. from Bandégo; but the town itself is well-shaded, and has, besides kórna and bíto, some wide-spreading umbrageous fig-trees, under one of which Mr. Richardson had been buried. His grave, well-protected with thorn bushes, appeared to have remained untouched, and was likely to remain so. The natives were well aware that it was a Christian who had died here; and they regarded the tomb with reverence. The story of his untimely end had caused some sensation in the neighbourhood. He arrived in a weak state in the evening, and early the next morning he died. The people had taken great interest in the matter; and the report they gave me of the way in which he was buried agreed in the main circumstances with that which I afterwards received from his servants, and of which I forwarded an account from Kúkawa. Unfortunately I had no means of bestowing gifts on the inhabitants of the place where my companion had died. I gave, however, a small present to a man who promised to take especial care of the grave; and I afterwards persuaded the vizier of Bórnu to have a stronger fence made round it.

## THE RUINS OF GAMBARU

*March* 28. Having made a short halt about noon to refresh ourselves and our animals, we continued our march through the forest, which here consisted principally of dúm-palms, faráón, kálgo, talha-trees, and a little siwák or *Capparis sodata*. The ground was covered with the heavy footprints of the elephant, and even at this season it retained many ponds in the channel-like hollows. A solitary maráya or mohhor (*Antilope Soemmeringii*) bounded through the thicket; indeed antelopes of any species are rare in these quarters, and on the whole road I had seen but a single gazelle, near the village Díggere-báre. But it seems remarkable that from the description of the natives there cannot be the least doubt that that large and majestic variety of antelope called *addax*, which is very much like a large stag, is occasionally found here. A fine open space with rich pastures and with hurdle-inclosures interrupted the thicket for about a mile, after which we had to traverse another thick covert, and emerging from it were agreeably surprised at beholding a lake of considerable dimensions on our left, and after a short interval another still more considerable approaching from the north and turning eastward, its surface furrowed by the wind and hurrying along in little billows which dashed upon the shore. On its eastern side lie the ruins of the celebrated town Ghámbarú, which although not the official residence of the kings of Bórnu, was nevertheless their favourite retreat during the flourishing period of the empire; and those two lakes, although connected with the komá-dugu and fed by it, were artificial basins, and seem to have considerable depth; else they could scarcely have presented such a magnificent sheet of water at this season of the year.

But at present all this district, the finest land of Bórnu in the proper sense of the word, which once resounded with the voices and bustle of hundreds of towns and villages, has become one impenetrable jungle, the domain of the elephant and the lion, and with no human inhabitants except a few scattered herdsmen or cattle-breeders, who are exposed every moment to the predatory inroads of the Tawárek. This condition of the finest part of the country is a disgrace to its present rulers, who have nothing to do but to transfer hither a few hundreds of their lazy slaves, and establish them in a fortified place, where-upon the natives would immediately gather round them and change this fine country along the komádugu from an impenetrable jungle into rich fields, producing not only grain but also immense quantities of cotton and indigo.

The town of Ghámbarú was taken and destroyed by the Jemáá of the Fúlbe or Felláta at the same time with Ghasréggomo, or Bírni, in the year of the Héjra 1224, or 1809 of our era, and has not been since reoccupied, so that the ruins are thickly overgrown and almost enveloped in the forest. Although I had not leisure to survey attentively the whole area of the town, I could not help dismounting and looking with great interest at a tolerably well preserved building, evidently part of a mosque, at the south-eastern corner of the wall. I knew, from the report of the last expedition, that there were here remains of brick buildings; but I did not expect to find the workmanship so good. The bricks are certainly not so regularly-shaped as in Europe, but in other respects they seemed quite as good. It is indeed a source of mournful reflection for the traveller to compare this solid mode of building practised in former times in this country, at least by its rulers, with the frail and ephemeral architecture of the present day.

## ENTRY INTO KUKAWA[2]

*April* 2. This was to be a most momentous day of my travels; for I was to reach that place which was the first distinct object of our mission, and I was to come into contact with those people on whose ill or good-will depended the whole success of our mission.

I was now approaching the residence of the chief whom the mission, of which I had the honour to form part, was especially sent out to salute, in a very poor plight, without resources of any kind, and left entirely by myself owing to the death of the director. I was close to this place, a large town, and was about to enter it without a single companion. The heat being just at its highest, no living being was to be seen either in the village or on the road; and I hesitated a moment, considering whether it would not be better to wait here for my camels. But my timid

[2] It is interesting to compare Barth's description with those of Denham, Nachtigal and Monteil on their respective entries into Kukawa; together they span three quarters of a century.

reluctance being confounded by the thought that my people might be far behind, and that if I waited for them we should find no quarters prepared for us, I spurred on my nag, and soon reached the western suburb of Kúkawa.

Proceeding with some hesitation towards the white clay wall which encircles the town, and which from a little distance could scarcely be distinguished from the adjoining ground, I entered the gate, being gazed at by a number of people collected here, and who were still more surprised when I inquired for the residence of the sheikh. Then passing the little daily market (the dyrríya), which was crowded with people, I rode along the déndal, or promenade, straight up to the palace, which borders the promenade towards the east. It is flanked by a very indifferent mosque, built likewise of clay, with a tower at its N.W. corner, while houses of grandees inclose the place on the north and south sides. The only ornament of this place is a fine chédia or caoutchouc-tree in front of the house of 'Ali Ladán, on the south side; but occasionally it becomes enlivened by interesting groups of Arabs and native courtiers in all the finery of their dress, and of their richly caparisoned horses.

The sheikh, though he usually resides in his palace in the eastern town, was at present here; and the slaves stared at me, without understanding, or caring to understand, what I wanted, until Díggama, the storekeeper, was called, who, knowing something of me as 'Abd el Kerím, ordered a slave to conduct me to the vizier. Though I had heard some account of the sheikh living out of the western town, I was rather taken by surprise at seeing the large extent of the double town; and I was equally astonished at the number of gorgeously-dressed horsemen whom I met on my way.

Considering my circumstances, I could not have chosen a more favourable moment for arriving. About two hundred horsemen were assembled before the house of the vizier, who was just about to mount his horse in order to pay his daily visit to the sheikh. When he came out, he saluted me in a very cheerful way, and was highly delighted when he heard and saw that I had come quite alone. He told me he had known me already, from the letter which I had sent to his agent in Zínder stating that I would come after I had finished my business, but not before. While he himself rode in great state to the sheikh, he ordered one of his people to show me my quarters. These were closely adjoining the vizier's house, consisting of two immense courtyards, the more secluded of which inclosed, besides a half-finished clay dwelling, a very spacious and neatly-built hut. This, as I was told, had been expressly prepared for the mission before it was known that we were without means.

## AUDIENCE WITH THE SHEHU OF BORNU

*April* 3. Thus strengthened, I went the next morning to pay my respects to the vizier, taking with me a small present of my own, the principal attractions of which lay in a thick twisted lace of silk of very handsome workmanship, which I had had made in Tripoli, and a leathern letter-case of red colour, which I had brought with me from Europe. Destitute as I was of any means, and not quite sure as yet whether Her Britannic Majesty's Government would authorize me to carry out the objects of the mission, I did not deem it expedient to assume too much importance, but simply told the vizier that, though the director of the mission had not been fortunate enough to convey to him and the sheikh with his own mouth the sentiments of the British Government, yet I hoped that, even in this respect, these endeavours would not be quite in vain, although at the present moment our means were so exhausted that, even for executing our scientific plans, we were entirely dependent on their kindness.

I found the sheikh ('Omár, the eldest son of Mohammed el Amín el Kánemy) a very simple, benevolent, and even cheerful man. He has regular and agreeable features, rather a little too round to be expressive; but he is remarkably black — a real glossy black, such as is rarely seen in Bórnu, and which he has inherited undoubtedly from his mother, a Bagirmaye princess.

He was very simply dressed in a light tobe, having a bernús negligently wrapped round his shoulder; round his head a dark-red shawl was twisted with great care; and his face was quite uncovered, which surprised me not a little, as his father used to cover it in the Tawárek fashion. He was reclining upon a diván covered with a carpet, at the back of a fine airy hall neatly polished.

My presents were very small, the only valuable article among them being a nice little copy of the Kurán, which on a former occasion I had bought in Egypt for five pounds sterling, and was now carrying with me for my own use. That I made a present of this book to the prince may perhaps be regarded with an unfavourable eye by some persons in this country; but let them consider it as a sign of an unprejudiced mind, and of the very high esteem in which he held me, that, although knowing me to be a Christian, he did not refuse to accept from my hands that which was most holy in his eyes. On the whole I could not have expected a more friendly reception, either from the sheikh or from his vizier. But there was a very delicate point which I was obliged to touch upon: what was to become of Mr. Richardson's property?

In the afternoon I went again to the vizier, and requested to see the inventory of all that my late companion had left; and he showed it to me and read it himself. He then ordered the box to be opened, which contained clothes and papers; and I was glad to see that not only the journals, upon the keeping of which Mr. Richardson had bestowed great care, but also all his other collectanea, were safe. Having taken the inventory with me, I sent Mohammed the following day to him with the request that Mr. Richardson's property should be delivered to me. Having been desired to call myself at noon, I went, but was surprised to find only Lamíno (properly El Amín), the vizier's confidential officer, of whom I shall have occasion to speak hereafter. I was still more surprised when only some of Mr. Richardson's boxes were brought in, and I was desired to select what I wanted, and leave the rest behind. This I refused to do, and asked where the other things were, when Lamíno did not hesitate to declare that the ornamented gun and the handsome pair of pistols had been sold. Upon hearing this, though I had been treated very kindly and hospitably on my arrival, and had received immense quantities of provision of every kind, I could not refrain from declaring that if in truth they had behaved so unscrupulously with other people's property I had nothing more to do here, and returned to my quarters immediately.

My firmness had its desired effect; and late in the evening I received a message from the vizier, that if I wanted to have a private interview with him I might come now, as during the daytime he was always troubled by the presence of a great many people. The person who brought me this message was Háj Edrís, a man of whom in the course of my proceedings I shall have to speak repeatedly. Satisfied with having an opportunity of conversing with the vizier without reserve, I followed the messenger immediately, and found Háj Beshír quite alone, sitting in an inner court of his house, with two small wax candles by his side. We then had a long interview, which lasted till midnight, and the result of which was that I protested formally against the sale of those things left by Mr. Richardson, and insisted that all should be delivered to me and to Mr. Overweg as soon as he should arrive, when we would present to the sheikh and to the vizier, in a formal manner, all those articles which we knew our companion had intended to give to them. Besides, I urged once more the necessity of forwarding the news of Mr. Richardson's death, and of my safe arrival as soon as possible, as, after our late misfortunes in Aïr, Her Britannic Majesty's Government, as well as our friends, would be most anxious about our safety. I likewise tried to persuade my benevolent and intelligent host that he might do a great service to the mission, if he would enable us to carry out part of our scientific purposes without delay, as Government would certainly not fail to honour us with their confidence, if they saw that we were going on. Having carried all my points, and being promised protection and assistance to the widest extent, I indulged in a more friendly chat, and, delighted by the social

7. A Kanembu Chief
From Barth's *Travels and Discoveries*.

## Article 5th

The Sovereign of Bornoo, El Emir Omar son of Mohammed el Kanemy, promises to do all he can to facilitate the passage of Couriers carrying Despatches to or from the English Nation within his Territories and to provide for their security. —

الشرط الخامس

حاكم برنوم الامير الشيخ عمر بن الشيخ محمد الامير الكانمي رهنه الوعد بان يعمل جهده ويسهل ما يحمله السيارة من مكاتيب اتباع دولة الانكليز التي تاتيهم والتي يرسلونها من وطنه ويكون ذلك بامان

## Article 6th

The Sovereign of the Kingdom of Bornoo will put in execution the present Treaty; will make it public, and cause it to be observed; and it shall not be violated. from this day forward for ever.

الشرط السادس

حاكم مملكة برنوم يعمل في انونا ليكرم هذه الشروط معمولا بها ويشهرها مراعيوم المستقبل الدائم

Written and Signed on the third day of September 1852 corresponding with the seventeenth day of Dhu il Kád 1268.

بتاريخ ضحوة الخميس لسبعة مشرون شهر الله ذي القعدة الحرام وثلث شهر سبتمبر ١٨٥٢ م

Dr. Barth

8. Final clauses, signatures and seals of the Treaty with Bornu, September 1852

*Crown copyright; reproduced by permission of the Controller of H.M. Stationery Office.*

character of my host, and full of the most confident hopes for
my future proceedings, withdrew a little after midnight.

Having in this way vindicated the honourable character of
the mission, and my own, I applied myself with more cheerfulness to my studies and inquiries, for which I found ample
opportunity; for many distinguished personages from distant
countries were staying here at this time, partly on their journey
to or from Mekka, partly only attracted by the fame of the
vizier's hospitable and bounteous character.

## HISTORY OF BORNU

Altogether, in the history of Bórnu we can distinguish the
following epochs. First, the rise of power in Kánem, Njímiye
being the capital of the empire, silent and imperceptible till we
see on a sudden, in the beginning of the 12th century, the
powerful prince Dúnama ben Humé start forth under the
impulse of Islám, wielding the strength of a young and vigorous
empire, and extending his influence as far as Egypt. The acme,
or highest degree of prosperity, of this period coincides with the
reign of Díbalámi Dúnama Selmámi, in the middle of the 13th
century, during the prime of the dynasty of the Beni Háfis in
Tunis. But this reign already engendered the germs of decay;
for during it the two cognate elements of which the empire
consisted, namely the Tedá and the Kanúri, were disunited,
and it yielded too much influence to the aristocratical element,
which was represented by the twelve great offices, an institution
which seems to deserve particular attention.

The consequence was, that a series of civil wars and regicides
ensued, interrupted only by the more tranquil reign of Ibrahím
Nikálemi in the first half of the 14th century, which was
followed, however, by the most unfortunate period of the
empire, when the great native tribe of the Soy burst forth and
killed four kings in succession. Then followed another respite
from turmoil, just at the time when Ebn Batúta visited Negroland; but the son of the very king who in the time of that
distinguished traveller ruled over Bórnu fell the first victim in

the struggle that ensued with a power which had arisen from the same root, had gained strength during the civil wars of Bórnu, and which now threatened to swallow it up altogether. This was the dynasty of the Bulála, which, originating with the fugitive Bórnu prince Jíl Shikomémi, had established itself in the district of Fíttri over the tribe of the Kúka, and from thence spread its dominion in every direction till, after a sanguinary struggle, it conquered Kánem, and forced the Kanúri dynasty to seek refuge in the western provinces of its empire, about the year 1400 of our era.

The Bórnu empire (if we may give the name of empire to the shattered host of a belligerent tribe driven from their home and reduced to a few military encampments) for the next seventy years seemed likely to go to pieces altogether, till the great king 'Ali Dúnamámi opened another glorious period; for having at length mastered the aristocratical element, which had almost overwhelmed the monarchy, he founded as a central point of government a new capital or 'bírni', Ghasréggomo, the empire having been without a fixed centre since the abandonment of Njímiye. It was in his time that Leo Africanus visited Negroland, where he found the Bulála empire (Gaoga) still in the ascendant; but this was changed in the beginning of the 16th century, even before the publication of his account; for in the hundred and twenty-second (lunar) year from the time when 'Omár was compelled to abandon his royal seat in Njímiye, ceding the rich country of Kánem, the very nucleus of the empire, to his rivals, the energetic king Edrís Katakarmábi entered that capital again with his victorious army, and from that time down to the beginning of the present century Kánem has remained a province of Bórnu, although it was not again made the seat of government.

Altogether the 16th century is one of the most glorious periods of the Bórnu empire, adorned as it is by such able princes as the two Edrís' and Mohammed, while in Western Negroland the great Sónghay empire went to pieces, and was finally subjugated by Mulay Hámed el Mansúr, the emperor of Morocco. Then followed a quieter period, and old age seemed gradually to gain on the kingdom, while pious and peaceful kings occupied the throne, till in the middle of the last century the energetic and enterprising king 'Ali 'Omármi began a violent struggle against that very nation from which the Bórnu dynasty had sprung, but which had now become its most fearful enemy — the Imóshagh or Tawárek. He made great exertions in every direction; but his efforts seem to have resembled the convulsions of death, and being succeeded by an indolent king, for such was Ahmed, the fatal hour which was to accomplish the extinction of the dynasty of the Séfuwa rapidly approached. At last, when the very centre of the empire had already fallen a prey to a new nation which had started forth on a career of glory, the Fúlbe or Felláta, there arose a stranger, a nationalized Arab, who, in saving the last remains of the kingdom, founded a new dynasty, that of the Kánemíyín.

## THE WAZIRI OF BORNU, HAJ BASHIR

*April.* But I must principally dwell upon my relations to the vizier el Háj Beshír ben Ahmed Tiráb, upon whose benevolent disposition the whole success of the mission depended, as he ruled entirely the mind of the sheikh, who was more sparing of words, and less intelligent.

Mohammed el Beshír, being the son of the most influential man in Bórnu after the sheikh, enjoyed all the advantages which such a position could offer for the cultivation of his mind, which was by nature of a superior cast. He had gone on a pilgrimage to Mekka in the year 1843, by way of Ben-Ghází, when he had an opportunity both of showing the Arabs near the coast that the inhabitants of the interior of the continent are superior to the beasts, and of getting a glimpse of a higher state of civilization than he had been able to observe in his own country.

Having thus learned to survey the world collectively from a new point of view, and with an increased eagerness after everything foreign and marvellous, he returned to his native country, where he soon had an opportunity of proving his talent, his father being slain in the unfortunate battle at Kúsuri, and

Sheikh 'Omár, a fugitive in his native country, having much need of a faithful counsellor in his embarrassed situation. The sheikh was beset by a powerful and victorious host, encamping in the largest of the towns of his kingdom, while the party of the old dynasty was rising again, and not only withdrawing from him the best forces wherewith to face the enemy, but threatening his very existence, at the same time that a brother was standing in fierce rivalry to him at the head of a numerous army. Sheikh 'Omár was successful, the host of Wadáy was obliged to withdraw, and, abandoning the purpose for which they had come, namely, that of re-establishing the old dynasty, commenced a difficult retreat of many hundred miles at the beginning of the rainy season; the partisans of the old dynasty were entirely crushed, the last prince of that family slain, the residence of the sultans levelled to the ground, and even the remembrance of the old times was almost effaced. There remained to be feared only his brother 'Abd e' Rahmán. 'Abd e' Rahmán was a good soldier, but a man of a very loose and violent character. When a youth he had committed all sorts of violence and injustice, carrying off young brides by force, to indulge his passions: he was besides a man of little intelligence. Being but a few months younger than 'Omár, he thought himself equally entitled to the succession; and if once admitted into a high position in the empire, he might be expected to abuse his influence on the very first opportunity.

Sheikh 'Omár, therefore, could not but choose to confide rather in the intelligent son of his old minister, the faithful companion in the field and counsellor of his father, than in his own fierce and jealous brother; and all depended upon the behaviour of Háj Beshír, and upon the discretion with which he should occupy and maintain his place as first, or rather only minister of the kingdom. Assuredly, his policy should have been to conciliate, as much as possible, all the greater 'kokanáwa' or courtiers, in order to undermine the influence of 'Abd e' Rahmán, whom it might be wise to keep at a respectful distance. But in this respect the vizier seems to have made great mistakes, his covetousness blinding him to his principal advantages; for covetous he certainly was — first, from the love of possessing, and also in order to indulge his luxurious disposition, for he was certainly rather 'kamúma', that is to say, extremely fond of the fair sex, and had a harím of from three to four hundred female slaves.

In assembling this immense number of female companions for the entertainment of his leisure hours, he adopted a scientific principle; in fact, a credulous person might suppose that he regarded his harím only from a scientific point of view; — as a sort of ethnological museum — doubtless of a peculiarly interesting kind — which he had brought together in order to impress upon his memory the distinguishing features of each tribe. I have often observed that, in speaking with him of the different tribes of Negroland, he was at times struck with the novelty of a name, lamenting that he had not yet had a specimen of that tribe in his harím, and giving orders at once to his servants to endeavour to procure a perfect sample of the missing kind. I remember, also, that on showing to him one day an illustrated ethnological work in which he took a lively interest, and coming to a beautiful picture of a Circassian female, he told me, with an expression of undisguised satisfaction, that he had a living specimen of that kind; and when, forgetting the laws of Mohammedan etiquette, I was so indiscreet to ask him whether she was as handsome as the picture, he answered only with a smile, at once punishing and pardoning my indiscreet question. I must also say that, notwithstanding the great number and variety of the women who shared his attention, he seemed to take a hearty interest in each of them; at least I remembered that he grieved most sincerely for the loss of one who died in the winter of 1851. Poor Háj Beshír! He was put to death in the last month of 1853, leaving seventy-three sons alive, not counting the daughters, and the numbers of children which may be supposed to die in such an establishment without reaching maturity.

But to return to his political character. I said that he neglected to attach to himself the more powerful of the courtiers, with whose assistance he might have hoped to keep the rival brother of Sheikh 'Omár at some distance; indeed, he even alienated them by occasional, and sometimes injudicious use of his almost unlimited power, obliging them, for instance, to resign to him a handsome female slave or a fine horse. If he had possessed great personal courage and active powers, he might have mastered circumstances and kept his post, notwithstanding the ill-will of all around him; but he wanted those qualities, as the result shows: and yet, well aware of the danger which threatened him, he was always on his guard, having sundry loaded pistols and carbines always around him, upon and under his carpet. Shortly before I arrived, an arrow had been shot at him in the evening, while he was sitting in his courtyard.

I have peculiar reason to thank Providence for having averted the storm which was gathering over his head during my stay in Bórnu, for my intimacy with him might very easily have involved me also in the calamities which befell him. However, I repeat that altogether he was a most excellent, kind, liberal, and just man, and might have done much good to the country, if he had been less selfish and more active. He was incapable, indeed, of executing by himself any act of severity, such as in the unsettled state of a semi-barbarous kingdom may at times be necessary; and, being conscious of his own mildness, he left all those matters to a man named Lamíno, to whom I gave the title of 'the shameless left hand of the vizier'.

I remonstrated with him on the shamefully neglected state of the shores of the lake, which contained the finest pasture-grounds, and might yield an immense quantity of rice and cotton. He entered with spirit into all my proposals; but in a short time all was forgotten. He listened with delight to what little historical knowledge I had of these countries, and inquired particularly whether Kánem had really been in former times a mighty kingdom, or whether it would be worth retaking. It was in consequence of these conversations that he began to take an interest in the former history of the country, and that the historical records of Edrís Alawóma came to light; but he would not allow me to take them into my hands, and I could only read over his shoulders. He was a very religious man; and though he admired Europeans very much on account of their greater accomplishments, he was shocked to think that they drank intoxicating liquors. However, I tried to console him by telling him that, although the Europeans were also very partial to the fair sex, yet they did not indulge in this luxury on so large a scale as he did, and that therefore he ought to allow them some other little pleasure.

## THE CITY OF KUKAWA

*April.* Having now a horse whereon to mount, I rode every day, either into the eastern town to pay a visit to the sheikh, or to the vizier, or roving around the whole circuit of the capital, and peeping into the varied scenes which the life of the people exhibited. The precincts of the town with its suburbs are just as interesting as its neighbourhood (especially during the months that precede the rainy season) is monotonous and tiresome in the extreme. Certainly, the arrangement of the capital contributes a great deal to the variety of the picture which it forms, laid out as it is in two distinct towns, each surrounded with its wall, the one, occupied chiefly by the rich and wealthy, containing very large establishments, while the other, with the exception of the principal thoroughfare which traverses the town from west to east, consists of rather crowded dwellings, with narrow winding lanes. These two distinct towns are separated by a space about half a mile broad, itself thickly inhabited on both sides of a wide open road which forms the connection between them, but laid out less regularly, and presenting to the eye a most interesting medley of large clay buildings and small thatched huts, of massive clay walls surrounding immense yards, and light fences of reeds in a more or less advanced state of decay, and with a variety of colour, according to their age, from the brightest yellow down to the deepest black. All around these two towns there are small villages or clusters of huts, and large detached farms surrounded with clay walls, low enough to allow a glimpse from horseback over the thatched huts which they inclose.

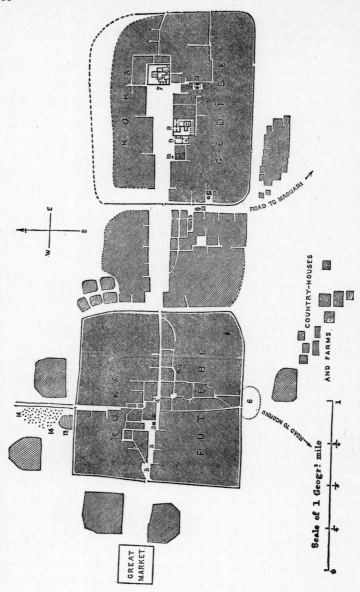

Fig. 4

In this labyrinth of dwellings a man, interested in the many forms which human life presents, may rove about at any time of the day with the certainty of finding never-failing amusement, although the life of the Kanúri people passes rather monotonously along, with the exception of some occasional feasting. During the hot hours, indeed, the town and its precincts become torpid, except on market-days, when the market-place itself, at least, and the road leading to it from the western gate, are most animated just at that time. For, singular as it is, in Kúkawa, as well as almost all over this part of Negroland, the great markets do not begin to be well attended till the heat of the day grows intense; and it is curious to observe what a difference prevails in this as well as in other respects between these countries and Yóruba, where almost all the markets are held in the cool of the evening.

The daily little markets, or durríya, even in Kúkawa, are held in the afternoon, and are most frequented between the áser (lásari) and the mughreb (almágribu) or sunset. The most important of these durríyas is that held inside the west gate of the billa futébe; and here even camels, horses, and oxen are sold in considerable numbers: but they are much inferior to

←        Fig. 4. The City of Kukawa

1. English house, [of which a special plan is given on page 168].
2. Palace, 'fáto maibe,' of the sheikh, in the western town or billa futébe, with the mosque, 'máshidí,' at the corner.
3. Minaret of mosque.
4. Square at the back of the palace, with a most beautiful caoutchouc-tree, the finest in Kúkawa.
5. Déndal, or principal street.
6. Area before the southern gate where all the offal and dead bodies of camels and cattle, and sometimes even of slaves, are thrown, and which, during the rainy season, is changed into a large and deep pond.
7. Palace of the sheikh in the eastern town, or billa-gedíbe.
8. Palace of the vizier el Háj Beshír.
9. House where I was first lodged on my arrival, afterwards occupied by Lamíno, the vizier's head man.
10. (The house west from this) Palace belonging to Abu-Bakr, the sheikh's eldest and favourite son, with a very large caoutchouc-tree in front.
11. House belonging to Abba Yusuf, second brother of the sheikh.
12. House occupied during my later stay by Lamíno.
13. Hollows from whence the clay has been taken for building material, and which, during the rainy season, are changed into deep pools of stagnant water.
14. Cemetery.

the large fair, or great market, which is held every Monday
on the open ground beyond the two villages which lie at a
short distance from the western gate. Formerly it was held on
the road to Ngórnu, before the southern gate; but it has been
removed from thence on account of the large pond of water
formed during the rainy season in the hollow close to this gate.

## THE MONDAY MARKET IN KUKAWA

*April.* I visited the great fair, 'kásukú letenínbe', every Monday
immediately after my arrival, and found it very interesting, as
it calls together the inhabitants of all the eastern parts of Bórnu,
the Shúwa and the Koyám, with their corn and butter, the
former, though of Arab origin and still preserving in purity his
ancient character, always carrying his merchandise on the back
of oxen, the women mounted upon the top of it while the
African Koyám employs the camel, if not exclusively, at least
with a decided preference; the Kánembú with their butter and
dried fish, the inhabitants of Mákari with their tobes (the kóre
berné): even Búdduma, or rather Yédiná, are very often seen
in the market, selling whips made from the skin of the hippopotamus, or sometimes even hippopotamus meat, or dried fish,
and attract the attention of the spectator by their slender
figures, their small handsome features unimpaired by any
incisions, the men generally wearing a short black shirt and a
small straw-hat, 'súni ngáwa', their neck adorned with several
strings of kúngona, or shells, while the women are profusely
ornamented with strings of glass beads, and wear their hair in
a very remarkable way, though not in so awkward a fashion as
Mr. Overweg afterwards observed in the island Belárigo.

On reaching the market-place from the town the visitor first
comes to that part where the various materials for constructing
the light dwellings of the country are sold, such as mats, of
three different kinds, the thickest, which I have mentioned
above as lágará, then síggedí, or the common coarse mat made
of the reed called kalkálti, and the búshi, made of dúm-leaves,
or 'ngílle', for lying upon; poles and stakes; the framework,

'léggerá', for the thatched roofs of huts, and the ridge-beam
or 'késkan súmo'; then oxen for slaughter, 'fé debáterám', or
for carrying burdens, 'knému lápterám'; further on, long rows
of leathern bags filled with corn, ranging far along on the south
side of the market-place, with either 'kéwa', the large bags
for the camel, a pair of which form a regular camel's load, or
the large 'jerábu', which is thrown across the back of the
pack-oxen, or the smaller 'fállim', a pair of which constitute
an ox-load, 'kátkun knémube'. These long rows are animated
not only by the groups of the sellers and buyers, with their
weatherworn figures and torn dresses, but also by the beasts of
burden, mostly oxen, which have brought the loads and which
are to carry back their masters to their distant dwelling-places;
then follow the camels for sale, often as many as a hundred or
more, and numbers of horses, but generally not first-rate ones,
which are mostly sold in private. All this sale of horses, camels,
etc., with the exception of the oxen, passes through the hands
of the dilélma or broker, who, according to the mode of announcement, takes his percentage from the buyer or the seller.

The middle of the market is occupied by the dealers in other
merchandise of native and of foreign manufacture, the 'amagdí'
or tob from Ujé, and the kóre, or rébshi; the farásh, or 'fetkéma',
and the 'selláma', the people dealing in cloths, shirts, túrkedís,
beads of all sizes and colours, leatherwork, coloured boxes of
very different shape and size, very neatly and elegantly made
of ox-hide. There are also very neat little boxes made of the
kernel, or 'náge', of the fruit of the dúm-tree. Then comes
the place where the kómbuli disposes of his slaves.

There are only a few very light sheds or stalls ('kaudi'),
erected here and there. In general, besides a few of the retail
dealers, only the dilélma or broker has a stall, which, on this
account, is called diléllam; and, no shady trees being found,
both buyers and sellers are exposed to the whole force of the
sun during the very hottest hours of the day, between eleven
and three o'clock, when the market is most full and busy, and
the crowd is often so dense that it is difficult to make one's way
through it: for the place not being regularly laid out, nor the

thoroughfares limited by rows of stalls, each dealer squats down
with his merchandise where he likes. There are often from
twelve to fifteen thousand people crowded together in the
market; but the noise is not very great, the Kanúri people being
more sedate and less vivacious than the Háusáwa, and not
vending their wares with loud cries. However, the wanzám or
barber, going about, affords amusement by his constant
whistling, 'kangádi'. In general, even amusements have
rather a sullen character in Bórnu; and of course, in a place
of business like the market, very little is done for amusement,
although sometimes a serpent-tamer ('kadíma') or a story-
teller ('kosgolíma') is met with. Also the luxuries offered to
the people are very few in comparison with the varieties of
cakes and sweetmeats in the market-places of Háusa; and
'kólché' (the common sweet groundnut), 'gángala' (the bitter
groundnut), boiled beans or 'ngálo', and a few dry dates
from the Tébu country, are almost the only things, besides
water and a little nasty sour milk, offered as refreshment to the
exhausted customer.

The fatigue which people have to undergo in purchasing
their week's necessaries in the market is all the more harassing,
as there is not at present any standard money for buying and
selling; for the ancient standard of the country, viz. the pound
of copper, has long since fallen into disuse, though the name,
'rotl', still remains. The 'gábagá', or cotton-strips, which
then became usual, have lately begun to be supplanted by
the cowries or 'kúngona', which have been introduced, as it
seems, rather by a speculation of the ruling people, than by a
natural want of the inhabitants, though nobody can deny that
they are very useful for buying small articles, and infinitely
more convenient than cotton strips. Eight cowries or kúngona
are reckoned equal to one gábagá, and four gábagá, or two-
and-thirty kúngona, to one rotl. Then, for buying larger objects,
there are shirts of all kinds and sizes, from the 'dóra', the
coarsest and smallest one, quite unfit for use, and worth six
rotls, up to the large ones, worth fifty or sixty rotls. But while
this is a standard value, the relation of the rotl and the Austrian

dollar, which is pretty well current in Bórnu, is subject to extreme fluctuation, due, I must confess, at least partly, to the speculations of the ruling men, and principally to that of my friend the Háj Beshír. Indeed, I cannot defend him against the reproach of having speculated to the great detriment of the public; so that when he had collected a great amount of kúngona, and wished to give it currency, the dollar would suddenly fall as low as to five-and-forty or fifty rotls, while at other times it would fetch as much as one hundred rotls, or three thousand two hundred shells; that is, seven hundred shells more than in Kanó. The great advantage of the market in Kanó is, that there is one standard coin, which, if a too large amount of dollars be not on a sudden set in circulation, will always preserve the same value.

But to return to the market. A small farmer who brings his corn to the Monday market, or the 'kásukú léteninbe', in Kúkawa, will on no account take his payment in shells, and will rarely accept of a dollar: the person, therefore, who wishes to buy corn, if he has only dollars, must first exchange a dollar for shells, or rather buy shells; then with the shells he must buy a 'kúlgu', or shirt; and after a good deal of bartering he may thus succeed in buying the corn, be it some kind of argúm, wheat, or rice. However, these two latter articles are not always to be got, while more frequently they are only in small quantities. The rice sold in Kúkawa is wild rice, the refuse of the elephants, and of a very inferior description.

The fatigue to be undergone in the market is such that I have very often seen my servants return in a state of the utmost exhaustion. Most of the articles which are sold at the great Monday fair may also be found in the small afternoon markets or durríya, but only in small quantity, and at a higher price, and some articles will be sought for there in vain. But while there is certainly a great deal of trouble in the market of Kúkawa, it must be acknowledged that the necessaries of life are cheaper there than in any other place which I have visited in Central Africa, almost half as cheap again as in Kátsena and Sókoto, a third cheaper than in Kanó, and about a fourth

cheaper than in Timbúktu. About the cheapness of meat and
corn in the latter place, which is indeed a very remarkable fact,
and struck me with the utmost surprise when I first reached
that celebrated town, I shall speak in the proper place. But I
must remark that dukhn, argúm móro, or millet (*Pennisetum
typhoïdeum*), is in greater quantity, and therefore cheaper, in
Kúkawa than the durra or sorghum, 'ngáberi', just as it is in
Timbúktu and Kanó, while in Bagírmi durra is much cheaper.
The ngáberi of Bórnu, however, particularly that kind of it
which is called matíya, and which is distinguished by its
whiteness, is most excellent; and the 'senásin', a kind of thin
pancake prepared from this grain, is the lightest and best food
for a European in this country.

Of course the price of corn varies greatly according to the
season, the lowest rates ruling about a month or two after the
harvest, when all the corn in the country has been thrashed, and
the highest rates just about the harvest time. In general, a
dollar will purchase in Kúkawa three ox-loads, 'kátkun
knémube', of argúm; a dollar and a half will buy a very good
ox of about six hundred pounds' weight; two dollars fetch a
pack-ox ('knému'), or a milch-cow ('fé mádarabé'); one
dollar, two good sheep; from seventeen to twenty rotls, a
'téndu' of butter, containing about four pounds' weight. For
wheat and rice the general rule in Negroland is, that they fetch
double the price of the native corn. Rice might seem to be
indigenous in Central Africa, growing wild everywhere, as well
in Bághena, in Western Africa, as in Kótoko or Bagírmi.
Wheat, on the contrary, was evidently introduced some
hundred years ago, together with onions, the favourite food of
the Arab, to the merits of which the native African is insensible,
although it is a most wholesome article of diet in this climate.

Of vegetables, the most common in the market are — beans
of various descriptions, which likewise form a very important
article of food in many districts, certainly as much as the third
of the whole consumption; onions, consumed in great quantity
by the Arabs, but not by the natives, who prefer to season their
food with the young leaves of the monkey-bread tree, 'kálu

kúka', or the 'karás', or with a sauce made from dried fish. There are no sweet potatoes and no yams in this part of Bórnu, the consequence of which is that the food of the natives is less varied than in Háusa, Kébbi, or Yóruba. Yams are brought to this country as rarities, and are given as presents to influential persons.

Camels sell at from eight to twenty dollars. When there is no caravan in preparation, a very tolerable beast may be about for the former price; but when a caravan is about to start, the best will fetch as much as twenty dollars — very rarely more; and a good camel may always be had for about fifteen dollars. Some camels may be bought for four or five dollars each, but cannot be relied on.

Very strong travelling horses for servants were during my first visit purchasable for from six to eight dollars, while an excellent horse would not fetch more than thirty dollars; but in the year 1854 the price had risen considerably, in consequence of the exportation of horses, which had formerly been forbidden, having been permitted, and great numbers having been exported to the west — chiefly to Múniyo, Kátsena, and Márádi. A first-rate horse of foreign race, however, is much dearer, and will sometimes fetch as much as three hundred dollars. I shall have another opportunity of speaking of the horses of Bórnu, which is rather an interesting and important subject, as the breed is excellent, and, besides being very handsome and of good height, they bear fatigue marvellously — a fact of which one of my own horses gave the best proof, having carried me during three years of almost incessant fatigue on my expedition to Kánem, to the Músgu country, to Bagírmi, to Timbúktu, and back to Kanó, where my poor dear companion died in December 1854: and let it be taken into consideration that, though I myself am not very heavy, I constantly carried with me a double-barrelled gun, one or two pairs of pistols, a quantity of powder and shot, several instruments, my journals, and generally even my coffee-pot and some little provision.

But to return to the picture of life which the town of Kúkawa presents. With the exception of Mondays, when just during

the hottest hours of the day there is much crowd and bustle
in the market-place, it is very dull from about noon till three
o'clock in the afternoon; and even during the rest of the day,
those scenes of industry, which in the varied panorama of
Kanó meet the eye, are here sought for in vain. Instead of
those numerous dyeing-yards or máriná full of life and bustle,
though certainly also productive of much filth and foul odours,
which spread over the town of Kanó, there is only a single, and
a very poor máriná in Kúkawa; no beating of tobes is heard,
nor the sound of any other handicraft.

There is a great difference of character between these two
towns; and, as I have said above, the Bórnu people are by
temperament far more phlegmatic than those of Kanó. The
women in general are much more ugly, with square short
figures, large heads, and broad noses, with immense nostrils,
disfigured still more by the enormity of a red bead or coral
work in the nostril. Nevertheless they are certainly quite as
coquettish, and, as far as I had occasion to observe, at least
as wanton also, as the more cheerful and sprightly Háusa
women. I have never seen a Háusa woman strolling about the
streets with her gown trailing after her on the ground, the
fashion of the women of Kúkawa, and wearing on her shoulders
some Manchester print of a showy pattern, keeping the ends
of it in her hands, while she throws her arms about in a
coquettish manner. In a word, their dress, as well as their
demeanour, is far more decent and agreeable. The best part
in the dress or ornaments of the Bórnu women is the silver
ornament (the 'fállafálle kélabé') which they wear on the
back of the head, and which in taller figures, when the hair is
plaited in the form of a helmet, is very becoming; but it is not
every woman who can afford such an ornament, and many a
one sacrifices her better interests for this decoration.

The most animated quarter of the two towns is the great
thoroughfare, which, proceeding by the southern side of the
palace in the western town, traverses it from west to east, and
leads straight to the sheikh's residence in the eastern town.
This is the 'déndal' or promenade, a locality which has its

9. Humbutudi Village
From Barth's *Travels and Discoveries*.

10. The River Benue
From Barth's *Travels and Discoveries*.

11. The Market in Sokoto
From Barth's *Travels and Discoveries*.

12. The River Niger
From Barth's *Travels and Discoveries*.

imitation, on a less or greater scale, in every town of the country. This road, during the whole day, is crowded by numbers of people on horseback and on foot; free men and slaves, foreigners as well as natives, every one in his best attire, to pay his respects to the sheikh or his vizier, to deliver an errand, or to sue for justice or employment, or a present. I myself very often went along this well-trodden path — this highroad of ambition; but I generally went at an unusual hour, either at sunrise in the morning, or while the heat of the mid-day, not yet abated, detained the people in their cool haunts, or late at night, when the people were already retiring to rest or, sitting before their houses, beguiling their leisure hours with amusing tales or with petty scandal. At such hours I was sure to find the vizier or the sheikh alone; but sometimes they wished me also to visit and sit with them, when they were accessible to all the people; and on these occasions the vizier took pride and delight in conversing with me about matters of science, such as the motion of the earth, or the planetary system, or subjects of that kind.

## EXCURSION TO LAKE CHAD

*April* 24. My stay in the town was agreeably interrupted by an excursion to Ngórnu and the shores of the lake.

Sheikh 'Omár, with his whole court, left Kúkawa in the night of the 23rd of April, in order to spend a day or two in Ngórnu, where he had a tolerably good house; and, having been invited by the vizier to go there, I also followed on the morning of the next day. This road to Ngórnu is strongly marked with that sameness and monotony which characterize the neighbourhood of Kúkawa. At first nothing is seen but the melancholy 'káwo', *Asclepias procera* or *gigantea;* then 'ngílle', low bushes of *Cucifera*, appear, and gradually trees begin to enliven the landscape, first scattered here and there, further on forming a sort of underwood. The path is broad and well-trodden, but consists mostly of deep sandy soil. There are no villages on the side of the road, but a good many at a little distance. In the rainy season some very large ponds are formed by its side. Two miles and a half before the traveller reaches Ngórnu the trees cease again, being only seen in detached clusters at a great distance, marking the sites of villages, while near the road they give way to an immense fertile plain, where beans are cultivated, besides grain. However, this also is covered at this season of the year with the tiresome and endless *Asclepias*. Among the sites of former towns on the east side of the road is that of New Bírni, which was built by the Sultan Mohammed, when residing in Berberuwá, about the year 1820, and destroyed by Háj Beshír in the year 1847, and does not now contain a living soul. Further on is a group of kitchen-gardens belonging to some grandees, and adorned with two or three most splendid tamarind-trees, which in this monotonous landscape have a peculiar charm.

It was about one o'clock in the afternoon when I entered Ngórnu, the town of 'the blessing'. The heat being then very great, scarcely anybody was to be seen in the streets; but the houses, or rather yards, were full of people, tents having been pitched to accommodate so many visitors, while fine horses looked forth everywhere over the low fences, saluting us as we passed by. Scarcely a single clay house was to be seen, with the exception of the house of the sheikh, which lies at the end of the déndal; but nevertheless the town made the impression of comfort and ease, and every yard was neatly fenced with new 'síggedí' mats, and well shaded by kórna-trees, while the huts were large and spacious.

Having in vain presented myself at the house of the vizier, where the people were all asleep, and wandered about the town for a good while, I at length took up my quarters provisionally with some Arabs, till the cool of the afternoon aroused the courtiers from their long midday slumber, which they certainly may have needed, inasmuch as they had been up at two o'clock in the morning. But even after I had the good fortune to see Háj Beshír, I found it difficult to obtain quarters, and I was obliged to pitch my tent in a courtyard.

Being tired of the crowd in the town, I mounted on horseback early next morning in order to refresh myself with a sight of the lake, which I supposed to be at no great distance, and indulged beforehand in anticipations of the delightful view which I fondly imagined was soon to greet my eye. We met a good many people and slaves going out to cut grass for the horses; and leaving them to their work we kept on towards the rising sun. But no lake was to be seen, and an endless grassy plain without a single tree extended to the furthest horizon. At length, after the grass had increased continually in freshness and luxuriance, we reached a shallow swamp, the very indented border of which, sometimes bending in, at others bending out, greatly obstructed our progress. Having struggled for a length of time to get rid of this swamp, and straining my eyes in vain to discover the glimmering of an open water in the distance, I at length retraced my steps, consoling myself with the thought that I had seen at least some slight indication of the presence of the watery element, and which seemed indeed to be the only thing which was at present to be seen here.

## ARRIVAL OF OVERWEG

*May* 7. I found Overweg in the shade of a nebek-tree near Kálilwá. He looked greatly fatigued and much worse than when I left him, four months ago, at Tasáwa; indeed, as he told me, he had been very sickly in Zínder — so sickly, that he had been much afraid lest he should soon follow Mr. Richardson to the grave. Perhaps the news which he just then heard of our companion's death made him more uneasy about his own illness. However, we were glad to meet again alive, and expressed our hopes to be able to do a good deal for the exploration of these countries. He had had an opportunity of witnessing, during his stay in Góber and Marádi, the interesting struggle going on between this noblest part of the Háusa nation and the Fúlbe, who threatened their political as well as religious independence; and he was deeply impressed with the charming scenes of unrestrained cheerful life which he had witnessed in those pagan communities; while I, for my part, could assure him that my reception in Bórnu seemed to guarantee success, although, under existing circumstances, there seemed to be very little hope that we should ever be able to make a journey all round the Tsád; but I thought that, with the assistance of those people in Bínder and Maduwári whom I had just visited, and who appeared to be on friendly terms with the islanders, it might be possible to explore the navigable part of the lagoon in the boat.

Mr. Overweg was, in some respects, very badly off, having no clothes with him except those which he actually wore, all his luggage being still in Kanó, though he had sent two men to fetch it. I was therefore obliged to lend him my own things,

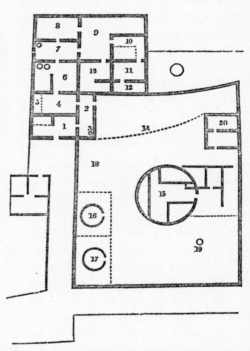

FIG. 5.   The English House at Kukawa

1.  Segífa, or 'soró chínnabe,' into which a person coming from the small yard before the house first enters through the principal gate. In the corner there is a spacious clay bench, ' dágali,' raised three feet from the ground.

2.  Small open courtyard, with a very fine chédia or caoutchouc-tree (3), in which we had generally a troop of monkeys, while at the bottom a couple of squirrels (*Sciurus*) were living in a hole.

and he took up his quarters in another part of our house, though it was rather small for our joint establishment. The vizier was very glad of his arrival, and, in fulfilment of his engagement to deliver all the things left by Mr. Richardson as soon as Mr. Overweg should arrive, he sent all the half-empty boxes of our late companion in the evening of the next day; even the gun and pistols, and the other things which had been sold, were returned, with the single exception of Mr. Richardson's watch, which, as the sheikh was very fond of it, and kept it near him night and day, I thought it prudent to spare him the mortification of returning.

4. A second courtyard with a henhouse. (5)

6. Inner segífa, where, in the beginning, the servants loitered, and which was afterwards changed into a simple dining-room. Here generally the water-jars were kept.

7. Small courtyard, with water-jar.

8. Inner room, where I used to live, and afterwards Mr. Vogel.

9. Inner large courtyard, where, in the corner, the kitchen was established.

10. Room with a large claybank, where Mr. Overweg used to recline in the daytime.

11. Bedroom of Mr. Overweg, and afterwards of the Sappers, Corporal Church and Macguire.

12. Small back courtyard.

13. Storeroom.

14. Outer enclosure of great courtyard in the beginning of our residence in Kúkawa. This wall we afterwards pulled down, when we obtained a very large yard for our horses and cattle. We, at times, had six horses and five or six cows.

15. Very large well-built conical hut, with clay wall and thatched roof. In the interior there were two spacious raised claybanks of the kind called 'dágali' and 'zinzin,' and in the background a raised recess, separated by a wall two feet high, for luggage or corn. This hut I occupied during my last stay in Kúkawa after my return from Timbúktu, when I built in front of it a large shed with that sort of coarse mats called síggedí.

16. Hut occupied by Maádi, a liberated slave, first in the service of Mr. Richardson, afterwards in that of Mr. Overweg, and lastly, Mr. Vogel's head servant. Having been wounded in the service of the expedition, a small pension has been granted to him.

17. Hut occupied by another servant.

18. Place for our cattle.

19. A well. The sandy soil, as I have said, obliged us to change the place of our well very often, and we had great trouble in this respect.

20. A clayhouse which, during the latter part of our stay, fell to ruins.

## THE TREATY WITH BORNU

*May* 9. Mr. Overweg and I, having then made a selection from the articles that remained to us, presented to the vizier, on the morning of the ninth, those destined for him, and in the afternoon we presented the sheikh with his share. These presents could not be now expected to please by their novelty, or to awaken a feeling of gratitude in the receivers, who had long been in possession of them; but although made to understand by Mr. Richardson's interpreters that he alone had been authorized by the British Government, Mr. Overweg and I not being empowered to interfere, and that consequently they might regard themselves as legitimate possessors of our deceased companion's property, they must yet have entertained some doubt about the equity of their claim; and as soon as I arrived, and began to act with firmness, they grew ashamed of having listened to intriguing servants. In short, though we had put them to shame, they esteemed us all the better for our firmness, and received their presents in a very gracious manner.

We now spoke also about the treaty, the negotiation of which, we said, had been specially intrusted to our companion, but now, by his death, had devolved on us. Both of them assured us of their ardent desire to open commercial intercourse with the English, but at the same time they did not conceal that their principal object in so doing was to obtain fire-arms. They also expressed their desire that two of their people might return with us to England, in order to see the country and its industry, which we told them we were convinced would be most agreeable to the British Government. Our conversation was so unrestrained and friendly, that the sheikh himself took the opportunity of excusing himself for having appropriated Mr. Richardson's watch.

But the following narrative will show how European travellers, endeavouring to open these countries to European intercourse, have to struggle against the intrigues of the Arabs; who are well aware that as soon as the Europeans, or rather the English, get access to Negroland, not only their slave-trade, but even their whole commerce, as they now carry it on, will be annihilated.

We had scarcely re-entered our house when, the rumour spreading through the Arab quarter of the manner in which we had been received, and of the matters talked of El Khodr, a native of Dar-Fúr, and the foremost of the native traders, went to the sheikh with the news that seven large vessels of the English had suddenly arrived at Núpe, and that the natives were greatly afraid of them. This announcement was soon found to be false, but nevertheless it served its purpose, to cool a little the friendly and benevolent feeling which had been manifested towards us.

The following day we went to pitch the large double tent, which we had given to the sheikh, on the open area before his palace in the eastern town; and having fully succeeded in arranging it, although a few pieces were wanting, it was left the whole day in its place, and made a great impression upon the people. At first it seemed rather awkward to the natives, whose tents, even if of large size, are mere bell-tents; but in the course of time it pleased the sheikh so much, that when I finally left the country, he begged me to entreat the British Government to send him another one like it.

## CHAPTER 6

# ADAMAWA (1851)

## SETTING OUT FROM KUKAWA

*May*. The much desired moment of my departure for Adamáwa drew nearer and nearer. The delay of my starting on this undertaking, occasioned by the late arrival of Mr. Overweg, had been attended with the great advantage that, meanwhile, some messengers of the governor of that country had arrived, in whose company, as they were returning immediately, I was able to undertake the journey with a much better prospect of success. The subject of their message was, that Kashella 'Alí Ladán, on his late predatory incursion into the Marghí country, had enslaved and carried away inhabitants of several places to which the governor of Adamáwa laid claim, and it was more in order to establish his right, than from any real concern in the fate of these unfortunate creatures, that he was pleased to lay greet stress upon the case. Indeed, as the sequel shows, his letter must have contained some rather harsh or threatening expressions, to which the ruler of Bórnu was not inclined to give way, though he yielded to the justice of the specific claim.

*May* 29. After much delay, and having twice taken official leave of the sheikh in full state, I had at length the pleasure of seeing our little band ready for starting in the afternoon of Thursday.

At four o'clock in the afternoon I left the 'chínna ánumbe', the southern gate of Kúkawa, on my adventurous journey to Adamáwa. My little troop was not yet all collected. For being extremely poor at the time, or rather worse than poor, as I had nothing but considerable debts, I had cherished the hope

that I should be able to carry all my luggage on one camel; but
when the things were all packed up, provisions, cooking utensils,
tent, and a few presents, I saw that the one weak animal which
I had was not enough, and bought another of Mr. Overweg,
which had first to be fetched from the pasture-ground. I therefore left two servants and my old experienced Háusa warrior,
the Mâllem Katúri, whom, as I have stated above, I had
expressly hired for this journey, behind me in the town, in
order to follow us in the night with the other camel.

The messengers from Adamáwa, as we proceeded onward,
gradually collected together from the hamlets about, where
they had been waiting for us, and the spearmen among them
saluted me by raising their spears just in my face, and beating
their small round hippopotamus shields; Mohámmedu was
armed with a sword and bow and arrows. They had not been
treated so well as, with reference to my prospects, the sheikh
ought to have treated them, and Ibrahíma, instead of a handsome horse which was promised to him, had received a
miserable poor mare, quite unfit for himself, and scarcely
capable of carrying his little son and his small provision bag.

As soon as I had left the town behind me, and saw that I
was fairly embarked in my undertaking, I indulged in the most
pleasant feelings. I had been cherishing the plan of penetrating
into those unknown countries to the south for so long a time,
that I felt the utmost gratification in being at length able to
carry out my design. At that time I even cherished the hope
that I might succeed in reaching Báya, and thus extend my
inquiries even as far as the equator; but my first design was,
and had always been, to decide by ocular evidence the question
with regard to the direction and the tributaries of the great
river which flowed through the country in the south.

## THE MARGHI COUNTRY

*June* 7. The storm luckily passing by, I walked through the
village, and visited several courtyards. The inhabitants, who,
at least outwardly, have become Mohammedans, go entirely

naked, with the exception of a narrow strip of leather, which they pass between the legs and fasten round their waist. But even this very simple and scanty covering they seem to think unnecessary at times. I was struck by the beauty and symmetry of their forms, which were thus entirely exposed to view, and by the regularity of their features, which are not disfigured by incisions, and in some had nothing of what is called the Negro type; but I was still more astonished at their complexion, which was very different in different individuals, being in some of a glossy black, and in others of a light copper, or rather rhubarb colour, the intermediate shades being almost entirely wanting. Although the black shade seemed to prevail, I arrived at the conclusion that the copper colour was the original complexion of the tribe, the black shade being due to intermixture with surrounding nations. But the same variety of shades has been observed in many other tribes, as well on this continent as in Asia.

Being allowed to stray about at my leisure, I observed in one house a really beautiful female in the prime of womanhood, who, with her son, a boy of about eight or nine years of age, formed a most charming group, well worthy of the hand of an accomplished artist. The boy's form did not yield in any respect to the beautiful symmetry of the most celebrated Grecian statues, as that of the praying boy, or that of the *diskophóros*. His legs and arms were adorned with strings of iron beads, such as I shall have occasion to describe more distinctly further on, made in Wándalá, which are generally worn by young people; his legs were as straight as possible: his hair, indeed, was very short, and curled, but not woolly. He, as well as his mother and the whole family, were of a pale or yellowish-red complexion, like rhubarb. His mother, who was probably twenty-two years of age, was a little disfigured by a thin pointed metal plate about an inch long, which was stuck through her under lip. This kind of barbarous ornament is called in the language of these people 'seghéum', and is very differently shaped, and generally much smaller than that worn by this woman; indeed it is often a mere thin tag. It is possible that its size varies according to the character of the females by whom it is worn. However small it may be it can hardly be fastened in the lip without being very inconvenient, and even painful, at least at first; at any rate it is less monstrous than the large bone which is worn by the Músgu women in the same way. These simple people were greatly amused when they saw me take so much interest in them; but while they were pleased with my approval, and behaved very decently, they grew frightened when I set about sketching them. This is the misfortune of the traveller in these regions, where everything is new, and where certainly one of the most interesting points attaches to the character of the natives, — that he will very rarely succeed in persuading one of them to stand while he makes an accurate drawing of him. The men are generally tall, and, while they are young, rather slender; some of the women also attain a great height, and in that state, with their hanging breasts, form frightful objects in their total nakedness, especially if they be of red colour.

In another courtyard, I saw two unmarried young girls busy at house-work: they were about twelve years of age, and were more decently clad, wearing an apron of striped cotton round their loins; but this was evidently a result of Mohammedanism. These also were of copper colour; and their short curled hair was dyed of the same hue by powdered camwood rubbed into it. They wore only thin tags in their under lips, and strings of red glass beads round their neck. Their features were pleasing, though less handsome than those of the woman above described. They were in ecstasies when I made them some little presents, and did not know how to thank me sufficiently.

*June* 8. It was one o'clock in the afternoon when we reached the first cluster of huts belonging to the village or district of I'sge, or I'ssege, which spread to a considerable extent over the plain, while horses and sheep were feeding on the adjacent pastures, and women were cultivating the fields. A first glance at this landscape impressed me with the conviction that I had at length arrived at a seat of the indigenous inhabitants, which, although it had evidently felt the influence of its overbearing and merciless neighbours, had not yet been altogether despoiled by their hands. Vigorous and tall manly figures, girt round the loins with a short leathern apron, and wearing, besides their agricultural tools, the 'danísko' (hand-bill), or a spear, were proudly walking about or comfortably squatting together in the shade of some fine tree, and seemed to intimate that this ground belonged to them, and that the foreigner, whoever he might be, ought to act discreetly. As for their dress, however, I almost suspected that, though very scanty, it was put on only for the occasion; for, on arriving at the first cluster of huts, we came abruptly upon a hollow with a pond of water, from which darted forth a very tall and stout bronze-coloured woman, totally naked, with her pitcher upon her head, — not only to my own amazement, but even to that of my horse, which, coming from the civilized country of Bórnu, which is likewise the seat of one of the blackest races in the interior, seemed to be startled by such a sight. However, I have observed that many of those simple tribes deem some sort of covering, however scanty it might be, more essential for the man than the woman.

At length we reached the eastern quarter; but the owners of the courtyards which were selected for our quarters, did not seem at all inclined to receive us. I had cheerfully entered with Bú-Sád the courtyard assigned to me, in order to take possession of it, and my servant had already dismounted, when its proprietor rushed furiously in, and raising his spear in a most threatening attitude, ordered me to leave his house instantly. Acknowledging the justice of his claims to his own hearth, I did not hesitate a moment to obey his mandate; but I had some difficulty in persuading my servant to go away peaceably, as he was more inclined to shoot the man. This dwelling in particular was very neatly arranged; and I was well able to sympathize with the proprietor, who saw that his clean yard was to be made a stable and littered with dirt. The yards contained from five to seven huts, each of different size and arrangement, besides a shed, and gave plain indications of an easy and comfortable domestic life.

Bíllama, that is to say, my guide, who seemed not to have

been more fortunate than myself in his endeavour to find a lodging, being rather crest-fallen and dejected, we thought it best to give up all idea of sheltered quarters, and, trusting to our good luck, to encamp outside. We therefore drew back altogether from the inhabited quarter into the open meadow, and dismounted beneath the wide-spreading shade of an immense kúka, or 'bokki', at least eighty feet high, the foliage of which being interwoven with numbers of climbing plants, such as I very rarely observed on this tree, formed a most magnificent canopy. While my tent was being pitched here, a number of natives collected round us, and squatting down in a semicircle eyed all my things very attentively, drawing each other's attention to objects which excited their curiosity. They were all armed; and as there were from thirty to forty, and hundreds more might have come to their assistance in a moment, their company was not so agreeable as under other circumstances it might have been. The reason, however, why they behaved so inhospitably towards me evidently was, that they took me for an officer of the king of Bórnu: but this impression gave way the longer they observed my manners and things; indeed, as soon as they saw the tent, they became aware that it was not a tent like those of their enemies, and they came to the same conclusion with regard to the greater part of my luggage. In many places in Negroland I observed that the bipartite tentpole was a most wonderful object to the natives, and often served to characterize the Christian. This time, however, we did not come to friendly terms; but the reader will be gratified to see how differently these people treated me on my return from Fúmbiná.

While our party was rather quietly and sullenly sitting near the tent, a number of Fúlbe, who had been staying in this district for some time, came to pay their respects to me. They were a very diminutive set of people, and, excepting general traits of resemblance and language, were unlike those proud fellow countrymen of theirs in the west; but I afterwards found that the Fúlbe in the eastern part of A'damáwa are generally of this description, while those about the capital have a far more noble and dignified appearance. I think this may be not so much a mark of a difference of tribe, as a consequence of the low circumstances of those settled at a great distance from the seat of government, who, being still engaged in struggling for their subsistence, have not raised themselves from their original condition of humble cattle-breeders, or 'berroróji', to the proud rank of conquerors and religious reformers. Their colour certainly was not the characteristic rhubarb-colour of the Fúta Púllo, nor the deep black of the Toróde, but was a greyish sort of black, approaching what the Frenchmen call the *chocolat-au-lait* colour, while their small features wanted the expressiveness which those of the light Púllo generally have. They all wore shirts, which however were deficient in that cleanliness which in general is characteristic of this race. These simple visitors might perhaps have proved very interesting companions, if we had been able to understand each other; but as they spoke neither Arabic, nor Háusa, nor Kanúri, while I was but a beginner in their language, our conversation flowed but sluggishly.

I had observed in all the dwellings of the natives a very large species of fish laid to dry on the roofs of the huts; and being not a little astonished at the existence of fish of such a size in this district, where I was not aware that there existed any considerable waters, I took the earliest opportunity of inquiring whence they were brought, and, having learnt that a considerable lake was at no great distance, I intimated to Bíllama my wish to visit it. I therefore mounted on horseback with him in the afternoon, and then passing behind the eastern quarter of I'ssege, and crossing a tract covered with excellent herbage, but so full of holes and crevices that the horses had great difficulty in getting over it, we reached a fine sheet of water of considerable depth, stretching from west to east, and full of large fish. All along the way we were met by natives returning from fishing, with their nets and their spoil. The fish measure generally about twenty inches in length, and seem to be of the same kind as that caught in the Tsád. The banks of the water, except on the west side, where we stood, were so hemmed in with rushes that I

could not form a satisfactory estimate of its magnitude and real
character; but it seems to be a hollow which is filled by the
rivulet or torrent which I surveyed in its upper course the
following day, and which seems to pass at a short distance to
the east of this lake. The latter, however, is said always to contain
water, which, as far as I know, is not the case with the river;
but certainly even the lake must become much shallower in
the dry season.

## THE TOWN OF UBA

*June* 10. Emerging from this rocky passage, we began gradually
to overlook the large valley stretching out to the foot of the
opposite mountain chain, which seemed from this place to be
uninterrupted. Its general elevation appeared to be about 800
feet above the bottom of the valley. We then again entered
upon cultivated ground, and turning round the spur of the
rocky chain on our right, on the top of which we observed the
huts of the pagans, we reached the wall of U'ba at two o'clock
in the afternoon.

The eastern quarter of this town, the northernmost Púllo
settlement in A'damáwa on this side, consisting of a few huts
scattered over a wide space, has quite the character of a new
and cheerless colony in Algeria; the earthen wall is low, and
strengthened with a light double fence of thorn bushes. The
western quarter, however, is more thickly and comfortably
inhabited; and each cluster of huts, which all consist of bongo,
or rather búkka bongo, 'jwarubokáru', is surrounded with a
little cornfield. It was pleasant to observe how the fences of
mats, surrounding the yards, had been strengthened and
enlivened by young living trees of a graceful slender appearance,
instead of dull stalks, giving to the whole a much more cheerful
character than is generally the case with the villages in other
parts of Negroland, particularly in Bórnu Proper, and promising
in a short time to afford some cool shade, which is rather
wanting in the place.

Passing the mosque, the 'judírde', a spacious quadrangular
building, consisting entirely of halls built of mats and stalks,

which must be delightfully cool in the dry season, but extremely damp during the rains, and including a large open space, we reached the lamórde (the house of the governor, or lámido); it lies on one side of a small square, or 'belbel'. Bíllama and Bú-Sád having here fired a couple of rounds we were soon shown into our quarters. These were of rather an indifferent description, but lying at the northern border of the inhabited quarter, and not far from the foot of the rocky ridge, they had the advantage of allowing us freedom of movement.

We had now reached the border of A'damáwa, the country after which I had been panting so long, and of which I had heard so many interesting accounts, a Mohammedan kingdom engrafted upon a mixed stock of pagan tribes, — the conquest of the valorous and fanatic Púllo chieftain, A'dama, over the great pagan kingdom of Fúmbiná.

I was musing over the fate of the native races of this country, when the governor, with a numerous suite, came to pay me a visit. Neither he nor any of his companions were dressed with any degree of elegance, or even cleanliness. I had endeavoured in vain to obtain information from my companions as to the period when the Fúlbe had begun to emigrate into this country; but they were unable to give me any other answer, than that they had been settled in the country from very ancient times, and that not only the fathers but even the grandfathers of the present generation had inhabited the same region as cattle-breeders, 'berroróji'. Neither the governor nor any of his people were able to give me more precise information, so that I was obliged to set my hopes upon the capital, where I was more likely to find a man versed in the history of the tribe. I then communicated to my visitor my wish to ascend the ridge, which overlooks the place, and on the top of which, according to Mohámmedu, a spring bubbled up between the rocks. The governor advised me to defer the excursion till the morrow, but as the weather was fine at the time, and as at this season it was very doubtful whether it would be so the next morning, I expressed a wish to obtain at once a view at least over the opposite mountain-chain. He then told me that I might do as

I liked, and followed me with his whole suite. The ridge, on this side at least, consisted entirely of enormous blocks of granite heaped one upon the other in wild confusion, and making the ascent extremely difficult, nay, impossible, without ropes, so that, with the utmost trouble, we reached the height of a little more than a hundred feet, which gave me, however, an advantageous position for obtaining a view over the broad valley and the mountain range beyond, of which, on my return journey, I made a sketch.

Some of the governor's people, however, were very agile in climbing these blocks, and they need to be so if they wish to subject the native inhabitants, who, when pursued, retire to these natural strongholds, which are scattered over nearly the whole of this country.

We had scarcely returned to our quarters, when a storm broke out, but it was not accompanied with a great quantity of rain. Our cheer was indifferent; and we passed our evening in rather a dull manner.

*June* 11. Seeing that the weather was gloomy, and being afraid of the fatigue connected with the ascent of the ridge even along a more easy path, as I was well aware how much my constitution had been weakened, I preferred going on, and gave orders for starting. On leaving the western gate of the town, which is formed of very large trunks of trees, we entered on a tract of corn-fields in a very promising condition, while at the same time a number of young jet black slave girls, well fed, and all neatly dressed in long aprons of white clean gábagá, and having their necks adorned with strings of glass beads, were marched out to their daily labour in the field.

The town formerly extended much further in this direction, till it was ransacked and plundered by Ramadhán, a slave and officer of the sheikh Mohammed el Kánemi. Before the Fúlbe occupied these regions, the slave-hunting expeditions of the people of Bórnu often extended into the very heart of A'damáwa. The Fúlbe certainly are always making steps towards subjugating the country, but they have still a great deal to do before they can regard themselves as the undisturbed possessors of the soil. Even here, at no great distance beyond the little range which we had on our right, an independent tribe called Gílle still maintains itself, and on my return journey I shall have to relate an unsuccessful expedition of the governor of U'ba against the Kilba-gáya.

## THE NJAI DISTRICT

*June* 12. We had now reached Mbutúdi, a village situated round a granite mount of about six hundred yards' circumference, and rising to the height of about three hundred feet. It had been a considerable place before the rise of the Fúlbe, encompassing on all sides the mount, which had served as a natural citadel; but it has been greatly reduced, scarcely more than one hundred huts altogether now remaining; and were it not for the picturesque landscape — the steep rocky mount overgrown with trees, and the slender deléb-palms shooting up here and there, and forming some denser groups on the southeast side, — it would be a most miserable place.

My companions were greatly astonished to find that, since they went to Kúkawa, some Fúlbe families had settled here: for formerly none but native pagans lived in the village. It was, therefore, necessary that we should address ourselves to this ruling class; and after we had waited some time in the shade of some caoutchouc-trees, a tall, extremely slender Púllo, of a very noble expression of countenance, and dressed in a snow-white shirt, made his appearance, and after the usual exchange of compliments, and due inquiry on the part of my companions after horse, cattle, mother, slaves, and family, conducted us to a dwelling not far from the eastern foot of the rock, consisting of several small huts, with a tall gigiña in the middle of its courtyard, which was never deserted by some large birds of the stork family, — most probably some European wanderers. However, it had the great disadvantage of being extremely wet, so that I preferred staying outside; and going to some distance from the huts, I laid myself down in the shade of a tree, where the ground was comparatively dry. The weather had been very cool and cheerless in the morning, and I was glad when the sun at length came forth, increasing the interest of the landscape, of which the accompanying view may give a slight idea.

I here tried, for the first time, the fruit of the deléb-palm, which was just ripe; but I did not find it worth the trouble, as it really requires a good deal of effort to suck out the pulp, which is nothing but a very close and coarse fibrous tissue, not separating from the large stone, and having a mawkish taste, which soon grows disagreeable. It cannot be at all compared with the banana, and still less with the fruit of the gonda-tree. It is, when full-grown, from six to eight inches long and four inches across, and of a yellowish brown colour; the kernel is about two inches and a half long and one inch thick. However, it is of importance to the natives, and, like the fruit of the dúm-palm, it yields a good seasoning for some of their simple dishes. They make use of the stone also, breaking and planting it in the ground, when, in a few days, a blade shoots forth with a very tender root, which is eaten just like the kelingoes; this is called 'múrrechi' by the Háusa people, 'báchul' by the Fúlbe, both of whom use it very extensively. But it is to be remarked that the gigiña, or deléb-palm, is extremely partial in its local distribution, and seems not at all common in A'damáwa, being, as my companions observed, here confined to a few localities, such as Láro and Song.

While resting here I received a deputation of the heads of families of the Fúlbe, who behaved very decently, and were not a little excited by the performances of my watch and compass. I then determined to ascend the rock, which commands and characterises the village, although, being fully aware of the debilitated state of my health, I was somewhat afraid of any great bodily exertion. It was certainly not an easy task, as the crags were extremely steep, but it was well worth the trouble, although the view over an immense expanse of country was greatly interrupted by the many small trees and bushes which are shooting out between the granite blocks.

After I had finished taking angles I sat down on this magnificent rocky throne, and several of the natives having followed me, I wrote from their dictation a short vocabulary of their language, which they call 'Záni', and which I soon found was intimately related to that of the Marghí. These poor creatures seeing, probably for the first time, that a stranger took real interest in them, were extremely delighted in hearing their words pronounced by one whom they thought almost as much above them as their god 'féte', and frequently corrected each other when there was a doubt about the meaning of the word. The rock became continually more and more animated, and it was not long before two young Fúlbe girls also, who from the first had cast a kindly eye upon me, came jumping up to me, accompanied by an elder married sister. One of these girls was about fifteen, the other about eight or nine years of age. They were decently dressed as Mohammedans, in shirts covering the bosom, while the pagans, although they had dressed for the occasion, wore nothing but a narrow strip of leather passed between the legs, and fastened round the loins, with a large leaf attached to it from behind; the women were, besides, ornamented with the 'kadáma', which is the same as the seghéum of the Marghí, and worn in the same way, stuck through the under-lip, but a little larger. Their prevailing complexion was a yellowish red, like that of the Marghí, with whom, a few centuries ago, they evidently formed one nation. Their worship, also, is nearly the same.

At length I left my elevated situation, and with a good deal of trouble succeeded in getting down again; but the tranquillity which I had before enjoyed was now gone, and not a moment was I left alone. All these poor creatures wanted to have my blessing; and there was particularly an old blacksmith, who, although he had become a proselyte to Islám, pestered me extremely with his entreaties to benefit him by word and prayer. They went so far as to do me the honour, which I of course declined, of identifying me with their god 'féte', who, they thought, might have come to spend a day with them, to make them forget their oppression and misfortunes. The pagans, however, at length left me when night came on, but the Fúlbe girls would not go, or if they left me for a moment, immediately returned, and so staid till midnight. The eldest of the unmarried girls made me a direct proposal of marriage, and I consoled her by stating, that I should have been happy to accept her offer if it were my intention to reside in the country. The manners of people who live in these retired spots, shut out from the rest of the world, are necessarily very simple and unaffected; and this poor girl had certainly reason to look out for a husband, as at fifteen she was as far beyond her first bloom as a lady of twenty-five in Europe.

## THE TOWN OF SORAU

*June* 14. Saráwu is the most elevated place on the latter part of this route, although the highest point of the water-partition, between the basin of the Tsád and that of the so-called Niger, as I stated before, seems to be at the pass north of U'ba. The difference between the state of the corn here and in Múbi and thereabout was very remarkable. The crop stood here scarcely a few inches above the ground. The soil also around the place is not rich, the mould being thin upon the surface of the granite, which in many places lies bare. The situation of Saráwu is very important on account of its being the point where the road from Logón and all the north-eastern part of A'damáwa, which includes some very considerable centres of industry and commerce, particularly Fátawel, the *entrepôt* of all the ivory trade in these quarters, joins the direct road from Kúkawa to the capital. Cotton is cultivated here to some extent. A'damáwa is a promising country of colonies.

Saráwu, too, was suffering from dearth from the same reason which I have explained above; the second crop, which is destined to provide for the last and most pressing period, while the new crop is ripening, not having been sown at all last year on account of the expedition, so that we had great difficulty in obtaining the necessary corn for our five horses. It would, however, have been very easy for me to obtain a sufficient supply if I had demanded a small fee for my medical assistance, as I had a good many patients who came to me for remedies;

but this I refrained from doing. I had here some very singular cases, which rather exceeded my skill; and among others there was a woman who had gone with child full two years, without any effort on the part of her imaginary offspring to come forth, and who came to me now with full confidence that the far-famed stranger would be able to help her to motherhood. Among the people who visited me there was also a Tébu, or rather Tedá, who in his mercantile rambles had penetrated to this spot; indeed these people are very enterprising, but in general their journeys lie more in the direction of Wándalá, where they dispose of a great quantity of glass beads. This man had resided here some time, but was not able to give me much information. He, however, excited my curiosity with regard to two white women, whom I was to see in Yóla, brought there from the southern regions of A'damáwa, and who he assured me were at least as white as myself. But, after all, this was not saying much; for my arms and face at that time were certainly some shades darker than the darkest Spaniard or Italian. I had heard already several people speak of these women, and the natives had almost made them the subject of a romance, spreading the rumour that my object in going to Yóla was to get a white female companion. I shall have occasion to speak about a tribe of lighter colour than usual in the interior, not far from the coast of the Cameroons, and there can be no doubt about the fact. My short and uncomfortable stay in the capital of A'damáwa deprived me of the opportunity of deciding with regard to the exact shade of these people's complexion, but I think it is a yellowish brown.

Having been busy in the morning writing Fulfúlde, I mounted my horse about ten o'clock, accompanied by Bíllama and Bú-Sád, in order to visit the market, which is held every Thursday and Sunday, on a little eminence at some distance from the Bórnu village, and close to the S.E. side of Saráwu Fulfúlde, separated from the latter by a ravine. The market was furnished with thirty-five stalls made of bushes and mats, and was rather poorly attended. However, it must be taken into consideration, that during the season of field-labours all markets in Negroland are much less considerable than at other seasons of the year. There were a good many head of cattle for sale, while two oxen were slaughtered for provision, to be cut up and sold in small parcels. The chief articles besides were ground-nuts, butter, a small quantity of rice, salt, and soap. Soap, indeed, is a very important article in any country inhabited by Fúlbe, and it is prepared in every household; while very often, even in large places inhabited by other tribes, it is quite impossible to obtain this article, so essential for cleanliness. No native grain of any kind was in the market, — a proof of the great dearth which prevailed throughout the country. A few túrkedí were to be seen; and I myself introduced a specimen of this article, in order to obtain the currency of the country for buying small matters of necessity.

The standard of the market is the native cotton, woven, as it is, all over Negroland, in narrow strips called 'léppi', of about two inches and a quarter in width, though this varies greatly. Shells ('kurdí', or 'chéde') have no currency. The smallest measure of cotton is the 'nánandé', measuring ten 'drá' or 'fóndudé' (sing. 'fóndukí'), equal to four fathoms, 'káme' or 'nándudé' (sing. 'nándukí'). Seven nánandé make one 'dóra' — meaning a small shirt of extremely coarse workmanship, and scarcely to be used for dress; and from two to five dóra make one thób or 'gaffaléul' of variable size and quality. The túrkedí which I introduced into the market, and which I had bought in Kanó for 1800 kurdí, was sold for a price equivalent to 2500 shells, which certainly is not a great profit, considering the danger of the road. However, it must be borne in mind that what I bought for 1800, a native certainly would have got for 1600, and would perhaps have sold for 2800 or more.

## FIRST SIGHT OF THE RIVER BENUE

*June* 18. It happens but rarely that a traveller does not feel disappointed when he first actually beholds the principal features of a new country, of which his imagination has composed a picture, from the description of the natives; but although

I must admit that the shape and size of the Alantíka, as it rose in rounded lines from the flat level, did not exactly correspond with the idea which I had formed of it, the appearance of the river far exceeded my most lively expectations. None of my informants had promised me that I should just come upon it at that most interesting locality — the Tépe — where the mightier river is joined by another of very considerable size, and that in this place I was to cross it. My arrival at this point, as I have stated before, was a most fortunate circumstance. As I looked from the bank over the scene before me, I was quite enchanted, although the whole country bore the character of a desolate wilderness; but there could scarcely be any great traces of human industry near the river, as, during its floods, it inundates the whole country on both sides. This is the general character of all the great rivers in these regions, except where they are encompassed by very steep banks.

The principal river, the Bénuwé, flowed here from east to west, in a broad and majestic course, through an entirely open country, from which only here and there detached mountains started forth. The banks on our side rose to twenty-five, and in some places to thirty feet, while just opposite to my station, behind a pointed headland of sand, the Fáro rushed forth, appearing from this point not much inferior to the principal river, and coming in a fine sweep from the south-east, where it disappeared in the plain, but was traced by me, in thought, upwards to the steep eastern foot of the Alantíka. The river, below the junction, keeping the direction of the principal branch, but making a slight bend to the north, ran along the northern foot of Mount Bágelé, and was there lost to the eye, but was followed in thought through the mountainous region of the Báchama and Zína to Hamárruwa, and thence along the industrious country of Korórofa, till it joined the great western river the Kwára or Niger, and, conjointly with it, ran towards the great ocean.[1]

[1] It was Barth's report of crossing the Benue so far north that decided the British Government to send out a further expedition and check whether this was indeed the same river as the Chadda penetrated by Laird and Oldfield in 1832. This was the origin of Baikie's expedition in the *Pleiad*, 1854.

I looked long and silently upon the stream; it was one of the happiest moments of my life.

I had now with my own eyes clearly established the direction and nature of this mighty river; and to an unprejudiced mind there could no longer be any doubt that this river joins the majestic watercourse explored by the gentlemen just mentioned. Hence I cherish the well-founded conviction, that along this natural highroad European influence and commerce will penetrate into the very heart of the continent, and abolish slavery, or rather those infamous slave-hunts and religious wars, destroying the natural germs of human happiness, which are spontaneously developed in the simple life of the pagans, and spreading devastation and desolation all around.

We descended towards the place of embarkation, which at this season of the year changes every week, or even more frequently. At present it was at the mouth of a small, deeply-worn channel, or dry watercourse, descending from the swampy meadow-grounds towards the river, and filled with tall reed-grass and bushes. Here was the poor little naval arsenal of the Tépe, consisting of three canoes, two in good repair, and a third one in a state of decay, and unfit for service.

It was now that for the first time I saw these rude little shells, hollowed out of a single trunk — for the boats of the Búdduma are more artificial, being made of a number of boards joined together; and I soon began to eye these frail canoes with rather an anxious feeling, as I was about to trust myself and all my property to what seemed to offer very inadequate means of crossing with safety a large and deep river. They measured from twenty-five to thirty feet in length, and only from a foot to a foot and a half in height, and sixteen inches in width; and one of them was so crooked, that I could scarcely imagine how it could stem the strong current of the river.

On the river itself two canoes were plying; but, notwithstanding our repeated hallooing and firing, the canoemen would not come to our side of the river; perhaps they were afraid. Roving about along the bushy watercourse, I found an old canoe, which being made of two very large trunks joined together, and had been incomparably more comfortable and spacious than the canoes now in use; although the joints being made with cordage just like the stitching of a shirt, and without pitching the holes, which were only stuffed with grass, necessarily allowed the water to penetrate continually into the boat; it, however, had the great advantage of not breaking if it ran upon a rock, being in a certain degree pliable. It was about thirty-five feet long, and twenty-six inches wide in the middle; but it was now out of repair, and was lying upside down. It was from this point, standing upon the bottom of the boat, that I made the sketch of this most interesting locality.

The canoemen still delaying to come, I could not resist the temptation of taking a river bath, a luxury which I had not enjoyed since bathing in the Eurymedon. The river is full of crocodiles; but there could be little danger from these animals after all our firing and the constant noise of so many people. I had not yet arrived at the conviction, that river-bathing is not good for an European in a tropical climate, but this was the first and last time that I bathed voluntarily, with a single exception, for when navigating the river of Logón on a fine day in March, 1852, I could not help jumping overboard, and on my return from Bagírmi, in August 1853, I was obliged to do it.

The bed of the river, after the first foot and a half, sloped down very gradually, so that at the distance of thirty yards from the shore I had not more than three feet and a half of water, but then it suddenly became deep. The current was so strong, that I was unable to stem it; but my original strength, I must allow, was at the time already greatly reduced. The only advantage which I derived from this feat was that of learning that the river carries gold with it; for the people, as often as I dipped under water, cried out that I was searching for this metal, and when I came out of the water, were persuaded that I had obtained plenty of it. However, the river was already too full for investigating this matter further.

At length a canoe arrived, the largest of the two that were actually employed, and a long bargaining commenced with the eldest of the canoemen, a rather short and well set lad. Of course as the chief of the caravan, I had to pay for all, and there being three camels and five horses to be carried over, it was certainly a difficult business. It cannot, therefore, be regarded as a proof of exorbitant demands, that I had to pay five 'dóras', a sum which in Kúkawa would buy two oxen-loads of Indian corn. I allowed all the people to go before me, in order to prevent the canoemen from exacting something more from them.

There was considerable difficulty with my large camel-bags, which were far too large for the canoes, and which several times were in danger of being upset; for they were so unsteady that the people were obliged to kneel down on the bottom, and keep their equilibrium by holding with both hands on the sides of the boat. Fortunately I had laid my tent-poles at the bottom of the canoe, so that the water did not reach the luggage; but owing to the carelessness of the Hajji's companions all his books were wetted, to his utmost distress; but I saw him after-wards shedding tears, while he was drying his deteriorated treasures on the sandy beach of the headland. The horses as they crossed, swimming by the sides of the canoe, had to undergo great fatigue; but desperate was the struggle of the camels, which were too obstinate to be guided by the frail vessels, and had to be pushed through alone, and could only be moved by the most severe beating; the camel of the Hajji was for a while given up in despair by the whole party. At length they were induced to cross the channel, the current carrying them down to a great distance, and our whole party arrived safe on the sandy beach of the headland, where there was not a bit of shade.

## ENTRY INTO YOLA

*June* 20. It was an unfavourable circumstance that we arrived on a Friday, and just during the heat of the day. The streets were almost deserted; and no person met us in order to impart to us, by a friendly welcome, a feeling of cheerfulness and confidence.

Yóla is a large open place, consisting, with a few exceptions, of conical huts surrounded by spacious courtyards, and even by corn-fields, the houses of the governor and those of his brothers being alone built of clay. Keeping along the principal street, we continued our march for a mile and a quarter before we reached the house of the governor, which lies on the west side of a small open area, opposite the mosque, a flat oblong building, or rather hall, inclosed with clay walls, and covered with a flat thatched roof a little inclined on one side. Having reached this place, my companions fired a salute, which, considering the nature of Bíllama's mission, and the peculiar character of the governor, which this officer ought to have known, and perhaps also since it happened to be Friday, was not very judicious.

Be this as it may, the courtiers or attendants of the governor, attracted by the firing, came out one after another, and informed us that their master must go to the mosque and say his mid-day prayers before he could attend to us or assign us quarters. We therefore dismounted and sat down in the scanty shade of a jéja or caoutchouc-tree, which adorns the place between the palace and the mosque, while a great number of people, amounting to several hundreds, gradually collected, all eager to salute me and shake hands with me. Fortunately, it was not long before Lowel came out from his palace and went into the mosque; and then I obtained a few moments' respite, the people all following him, with the exception of the young ones, who very luckily found the camels a worthier object of their curiosity than me. It had been my intention to salute the governor when he was crossing the place, but I was advised not to do so, as it might interfere with his devotional feelings.

## AUDIENCE WITH THE LAMIDO OF ADAMAWA

*June* 22. We then entered the palace; and having waited a short time in the segífa or záure, which here was formed by a spacious flat-roofed room supported by massive square pillars, we were called into the presence of the governor.

Mohammed Lowel, son of Mállem A'dama, was sitting in a separate hall, built of clay, and forming, for this country, quite a noble mansion. From without especially, it has a stately, castle-like appearance, while inside, the hall was rather encroached upon by quadrangular pillars two feet in diameter, which supported the roof, about sixteen feet high, and consisting of a rather heavy entablature of poles, in order to withstand the violence of the rains. The governor was very simply dressed, and had nothing remarkable in his appearance, while his face, which was half-covered by a somewhat dirty shawl, had an indifferent expression. Besides him there were none present but Mansúr and a mállem.

Having, as the first European that had ever visited his country with the distinct purpose to enter into friendly relations with him, paid him my respects on behalf of my countrymen, I delivered my letter of introduction from Sheikh 'Omár, who in a few but well-chosen lines introduced me to him as a learned and pious Christian, who wandered about to admire the works of the Almighty Creator, and on this account cherished an ardent desire to visit also A'damáwa, of the wonders of which I had heard so much. Lowel read it, and, evidently not quite displeased with its contents, although he took umbrage at some of the expressions, handed it silently over to the mállem and Mansúr. Hereupon Bíllama delivered his letters, of which not only the contents, but even the very existence had been totally unknown to me.

As soon as these various letters were read, all of which laid claim, on the side of Bórnu, to the territory of Kófa and Kóbchi, a storm arose, and in a fit of wrath Lowel reproached my companion with daring to come forward with such pretensions — he, who was himself well acquainted with the country and with the point in dispute. If Sheikh 'Omár wished for discord, well: he was ready; and they would harass each other's frontier-provinces by reciprocal incursions. Having given vent to his feelings towards Bíllama, his anger turned upon me; and he told me to my face that I had quite different reasons for coming into his country from those stated in Sheikh

'Omár's letter; referring to some ambiguous words in Malá
Ibrám's writing, in which that officer stated 'that, with regard
to me, the objects of my journey to A'damáwa were a perfect
secret to him'. Now I must confess, after all my acquaintance
with the politics of these people, and notwithstanding all Háj
Beshír's kindness and benevolence towards me, that I think
the Bórnu diplomatists quite capable of a little double dealing;
that is to say, I suspect that they were willing to make use of
me to frighten the governor of A'damáwa. Perhaps also they
were afraid lest, if I should succeed in A'damáwa, I might not
return to their country.

Be this as it may, after a long dispute with regard to the
boundaries, in which my friend from Mokha, and a learned
native of Wadáy, Móde 'Abd Alláhi, who was employed by
Lowel as a sort of secretary of state for foreign affairs, took part,
I, with my party, was ordered to withdraw for a time. After
sitting for full two hours on the damp ground outside, we received
an intimation that we might return home. Thus I had to return
with my presents a second time to my quarters; and of course
I was greatly vexed. However, several people who saw my
emotion endeavoured to console me; and Mansúr, who before
we left came out of his brother's audience-hall, entered into
conversation with me, and assured me that this unkind treatment in no way related to me, but that it was only intended
for Bíllama, the officer of Bórnu. There was present also the
very amiable mállem whom I had met in Saráwu Fulfúlde,
and who had come after us; and I felt sorry that I was not
disposed to answer his well-meant discourse in the manner it
deserved.

When we reached Mansúr's house, he invited us to dismount,
and entering the interior of his wide and neat dwelling we had
a long and animated conversation, when I explained to him
in a deliberate manner that such treatment did not offend me
on my own account, but on account of the government — the
very first and most powerful in the world — which had sent me;
that instead of coming with hostile intentions, as was imputed
to me, I had come with the friendly design of paying my

respects to the governor on behalf of the British sovereign, and to present him with a few specimens of our products and manufactures; that I had, no doubt, at the same time an intense desire to see their country, as it was the avowed purpose of Europeans in general, and of the English in particular, to become acquainted, and to open intercourse, with all parts of God's creation.

Mansúr explained to me, in return, that they well knew that I had not come to make war upon them, although Lowel, in the first fit of his anger, scarcely seemed to suspect anything less than that, 'but that they were vexed because I had come to them under the protection of the Bórnu people, their enemies'.

## EXPULSION FROM YOLA

*June* 24. I felt tolerably well in the morning, but afterwards became very ill, and unfortunately took too weak a dose of medicine.

After some other visitors had come and gone, I received, about ten o'clock, a formal visit from Móde 'Abd-Alláhi, the foreign secretary, and my friend from Mokha, in the name of the governor. Having moistened their organs with a cup of coffee, they acquitted themselves of their message in the following terms: 'The sultan' — all these provincial governors bear the title of sultan — 'had ordered them', they said, 'to beg me to accept his most respectful regards, and to inform me that he was nothing but a slave of the sultan of Sókoto, and that I was a far greater man than himself. As such a man had never before come to his country, he was afraid of his liege lord, and begged me to retrace my steps whither I had come; but if in course of time I should return with a letter from Sókoto, he would receive me with open arms, would converse with me about all our science, and about our instruments, without reserve, and would show me the whole country.'

To this message, which was certainly couched in very modest and insinuating terms, I answered that Mohammed Lowel, so far from being a slave of the sultan of Sókoto, was renowned far and wide as the almost independent governor of a large province; that the fame of his father A'dama, as a nobly-born, learned Púllo, extended far and wide throughout Tekrúr, or Negroland, and had even reached our own country; that it was absurd to argue that I was greater than himself, and that on this account he could not receive me on his own responsibility, but was obliged to refer my suit to his liege lord in Sókoto. I brought forward the examples of Kátsena and Kanó, expecially the latter place, in which, though it was the seat of a governor dependent on the Emír el Múmenín, in the same way as the governor of A'damáwa, I had long resided, without any representations being made to the sovereign lord. 'Oh! but the relations of Kátsena and Kanó', said the messengers of the governor, 'are entirely different from those of this province. These are large and busy thoroughfares for all the world, while A'damáwa is a distant territory in the remotest corner of the earth, and still a fresh unconsolidated conquest'. There was certainly some truth in this last remark; and whatever I might say to the contrary, the question was decided, and all reasoning was vain.

## HISTORY OF ADAMAWA

But, before proceeding further on my journey back, I must try to make the reader better acquainted with the country, though the abrupt way in which I was obliged to leave it allows me only, in most cases, to speak from the information of the natives.

Yóla is the capital of an extensive province, called by foreigners generally, and by the conquering Fúlbe in diplomatic language, A'damáwa, but the real name of which is Fúmbiná. Indeed A'damáwa is quite a new name given to the country (exactly as I stated in my report sent to Europe some years ago) in honour of Mâllem A'dama, the father of the present governor, who succeeded in founding here a new Mohammedan empire on the ruins of several smaller pagan kingdoms, the most considerable of which was that of Kókomi.

Whether what the people used to say be true, that the name of the wife of this officer was A'dama too, I am not able positively to decide.

Yóla is quite a new settlement, called by this name after the princely quarter of the town of Kanó, — the former capital, of which Denham's expedition heard some faint report, being Gúrin. Yóla is situated in a swampy plain, and is bordered on the north side by an inlet of the river, the inundation of which reaches close to that quarter where I was living. The town is certainly not less than three miles long from east to west. It seems probable that there are different names for the different quarters; but my stay was too short to allow me to learn them. The courtyards are large and spacious, but often contain only a single hut, the whole area being sown with grain during the rainy season. All the huts are built with clay walls, on account of the violence of the rains, and are tolerably high. Only the governor and his elder brothers possess large establishments, with dwellings built entirely of clay. Notwithstanding its size, the place can hardly contain more than twelve thousand inhabitants.

It has no industry; and the market, at least during the time of my stay there, was most insignificant and miserably supplied: but certainly during the season of field labours, as I have already had occasion to observe, all the markets in Negroland are less important than at other times of the year. The most common objects in the market, which find ready sale, are túrkedí, beads, and salt, while other articles, such as striped Manchester, calico, cloth bernúses, are generally sold privately to the wealthier people. The only articles of export at present are slaves and ivory. Four good túrkedí, bought in Kanó for 1800 or 2000 kurdí each, will generally purchase a slave; and a túrkedí will often buy an elephant's tusk of tolerable size.

Slavery exists on an immense scale in this country; and there are many private individuals who have more than a thousand slaves. In this respect the governor of the whole province is not the most powerful man, being outstripped by the governors of Chámba and Kóncha — for this reason, that Mohammed

Lowel has all his slaves settled in rúmde or slave-villages, where they cultivate grain for his use or profit, while the above-mentioned officers, who obtain all their provision in corn from subjected pagan tribes, have their whole host of slaves constantly at their disposal; and I have been assured that some of the head slaves of these men have as many as a thousand slaves each under their command, with whom they undertake occasional expeditions for their masters. I have been assured also that Mohammed Lowel receives every year in tribute, besides horses and cattle, about five thousand slaves, though this seems a large number.

The country of Fúmbiná is about two hundred miles long in its greatest extent, running from south-west to north-east, while its shortest diameter seems to reach from north-west to south-east, and scarcely ever exceeds seventy or eighty miles; but this territory is as yet far from being entirely subjected to the Mohammedan conquerors, who in general are only in posses-sion of detached settlements, while the intermediate country, particularly the more mountainous tracts, are still in the hands of the pagans. The people in this part of the country are engaged in constant warfare. While the country north from the Bénuwé, between Yóla and Hamárruwa, is entirely independent, and inhabited by warlike pagan tribes, the best-subjected tract seems to be that between the Wándalá and the Músgu country, where the settlements of the conquering tribe are very compact.

The country is certainly one of the finest of Central Africa, irrigated as it is by numerous rivers, among which the Bénuwé and the Fáro are the most important, and being diversified with hill and dale. In general, however, it is flat, rising gradually towards the south, from an elevation of about eight hundred feet, along the middle course of the Bénuwé, to fifteen hundred feet or more, and broken by separate hills or more extensive groups of mountains; but, as far as I know, there is not here a single example of large mountain masses. Mount Alantíka, of which I had a fine view from several points, though at a considerable distance, is considered as the most massive and elevated mountain in the whole country; and this is an entirely detached mountain, at the utmost fifty miles in circumference, and elevated certainly not more than eight thousand five hundred or nine thousand feet above the plain from which it rises. No doubt the Bénuwé may be presumed to have its sources in a mountainous tract of country; but of the uppermost course of this river I was not able to obtain the least information, while [I] have been able to lay down its lower course with great approximative certainty. Yet, although the elevation of the country is in general the same, the nature of the different districts varies greatly: thus in Chámba, apparently on account of the neighbourhood of Mount Alantíka, which attracts the clouds, the rainy season is said to set in as early as January, so that by the end of April or beginning of May the first crop is ripe, while in Yóla, and in the country in general, the rains rarely begin before March.

The grain most commonly grown in the country is *Holcus sorghum;* but in this respect also there is a great difference between the districts. Thus, the country of the Mbúm round Ngáundere scarcely produces anything but rógo, or yams, which form the daily, and almost sole food of the inhabitants. Meat is so dear there that a goat will often fetch the price of a female slave. Ground-nuts (*Arachis hypogœa*) are plentiful both in the eastern and the western districts. A tolerable quantity of cotton, called 'póttolo' in A'damáwa, is cultivated; but indigo or 'chachári' is very rare, and is hardly cultivated anywhere but in Saráwu and Máruwa; and this is very natural, as the Fúlbe do not value coloured shirts.

With regard to exuberance of vegetation, Tibáti seems to be one of the richest places; there both kinds of the banana, or ayabáje, the gonda, or papaya, 'dukúje', several species of the gúro tree, the *Pandanus*, the *Kajilia*, the monkey-bread tree, or *Adansonia*, the 'rími', or *Bombax*, and numerous other kinds are found. Of the palm tribe, the deléb-palm, or gigiña, and the *Elaïs Guineensis*, are frequent, but strictly limited to certain localities, while the date-tree (called by the Fúlbe of A'damáwa by the beautiful name 'tannedaráje') is very rare, and, except a few specimens in Yóla and Búndang, scarcely to be met with. Among the bushes, the *Palma Christi*, or *Ricinus*, is extremely common. Altogether, the predominant tree in the southern provinces of A'damáwa seems to be the banana. There are hot springs in the country of the Bakr Yemyem, about three days south from Kóncha, which are said to issue from the west foot of a mountain stretching from east to west, and to have a very high temperature; the water is reported to be palatable.

Of animals, the elephant is exceedingly frequent, not only the black or grey, but also a yellow species. The rhinoceros is often met with, but only in the eastern part of the country. East from the Bénuwé the wild bull is very common. The most singular animal seems to be the ayú,[2] which lives in the river, and in some respects resembles the seal; it comes out of the river in the night, and feeds on the fresh grass growing on its banks.

With regard to domestic animals, cattle were evidently introduced by the Fúlbe some two or three hundred years ago. There is an indigenous variety of ox, but quite a distinct species, not three feet high, and of dark-grey colour; this is called máturú. The native horse is small and feeble; the best horses are brought from the northern districts, chiefly from U'ba.

[2] Manatee.

## CHAPTER 7

# A BASE IN BORNU (1851–1852)

## RETURN TO KUKAWA

*July*. I had left Kúkawa on my journey to A'damáwa in the best state of health, but had brought back from that excursion the germs of disease; and residence in the town, at least at this period of the year, was not likely to improve my condition. It would certainly have been better for me, had I been able to retire to some more healthy spot; but trivial though urgent business obliged me to remain in Kúkawa.

It was necessary to sell the merchandize which had at length arrived, in order to keep the mission in some way or other afloat, by paying the most urgent debts and providing the necessary means for further exploration. There was merchandize to the value of one hundred pounds sterling; but, as I was obliged to sell the things at a reduced rate for ready money, the loss was considerable; for all business in these countries is transacted on two or three months' credit, and, after all, payment is made, not in ready money, but chiefly in slaves. It is no doubt very necessary for a traveller to be provided with those various articles which form the presents to be made to the chiefs, and which are in many districts required for bartering; but he ought not to depend upon their sale for the supply of his wants. Altogether it is difficult to carry on trade in conjunction with extensive geographical research, although a person setting quietly down in a place, and entering into close relations with the natives, might collect a great deal of interesting information, which would probably escape the notice of the roving traveller, whose purpose is rather to explore distant regions. Besides, I was obliged to make numerous presents to my friends, in order to keep them in good humour, and had very often not only to provide dresses for themselves and their wives, but even for their domestic retainers; so that, all things considered, the supply of one hundred pounds' worth of merchandize could not last very long.

*August.* On the 5th of August rain fell for the first time unaccompanied by a storm, though the rainy season in general sets in with dreadful tornadoes. The watery element disturbed the luxurious existence of the 'kanám galgálma', the large termites, which had fed on sugar and other supplies, and on the 6th they all of a sudden disappeared from the ground, and filled the air as short-lived winged creatures, in which state they are called by the people 'tsútsu', or 'dsúdsu', and, when fried, are used as food. Their tenure of life is so precarious, and they seem to be so weak, that they become very troublesome, as they fall in every direction upon man and his food. Of each swarm of these insects only one couple seems destined to survive; all the rest die a violent death.

The town now began to present quite a different appearance; but while it was agreeable to see the dryness relieved, and succulent grass and fresh crops springing up all around, and supplanting the dull uniformity of the *Asclepias gigantea*, on the other hand, the extensive waterpools formed everywhere in the concavities of the ground, were by no means conducive to health, more especially as those places were depositories of all sorts of offal, and of putrefying carcasses of many kinds. The consequence was that my health, instead of improving, became worse, although I struggled hard, and as often as possible rode out on horseback. All the people were now busy in the labours of the field, although cultivation in the neighbourhood of the town is not of a uniform, but of a varied character; and a large portion of the ground, consisting of 'ánge' and 'fírki', is reserved for the culture of the masákuwá (*Holcus cernuus*), or winter-corn, with its variety the kérirám.

On the 8th of August the neighbourhood presented a very animated spectacle, the crownlands in Gawánge being then cultivated by a great number of people, working to the sound of a drum. Their labours continued till the 15th; on which day Mr. Overweg had the honour of presenting his Búdduma friends to the sheikh of Bórnu. All nature was now cheerful; the trees were putting forth fresh leaves, and the young birds began to fledge. I took great delight in observing the little household of a family of the feathered tribe; there were five young ones, the oldest and most daring of which began to try his strength on the 12th August, while the other four set out together on the 14th.

My friend, the vizier, whose solicitude for my health I cannot acknowledge too warmly, was very anxious that I should not stay in the town during the rainy season; and knowing that one of our principal objects was to investigate the eastern shore of lake Tsád, sent me word, on the 11th of August, that I might now view the bahár el ghazál, an undertaking which, as I have already mentioned, he had at first represented as impossible.

I had the inexpressible delight of receiving by the courier, who arrived on the 6th of August, a considerable parcel of letters from Europe, which assured me as well of the great interest which was generally felt in our undertaking, although as yet only very little of our first proceedings had become known, as that we should be enabled to carry out our enterprise without too many privations. I therefore collected all the little energy which my sickly state had left me, and concluded the report of my journey to A'damáwa, which caused me a great deal of pain, but which, forwarded on the 8th of August, together with the news of Mr. Overweg's successful navigation,[1] produced a great deal of satisfaction in Europe. Together with the letters and sundry Maltese portfolios, I had also the pleasure of receiving several numbers of the 'Athenæum', probably the first which were introduced into Central Africa, and which gave me great delight.

Altogether our situation in the country was not so bad. We were on the best and most friendly terms with the rulers: we were not only tolerated, but even respected by the natives, and we saw an immense field of interesting and useful labour open

[1] of Lake Chad.

to us. There was only one disagreeable circumstance besides the peculiar nature of the climate; this was the fact that our means were too small to render us quite independent of the sheikh and his vizier, for the scanty supplies which had reached us were not sufficient to provide for our wants, and were soon gone. We were scarcely able to keep ourselves afloat on our credit, and to supply our most necessary wants. Mr. Overweg, besides receiving a very handsome horse from them, had also been obliged to accept at their hands a number of tobes, which he had made presents of to the chiefs of the Búdduma, and they looked upon him as almost in their employment. He lost a great deal of his time in repairing, or rather trying to repair, their watches and other things. Such services I had declined from the beginning, and was therefore regarded as less useful; and I had occasionally to hear it said, "Abd el Kerím faidanse bágo', — "Abd el Kerím is of no use whatever;' nevertheless, I myself was not quite independent of their kindness, although I sacrificed all I could in order to give from time to time a new impulse to their favour by an occasional present.

## ID EL FITR IN KUKAWA

*September.* The business of the town went on as usual, with the exception of the áid el fotr, the ngúmerí ashám, the festival following the great annual fast, which was celebrated in a grand style, not by the nation, which seemed to take very little interest in it, but by the court. In other places, like Kanó, the rejoicings seem to be more popular on this occasion; the children of the butchers or 'masufauchi' in that great emporium of commerce mounting some oxen, fattened for the occasion, between the horns, and managing them by a rope fastened to the neck, and another to the hind leg. As for the common people of Bórnu, they scarcely took any other part in this festivity than by putting on their best dresses; and it is a general custom in larger establishments that servants and attendants on this day receive a new shirt.

I also put on my best dress, and mounting my horse, which

had recovered a little from the fatigue of the last journey, though it was not yet fit for another, proceeded in the morning to the eastern town or 'billa gedíbe', the great thoroughfare being crowded with men on foot and horseback, passing to and fro, all dressed in their best. It had been reported that the sheikh was to say his prayers in the mosque, but we soon discovered that he was to pray outside the town, as large troops of horsemen were leaving it through the north gate or 'chinna yalábe'. In order to become aware of the place where the ceremony was going on, I rode to the vizier's house and met him just as he came out, mounted on horseback, and accompanied by a troop of horsemen.

At the same time several cavalcades were seen coming from various quarters, consisting of the kashéllas, or officers, each with his squadron, of from a hundred to two hundred horsemen, all in the most gorgeous attire, particularly the heavy cavalry; the greater part being dressed in a thick stuffed coat called 'degíbbir', and wearing over it several tobes of all sorts of colours and designs, and having their heads covered with the 'búge' or casque, made very nearly like those of our knights in the middle age, but of lighter metal, and ornamented with most gaudy feathers. Their horses were covered all over with the thick clothing called 'líbbedí', with various coloured stripes, consisting of three pieces, and leaving nothing but the feet exposed, the front of the head being protected and adorned by a metal plate. Others were dressed in a coat of mail, 'síllege', and the other kind called 'komá-komí-súbe'. The lighter cavalry was only dressed in two or three showy tobes and small white or coloured caps; but the officers and more favoured attendants wore bernúses of finer or coarser quality, and generally of red or yellow colour, slung in a picturesque manner round the upper part of their body, so that the inner wadding of richly coloured silk was most exposed to view.

All these dazzling cavalcades, amongst whom some very excellent horses were seen prancing along, were moving towards the northern gate of the 'billa gedíbe', while the troop of the sheikh himself, who had been staying in the western town, was coming from SW. The sight of this troop, at least from a little distance, as is the case in theatrical scenery, was really magnificent. The troop was led by a number of horsemen; then followed the livery slaves with their matchlocks; and behind them rode the sheikh, dressed as usual in a white bernús, as a token of his religious character, but wearing round his head a red shawl. He was followed by four magnificent chargers clothed in líbbedí of silk of various colours, that of the first horse being striped white and yellow, that of the second white and brown, that of the third white and light green, and that of the fourth white and cherry red. This was certainly the most interesting and conspicuous part of the procession. Behind the horses followed the four large álam or ensigns of the sheikh, and the four smaller ones of the musketeers, and then a numerous body of horsemen.

This cavalcade of the sheikh's now joined the other troops, and the whole body proceeded in the direction of Dawerghú to a distance of about a mile from the town. Here the sheikh's tent was pitched, consisting of a very large cupola of considerable dimensions, with blue and white stripes, and curtains, the one half white and the other red; the curtains were only half closed. In this tent the sheikh himself, the vizier, and the first courtiers were praying, while the numerous body of horsemen and men on foot were grouped around in the most picturesque and imposing variety.

Meanwhile I made the round of this interesting scene, and endeavoured to count the various groups. In their numbers I was certainly disappointed, as I had been led to expect myriads. At the very least, however, there were 3000 horsemen, and from 6000 to 7000 armed men on foot, the latter party with bow and arrow. There were besides a great multitude of spectators. The ceremony did not last long; and as early as nine o'clock the ganga summoned all the chiefs to mount, and the dense mass of human beings began to disperse and range themselves in various groups. They took their direction round the north-western corner of the east town, and entered the latter by the western gate; but the crowd was so great that I chose to forego taking leave of the sheikh, and went slowly back over the intermediate ground between the two towns in the company of some very chevaleresque and well-mounted young Arabs from Ben-Gházi, and posted myself at some distance from the east gate of the western town, in order to see the kashéllas, who have their residence in this quarter, pass by.

There were twelve or thirteen, few of whom had more than one hundred horsemen, the most conspicuous being Fúgo 'Ali, 'Ali Marghí, 'Ali Déndal, 'Ali Ladán, Belál, Sálah Kandíl and Jerma. It was thought remarkable that no Shúwa had come to this festivity; but I think they rarely do, although they may sometimes come for the 'Aid-el-kebír, or the 'ngúmerí layábe'. It is rather remarkable that even this smaller festivity is celebrated here with such *éclat*, while in general, in Mohammedan Negroland only the 'láya' is celebrated in this way; perhaps this is due to Egyptian influence, and the custom is as old at least as the time of the King Edrís Alawóma.

## THE OUTPOST AT YO

From 11 September till 14 November 1851, Barth and Overweg accompanied an expedition to Kanem, travelling beyond the boundaries of what is today Nigeria. They left modern Bornu at the frontier town of Yo.

*September* 16. I felt tolerably strong. Soon after we had started, we met a great many horses which had been sent here for pasturage, and then encountered another fish kafla. My horseman wanted me all at once to proceed to the town of Yó, from whence he was to return; and he continued on without stopping, although I very soon felt tired, and wanted to make a halt. The country, at the distance of some miles south from the komádugu, is rather monotonous and barren, and the large tamarind-tree behind the town of Yó is seen from such a distance that the traveller, having the same conspicuous object before his eyes for such a length of time, becomes tired out before he reaches it. The dúm-palm is the principal tree in this flat region, forming detached clusters, while the ground in general is extremely barren.

Proceeding with my guardian in advance, we at length reached the town, in front of which there is a little suburb; and being uncertain whether we should take quarters inside or outside, we entered it. It consisted of closely-packed streets, was extremely hot, and exhaled such an offensive smell of dried fish, that it appeared to me a very disagreeable and intolerable abode. Nevertheless we rode to the house of the shitíma, or rather, in the full form, Shitíma Yóma (which is the title the governor bears), a large building of clay. He was just about taking another wife; and large quantities of corn, intended as provision for his new household, were heaped up in front of it. Having applied to his men for quarters, a small courtyard with a large hut was assigned to us in another part of the town, and we went there; but it was impossible for me to make myself in any way comfortable in this narrow space, where a small gáwo afforded very scanty shade. Being almost suffocated, and feeling very unwell, I mounted my horse again and hastened out of the gate, and was very glad to have regained the fresh air. We then encamped about 600 yards from the town, near a shady tamarind-tree; and I stretched my feeble limbs on the ground, and fell into a sort of lethargy for some hours, enjoying a luxurious tranquillity; I was so fatigued with my morning's ride, that I thought with apprehension on what would become of me after my companions had joined me, when I should be obliged to bear fatigue of a quite different description.

As soon as I felt strong enough to rise from my couch, I walked a few paces in order to get a sight of the river or 'komádugu'.

## THE BORNU ARMY ON THE MARCH

After only ten days' rest back in Kukawa, Barth set out again, this time involved in a full-scale military campaign against Mandara. The army's first camp was just outside Ngornu.

*November* 25. The 'ngáufate' having its fixed arrangements, our place was assigned near the tents of Lamíno, at some

distance east from those of Háj Beshír. As the greater part of
the courtiers were taking at least a portion of their harím with
them to the 'kerígu', a simple tent was not sufficient for them;
but by means of curtains made of striped cotton-stuff a certain
space is encompassed in order to insure greater privacy. For
the sheikh and the vizier, as long as we remained in the Bórnu
territories, at every new encampment an inclosure of matting
was erected; for it is not the custom, as has been asserted, to
separate the royal camp from that of the rest, at least not on
expeditions into a hostile country, nor has it been so in former
times. The common soldiers had no further protection, except
some light and small huts with high gables, which some of them
had built with the tall stalks of the Indian corn, which lay in
great abundance on the stubble-fields.

*November* 26. Early in the morning the signal for the decamp-
ment of the army was given in front of the tent of the sheikh,
by the sound of the great drum; and in broad battle-array
('báta') the army with its host of cavalry moved onwards
over the plain, which was covered with tall reeds, and showed
only here and there a few signs of cultivation.

This time I still remained with the camels and the train-oxen,
which, mixed with pedestrians and some single horsemen in
long unbounded lines, kept along the road, while single troops
of Kánembú spearmen, in their light fanciful garments, mostly
consisting of a small apron of rags, or a hide tied round the
loins, and armed with their light wooden shields, passed the
luggage-train, shouting out in their wild native manner.

## THE WAR CAMP AT MARTE

*November* 28. The ngáufate advanced as far as the town of
Márte. Not far from Yédi there extends, in a southerly direction,
a very expansive plain devoid of any sort of vegetation except
some mimosas. This is the beginning of the 'fírki' ground,
which comprises so large a space in the southern regions of
Bórnu, and of which I have repeatedly spoken on former
occasions; but the plantation of the *Holcus cernuus*, called

'másakwá' or 'mósogá' (which is limited to this peculiar territory), had not turned out well this year, in consequence of the scarcity of rain.

I had marched in advance with my camel, when the vizier got sight of me, and begged me to come to the sheikh. After having saluted me in the most friendly way, he asked me why I always wore my pistols in my belt round the waist, instead of fixing them at the saddle-bow; but he praised my foresight when I appealed to the example of Ráís Khalíl,[2] who, when thrown from his horse, on his unlucky expedition to Mándará, remained without a weapon in his hand. However, he was of opinion that at present, with such a large army, no danger of this kind was to be feared. He showed me also, in the most flattering manner, that he had imitated my example of having my chronometer continually girded around my waist; and he assured me that he found it very convenient.

The troop was here proceeding in stately order, and a broad line of battle deployed, one officer, with the title of jérma, riding in advance, and being followed by the four fan-bearers of the sheikh, in full array; but a little further on, a small tract of underwood compelled them to change their order of march, and proceed in one long line. The vizier was kind enough to send me a message to the effect that I had better get in front, so as not to be in the midst of the confusion.

The place of encampment was chosen on the north-west side of the town of Márte; and when the sheikh had dismounted, in order to take possession of the mat house which had been prepared for him, the whole host of cavalry galloped up in the fiercest manner, before I was able to get out of their way, so that I received a very severe shock from a horseman, who struck against me with great violence.

In the afternoon my friend and companion on my journey to A'damáwa, Kashélla Bíllama, called on me; and we mounted on horseback, in order to pay a visit to the market, which is held every Friday outside the western gate of the town, where an open area surrounded by several wells spreads out. But the

---

[2] Denham.

market, at least that day, was very insignificant: it was not furnished with a single shed or stall, and not a single article of manufacture was exposed, Negro millet, butter, and wooden bowls being almost the only articles offered for sale; and sellers, as well as buyers, were very few in number. The town contains about four thousand inhabitants, and, taking into account the strategetical art of this country, possesses proper defences, the clay wall being in a good state of repair, and having a gate on each side excepting the side of the market, where there are two. Towards the east there is a little cultivated ground, and on the north a small suburb, consisting of large, conical, thatched huts, where, besides Kanúri, several Fúlbe or Felláta families are living. The interior of the town consists of narrow lanes; and most of the houses are clay buildings. There was nothing interesting to be seen; but I was agreeably surprised when my companion, who was a native of this place, took me to pay my compliments to his mother, who kept a small shed, or rather, as we should say, a shop, in the little market-place inside the town. It was certainly a trait of a good-natured and friendly disposition.

## THE TOWN OF ALA

*November* 30. Our march, however, was very short, the encampment having been chosen on the west side of the town of Alá. This town also is of some importance, and surrounded by a wall in good repair, with two gates on the north and west sides and only one on the south and east. The interior is enlivened by large trees, consisting of chédia (elastic gum), and kúrna trees, while the huts are remarkable for their high conical roof, the thatch of which, in a great many instances, is interlaced by the clasps of the *Cucurbita lagenaria*, the whole looking very cheerful. The sheikh having requested me repeatedly to give my compass up to him, as he imagined it would be sufficient for one of us to possess such an instrument, I thought it prudent to offer him my musical-box as a present, remarking that I would willingly give away such articles, but not scientific instruments. Several hares had been caught in the course of the day; and in the evening we had some of them very palatably dressed by the experienced female slave of Lamíno.

## DESCRIPTION OF DIKWA

*December* 1. Soon after starting, early in the morning we had to traverse some underwood, which caused a great rush and much confusion among the undisciplined army, so that two or three horsemen were seriously injured. On such occasions, as well as in the thick covert of the forest, I had a full opportunity of testing the valuable properties of the Arab stirrups, which protect the whole leg, and, if skilfully managed, keep every obtruder at a respectful distance; indeed I am almost sure that if, on these my African wanderings, I had made use of English stirrups I should have lost both my legs. Our way afterwards led over monotonous fírki ground, where we were cheered by the sight of some fine crops of sorghum. Detached hamlets were seen in every direction, even where the country did not present any traces of cultivation; but, with the exception of the Shúwa villages, this province does not contain many small hamlets, the population being concentrated in larger places. Underwood succeeded to the fírki ground, and extended to the very walls of the large town of Díkowa.

The sight of this town, with its walls over-towered by the regularly-shaped crowns of magnificent fig-trees, was very imposing. The western wall, along which our road lay, was covered with women and children, and we met a numerous procession of females in their best attire, who were going to salute their sovereign upon his arrival at the encampment; and coming from the capital, which is distinguished by the ugliness of its female inhabitants, I was agreeably surprised at their superior countenance and figure. But though the observer might be gratified with the personal appearance of the natives, their industry was questionable; for only a small tract of cultivated ground was to be seen on this side of the town, girt by a forest of mighty trees.

The encampment, or 'ngáufate', began to form close to the southern wall of the town, amidst sandy ground free from trees, and completely surrounded by a thick covert. Although it was December, the sun was very powerful; and, until the camels arrived, I sat down in the shade of a 'bíto' or *Balanites*, while the encampment was spreading out in all directions, and approached the edge of the covert. I then gave up my shady place to Kashélla Játo, an officer of the musketeers, who, in acknowledgement, offered me a clear piece of delicious gum, just taken from the tree and full of sweet fluid; in which state it is certainly a delicacy, and is so esteemed here as well as in Western Negroland. The encampment springing up gradually from the ground, with its variety of light dwellings built only for the moment — the multifarious appearance of armed people — the numbers of horses of all colours, some of the most exquisite beauty — the uninterrupted train of beasts of burden, camels, and pack-oxen, laden with the tents, furniture, and provisions, and mounted by the wives and concubines of the different chiefs, well dressed and veiled, — altogether presented a most interesting picture; for now almost the whole host or 'kebú', had collected, and twenty thousand men, with ten thousand horses, and at least as many beasts of burden, were no doubt assembled on this spot.

At length our two tents also were pitched, and we could make ourselves as comfortable as the scanty shade which they afforded allowed us.

In the evening, our conversation with the vizier turning upon the means which remained for Bórnu to attain once more to her former greatness, these devastating expeditions and slave-hunts fell under discussion; and I took the liberty to indicate, in opposition to such a system, the necessity of a well-established government, with a strong military force capable of extending their dominion. I also called the attention of the vizier to the point, that, as they could never rely upon the Turks, who might easily cut off all supplies of foreign merchandise, it was greatly to their interest to keep open to themselves that large river which passed a short distance to the south of their dominions, and which would enable them to supply themselves with every kind of European manufacture at a much cheaper rate than they were able to obtain them by the northern route. He did not hesitate to throw the whole blame upon the former sultans; but those poor men, when they possessed the dominion of the Kwána tribe, probably had no idea that the river which ran through their territory joined the sea; and even if they had, the relation between Islám and Christianity at that period was of so hostile a character, that, for the very reason that this stream might open to the Christians a more easy access to their country, they shunned any nearer connection with it as dangerous. However, under the present entirely altered state of affairs, there is no question that an energetic native chief, basing his power on a supply of European merchandise, as facilitated by the river Bénuwé, might easily dominate a great part of Central Africa.

On the first day of our arrival, our encampment was very comfortable; but every day that we stayed here it became more confined, owing principally to the numerous cavalry of these Arab tribes, almost all of whom are mounted; and many a new-comer was seen hurrying about without being able to find a spot to lie down, or to meet with friends to treat him. I myself had to entertain a respectable man among these Shúwa, of the name of Háj Hamadán, belonging to the tribe of the Hasúnna.

This man, who generally had his settlement far to the east, in the Wádi Guskáb, had come some time previously to Logón in order to pay a visit to some relations of his, and had now joined this expedition. But one must be very careful with these Shúwa; for, to use a common expression, if you give them an inch, they are wont to take an ell. But for their Jewish character, I should have liked to enter into more intimate relations with them than I actually did.

Their emigration into these regions, at least several centuries ago, is certainly not without interest; and, as I have already had occasion to observe in another place, they preserve the characteristic type of their race very distinctly — a middle-sized, slender figure (which, however, is apt to become fuller as they advance in years), small pleasing features, and a dark olive complexion. Their dialect is very peculiar; and while it lays claim to a far greater purity than belongs to the dialects of the coast, by the profusion of vowels which it has preserved, its character is deteriorated, and becomes nearly ridiculous, by the continued repetition and insertion of certain words. A Shúwa is not able to say three words without inserting his favourite term 'kúch, kúch', which corresponds to the English word 'thorough', but which is not Arabic at all. When they omit the word 'kúch', they make use of another term, 'bérketek', 'your worship', which at once bears testimony to the servile and degraded position which they occupy in Negroland, although in Bórnu they are still treated with some indulgence and lenity, especially since the time when Mohammed Tiráb, the father of the present vizier, who belonged to the tribe of the Sálamát, attained the highest degree of power and influence in the country.

While the encampment itself presented considerable interest, as being the temporary abode of so many people, the town of Díkcwa, near which we were encamped, seemed well deserving some attention, as having been repeatedly the residence of the rulers of the country, and being still one of the largest towns in the kingdom. I therefore paid a visit to it in the afternoon of the second day of our stay, being accompanied by my friend Bíllama. We entered the town by the western gate; and I saw that the walls were about thirty feet high, and terraced on the inside like those of the capital, and of considerable breadth at the base: they were in a state of good repair. I was struck by the height and round shape of the huts, which entirely wanted the characteristic top, or, as the Kanúri people call it, kógi ngímbe, and were of the same kind as I had observed in the other towns of this southern province. Every hut had its little courtyard, in some of which vegetation was seen, mostly karás.

The further we proceeded, the more I was pleased with the general appearance of the town, the exterior of which had made a favourable impression upon me on our first arrival. Large, beautiful, wide-spreading fig-trees, ngábore, chédia or elastic gum-trees, and kórna-trees, spread their shade all around, and two or three isolated papaw-trees, or, as the Kanúri call them, bambús-másarbe, with their remarkable feathery crowns and their smooth virgin-like stems, formed a lively contrast to the broad-leafed canopy of the other trees, while the hedges and fences of the courtyards were partly enlivened by a luxurious creeper called 'dagdágel' by the natives. The real nucleus of the town seemed to consist entirely of clay houses.

After a very pleasant ride, we reached the house of the 'mainta', or governor, who still enjoys a certain degree of independence. The chief ornament of the place in front of his house was the most splendid caoutchouc-tree I have ever seen; indeed I can scarcely imagine that the diameter of its crown, which was so regularly and symmetrically shaped that it appeared as if effected by art, measured less than from seventy to eighty feet. It really formed a beautiful fáge, or, as the Háusa people call it, íchenbatú, or open council-hall, such as are common in these places; but at present no political business of any importance was transacted here, and it formed a favourite lounge for idle people, amongst whom there was a troop of musicians, playing lustily upon their instruments to console the petty chief for the loss of his former power, which had dwindled away to a mere shadow. I would gladly have paid him a visit; but, poor as I was at the time, and without a single article worthy of his acceptance, I was rather glad that I was under no obligation to him. The interruption in the daily course of life of the inhabitants, by the presence of the army, was the more to be lamented as it prevented me from becoming an eye-witness to the chief industry of the natives, which consists in weaving and manufacturing into shirts the cotton which they grow; for they are almost exclusively cotton-growers, and have very little corn. But, although they are able to produce a fine sort of texture, they are very badly off for dyeing, and in this respect are far outstripped by the inhabitants of Ujé and Mákari. Instead of the beating of shirts, which forms so pleasant a sound in many other industrial towns of Negroland, there was nothing to be heard but the sound which proceeded from the powder-mill, if I may be allowed to give this grand name to a yard in which eight slaves were employed in pounding powder in large wooden mortars; for this is the way in which powder is prepared in Negroland, and during my stay in Bagírmi every time I had my coffee pounded (as I did not possess a coffee-mill), I excited the suspicion that I was preparing powder. Of course the presence of the army was the reason why so little activity was to be seen at present, and the little market, or durríya, which is held in the afternoon, was very badly attended; but the size and populousness of the town made such an impression upon me, that I thought myself justified in rating the number of inhabitants at about twenty-five thousand.

Having heard that the wealth of the inhabitants of Díkowa consisted of cotton, I expected to find extensive well-kept cotton-plantations; but, although the article was cultivated to a great extent, I was astonished at the neglected appearance which it exhibited, the cotton-fields being almost buried beneath the thicket, and overgrown not only with rank grass, but even with trees and bushes, so that scarcely any space was left for the plants to spread out; nevertheless their luxuriant growth bore ample testimony to the rich nature of the soil, and gave an idea of the wealth that lies buried in these regions. I have already observed, on another occasion, that the natives of Negroland take very little care of their cotton-plantations; and there is no doubt that, if sufficient care was bestowed, quite a different quality might be produced.

I roved about in this wild and fertile region till I was entirely hemmed in by an impenetrable thicket. While returning hence to our encampment by a more westerly path, I was ruminating in my mind how the former rulers of this country had evinced so much more feeling for the bounty and beauty of nature than its present possessors; for, while these have chosen for their residence the most monotonous district of the empire, the former selected those parts which nature itself had embellished — the shores of the so-called Yeou, or the komádugu Wáube, and this fine watercourse of Díkowa; and they not only chose the most interesting spots, but they even embellished them by art, as the large artificial basins in the neighbourhood of Ghasréggomo, Ghámbarú, and Dámasak amply testify. In this respect it is not uninteresting that we are informed by the imám A'hmed, the historian of the king Edrís Alawóma, that his master, when he visited the town of Fíka, could not forego the pleasure of paying a visit to the famous little alpine lake which lies at some distance from that town. Although the country of Bórnu is far from being the most favoured part of Negroland, yet the shores of these watercourses are very rich indeed, and capable of maintaining a numerous population.

In returning to our encampment, I passed the market, or durríya, which was held every afternoon on the west side of the encampment. It was really a busy scene, not yielding in importance to the little daily market of the capital; and this was not at all marvellous, as a greater crowd of people, and a far greater number of horses, were gathered here than the average population of Kúkawa. Not only were provisions, such as meat, grain, beans, ground-nuts, and other articles of a like description, offered for sale; but even small luxuries; and there was a good deal of bartering, as the buyers were destitute of currency—kúngona, or cowries, as well as gábagá or cotton strips. I also observed that the encampment, especially on this side, where it was skirted by a thick covert of trees, was encircled by a living wall of light Kánembú spearmen, who were keeping watch; for although the army was still in its own territory, yet, in the weak state of the government, a certain degree of insecurity already commences here; and the very first evening of our being encamped on this spot, the ngáufate was roused by the gangéma, or announcement by beat of drums, to the effect that everybody should be on his guard against horse-stealers.

While the country around presented interesting features, and the encampment itself exhibited a scene of great variety, the time we spent here passed away comfortably and agreeably, with the sole exception that the space allotted to us was too confined to be comfortable. We were on the most friendly terms with the sheikh as well as with his vizier; and all court etiquette was dispensed with. This went so far that I and my

companion accommodated our noble and princely friends with
our woollen jackets and drawers; for they began to feel the
cold at night very severely, and on these occasions the very
respectable Háj Edrís had to play the part of a royal laundress.

Already, during our hibernal stay in the country of Aïr, we
had been obliged to accommodate our old and austere friend
A'nnur and his numerous relatives with our Turkish waistcoats:
but we had not yet condescended to give away our under-
clothing; and being ourselves extremely poor and destitute in
every respect, it was certainly not a little privation we imposed
upon ourselves. The clothes of the sheikh and his vizier were all
very wide, and not fit for keeping out the cold. I have repeatedly
had occasion to mention how sensitive the Africans are to cold;
and I am persuaded that, in the burning regions of Central
Africa, a good cargo of warm under-clothing would find a ready
sale, especially if it should arrive in the months of December and
January. But neither did our noble hosts, on their part, fail to do
everything in their power to render our situation as comfortable
as possible; and it was very satisfactory to see how anxious the
vizier was to supply us with all desirable information.

## THE TOWN OF NGALA

From December 1851 until February 1852 Barth was exploring
out of Nigeria, in the Logone, Musgu, Mandara and Tuburi
regions. After barely a month back in Kukawa, he again set forth
on his travels — this time a courageous, lone thrust to the Kotoko
and Bagirmi country. On the way he stopped at Ngala.

We passed several towns in a state of the utmost decay and
entirely deserted; and traversing a dense underwood, which we
scarcely expected to see in the neighbourhood of a large town,
reached at five o'clock the clay walls of Ngála.

The interior of this town has a very peculiar character, and
nothing similar to it is seen in any part of Negroland, although
the place at present is in a state of great decay; for all the
ancient quarter of the town consists of clay houses, built on an
imposing and elevated terrace. The palace of the governor is
indeed something quite stupendous for these regions, having,

with its immense substructure, and its large and towering walls, the appearance of a large citadel. We were quartered in the extensive mansion of the gedádo or delátu, in which Mr. Tully[3] died; but it, as well as the whole of the town, was in the utmost state of decay. The times of Méram, the beloved wife of the sheikh Mohammed el Amín el Kánemy, had gone by; and the wealth of Ngála had been consumed by the slaves of the present sheikh and his vizier. The once magnificent palace of Méram itself is nothing but a large, desolate heap of ruins.

The quarters, however, which were assigned to me were in a tolerable state of repair, consisting, as they did, of an upper story, which afforded me sufficient protection against the numbers of mosquitoes which infest the place. We remained here the following day, when I went to pay a visit to the governor at his residence; but I felt rather sorry for it, as the good impression which the imposing exterior of the palace had made upon me, was destroyed by the ruinous and desolate state of the interior. The whole province is now in a very neglected condition, such as would indicate that the ruler of the country himself acknowledged his incapability of defending his subjects against another inroad of the Wádáy.

The governor was not a very intelligent man; but it was he who first called my attention to the fact that the town of Ngála has its own peculiar idiom, quite distinct from the Kanúri, and I afterwards found that it is even different from the dialects of the other principal places in the province of Kótokó, though it is very closely related to the idioms spoken by the islanders of the Tsád (the so-called Búdduma, but whose real name is Yédiná) on the one side, and to that of the Músgu on the other. At some distance from Ngála is the town of Ndíffu, or Ndifú, which is said to have been one of the latest strongholds of the tribe of the Soy, or Só, whom I have repeatedly mentioned in my historical sketch of the empire of Bórnu; and sundry remarkable ornaments are said to be dug up frequently in that place.

[3] Ensign Toole, who died at Ngala on February 26 1824, only two months after he had reached Bornu to reinforce the Denham–Clapperton–Oudney expedition.

I had seen scarcely any traces of cultivation on the western side of the town; and when we set out again I found as little on the other sides. Nevertheless, the environs of Ngála, especially the north-east side, are of great interest in the eyes of the Bórnu people, as having been the scene of two important battles fought with the Bagírmi, in the first of which, in the year of the Hejra 1233, the sultan Dúnama was slain; and my companions, who remembered all the incidents of that struggle, pointed out with patriotic enthusiasm the various positions which each body of the combatants had occupied.

## DEATH OF OVERWEG

Barth did not regain Kukawa till August 1852, having spent several weeks as a prisoner of the Sultan of Bagirmi in Masena. On his return he found Overweg grievously ill. He managed to take him out to Maduwari, on the shores of Lake Chad, for a change of air. He left him in the house of his friend Fugo Ali.

*September* 25. The same evening one of the servants whom I had left with Mr. Overweg came and informed me that he was much worse, and that they were unable to understand a single word he said. I mounted immediately, and found my friend in a most distressing condition, lying outside in the courtyard, as he had obstinately refused to sleep in the hut. He was bedewed with a cold perspiration, and had thrown off all his coverings. He did not recognize me, and would not allow me or any one else to cover him. Being seized with a terrible fit of delirium, and muttering unintelligible words, in which all the events of his life seemed to be confused, he jumped up repeatedly in a raging fit of madness, and rushed against the trees and into the fire, while four men were scarcely able to hold him.

At length, towards morning, he became more quiet, and remained tranquilly on his couch; and, not becoming aware that his strength was broken, I thought I might return to the town. After asking him if he had any particular desire, he said that he had something to tell me; but it was impossible for me to understand him, and I can only fancy, from what happened, that, being aware that death was at hand, he wanted to recommend his family to me.

At an early hour on Sunday morning, Mr. Overweg's chief servant came to me with the sad news that the state of my friend was very alarming, and that since I had left him he had not spoken a word, but was lying motionless. I mounted immediately on horseback; but before I reached the place, I was met by a brother of Fúgo 'Alí, who, with tears in his eyes, told me that our friend was gone. With the dawn of day, while a few drops of rain were falling, after a short struggle, his soul had departed.

In the afternoon I laid him in his grave, which was dug in the shade of a fine hájilíj, and well protected from the beasts of prey. Thus died my sole friend and companion, in the thirtieth year of his age, and in the prime of his youth. It was not reserved for him to finish his travels, and to return home in safety; but he met a most honourable death, as a martyr to science; and it is a remarkable fact that he found himself a grave on the very borders of that lake by the navigation of which he has rendered his name celebrated for ever. It was certainly a presentiment of his approaching death which actuated him in his ardent desire to be removed to this place, where he died hard by the boat in which he had made his voyage. Many of the inhabitants of the place, who had known him well during his repeated visits to the village, bitterly lamented his death; and no doubt the 'tabíb', as he was called, will be long remembered by them.

Dejected, and full of sad reflections on my lonely situation, I returned into the town in the evening; but our dwelling, which during my stay in Bagírmi my companion had greatly improved, and embellished by white-washing it with a kind of gypsum, of which he found a layer in our courtyard, now appeared to me desolate and melancholy in the extreme. While, therefore, originally it had been my plan to make another trial along the eastern shores of the Tsád, any longer stay in this place had now become so intolerable to me, that I determined to set out as soon as possible on my journey towards the Niger — to new countries and new people.

## CHAPTER 8

# FROM BORNU TO KATSINA (1852–1853)

## DEPARTURE FROM KUKAWA

*November* 19. At length, after a long series of delays, the road to the west became open, and I took leave of the sheikh on the 19th of November, in a private audience, none but the vizier being present. I then found reason to flatter myself that, from the manner in which I had explained to them the motives which had induced me to undertake a journey to the chiefs of the Fúlbe or Felláta, there were no grounds of suspicion remaining between us, although they made it a point that I should avoid going by Kanó; and even when I rejected their entreaty to remain with them after my successful return from Timbúktu, they found nothing to object, as I assured them that I might be more useful to them as a faithful friend in my own country, than by remaining with them in Bórnu. At that time I thought that Her Majesty's Government would be induced to send a consul to Bórnu, and, in consequence, I raised their expectations on that point.

*November* 25. It was half-past ten in the morning when I left the town of Kúkawa, which for upwards of twenty months I had regarded as my head quarters, and as a place upon which, in any emergency, I might safely fall back upon; for although I even then expected that I should be obliged to return to this place once more, and even of my own free will made my plans accordingly, yet I was convinced that, in the course of my proceedings, I should not be able to derive any further aid from the friendship and protection of the sheikh of Bórnu, and I likewise fully understood that circumstances might oblige me to make my return by the western coast.

My little troop consisted of the following individuals. First, Mohammed el Gatróni, the same faithful young lad who had accompanied me as a servant all the way from Fezzán to Kúkawa, and whom, on my starting for A'damáwa, I had sent home, very reluctantly, with my despatches and with the late Mr. Richardson's effects, on condition that, after having staid some time with his wife and children, he should return. He had lately come back with the same caravan which had brought me the fresh supplies. Faithful to my promise, I had mounted him on horseback, and made him my chief servant, with a salary of four Spanish dollars per month — and a present of fifty dollars besides, in the event of my enterprise being successfully terminated. My second servant, and the one upon whom, next to Mohammed, I relied most, was 'Abd-Alláhi, or rather, as the name is pronounced in this country, 'Abd-Alléhi, a young Shúwa from Kótokó, whom I had taken into my service on my journey to Bagírmi, and who, never having been in a similar situation, and not having dealt before with Europeans, at first had caused me a great deal of trouble, especially as he was laid up with the small pox for forty days during my stay in that country. He was a young man of very pleasing manners and straightforward character, and, as a good and pious Moslim, formed a useful link between myself and the Mohammedans; but he was sometimes extremely whimsical, and, after having written out his contract for my whole journey to the west and back, I had the greatest trouble in making him adhere to his own stipulations. I had unbounded control over my men, because I agreed with them that they should not receive any part of their salary on the road, but the whole on my successful return to Haúsa. 'Abd-Alláhi was likewise mounted on horseback, but had only a salary of two dollars, and a present of twenty dollars. Then came Mohammed ben A'hmed, the fellow of whom I have already spoken on my journey to Kánem, and who, though a person of very indifferent abilities, and at the same time very self-conceited on account of his

Islám, was yet valued by me for his honesty, while he, on his part, having been left by his countrymen and co-religionists in a very destitute situation, became attached to myself.

I had two more freemen in my service, one, a brother of Mohammed el Gatróni, who was only to accompany me as far as Zínder; the other an Arab from the borders of Egypt, and called Slimán el Ferjáni, a fine, strong man, who had once formed part of the band of the Welád Slimán in Kánem, and who might have been of great service to me, from his knowledge of the use of firearms and his bodily strength; but he was not to be trusted, and deserted me in a rather shameful manner a little beyond Kátsena.

Besides these freemen, I had in my service two liberated slaves, Dýrregu, a Haúsa boy, and A'bbega, a Marghí lad, who had been set free by the late Mr. Overweg, — the same young lads whom on my return to Europe I brought to this country, where they promised to lay in a store of knowledge, and who on the whole have been extremely useful to me, although A'bbega not unfrequently found some other object more interesting than my camels, which were intrusted to his care, and which in consequence he lost repeatedly.

## THE KOYAM DISTRICT

*November* 27. I now entered Koyám, with its straggling villages, its well-cultivated fields, and its extensive forests of middle-sized mimosas, which afford food to the numerous herds of camels constituting the wealth of the African tribe, who in former times, before the Bórnu dynasty was driven away from its ancient capital Njímiye by the rival family of the Bulála, led a nomadic life on the pasture-grounds of Kánem. Having thus traversed the district called Wódomá, we encamped about noon, at a short distance from a well in the midst of the forest, belonging to a district called Gágadá. The well was twenty-five fathoms deep, and was frequented during the night by numerous herds of cattle from different parts of the neighbourhood.

While making the round in the night in order to see whether

my people were on the look-out, as a great part of the security of a traveller in these regions depends on the vigilance exercised by night, I succeeded in carrying away secretly the arms from all my people, even from the warlike Ferjáni Arab, which caused great amusement and hubbub when they awoke in the morning, and enabled me to teach them a useful lesson of being more careful for the future.

## THE RUINS OF BIRNI NGAZARGAMU

*December* 1. I took a long walk in the afternoon along the sheet of water, which was indented in the most picturesque manner, and was bordered all around with the richest vegetation, the trees belonging principally to the species called karáge and baggarúwa. Further on dúm palms became numerous; and it was the more interesting to me, as I had visited this district, only a few miles further north, during the dry season. Guinea fowl were here so numerous that one could hardly move a step without disturbing a group of these lazy birds, which constitute one of the greatest delicacies of the traveller in these regions. A sportsman would find in these swampy forests not less interesting objects for his pursuits than the botanist; for elephants, several species of antelopes, even including the *oryx* or tétel, nay, as it would seem, even the large *addax*, the wild hog, besides an unlimited supply of water fowl, Guinea fowl, and partridges, would prove worthy of his attention, while occasional encounters with monkeys would cause him some diversion and amusement.

There was a great deal of cultivation along this luxuriant border, and even a little cotton was grown; but a very large amount of the latter article might be obtained here with a greater degree of industry. Besides a village at a short distance to the S.E., inhabited by Koyám, and which bears the same name as this branch of the river, there is a hamlet, consisting of about thirty cottages, inhabited by Fúlbe, or Felláta, of the tribe of the Híllega, the same tribe whom we have met in A'damáwa. They seemed to possess a considerable number of cattle, and appeared to lead a contented and retired life in this fertile but at present almost desolate region. But, unfortunately, they have been induced, by their close contact with the Kanúri, to give up the nice manner of preparing their milk which so distinguishes the Fúlbe in other provinces; and even the cheerful way in which the women offered us their ware could not induce me to purchase of them their unclean species of sour milk, which is prepared by means of the urine of cattle.

Beautiful and rich as was the scenery of this locality, it had the disadvantage of harbouring immense swarms of mosquitoes; and our night's rest, in consequence, was greatly disturbed.

*December* 2. Winding round the swamp (for the nature of a swamp or kulúgu was more apparent, at present, than that of a branch of the river), we reached, after a march of about three miles, the site of the ancient capital of the Bórnu empire, Ghasr-éggomo, which, as I have stated on a former occasion, was built by the king 'Alí Ghajidéni, towards the end of the fifteenth century, after the dynasty had been driven from its ancient seats in Kánem, and, after a desperate struggle between unsettled elements, began to concentrate itself under the powerful rule of this mighty king. The site was visited by the members of the former expedition, and it has been called by them by the half-Arabic name of Birni-Kadím, the 'old capital', — even the Bórnu people in general designating the place only by the name birni, or burni. The town had nearly a regular oval shape, but, notwithstanding the great exaggerations of former Arab informants, who have asserted that this town surpassed Cairo (or Masr el Káhira) in size, and was a day's march across, was little more than six English miles in circumference, being encompassed by a strong wall, with six or seven gates; which, in its present dilapidated state, forms a small ridge, and seems clearly to indicate that, when the town was conquered by the Fúlbe or Felláta, the attack was made from two different sides, viz., the south-west and north-west, where the lower part of the wall had been dug away. The interior of the town exhibits very little that is remarkable. The principal buildings consist of baked bricks; and in the present capital not the smallest approach is made to this more solid mode of architecture. The dimensions of the palace appear to have been very large, although nothing but the ground plan of large empty areas can be made out at present, while the very small dimensions of the mosque, which had five aisles, seem to afford sufficient proof that none but the people intimately connected with the court used to attend the service, just as is the case at the present time; and it serves, moreover, clearly to establish the fact that even in former times, when the empire was most flourishing, there was no such thing as a médresé, or college, attached to the mosque. The fact is, that although Bórnu at all times has had some learned men, study has always been a private affair, amongst a few individuals, encouraged by some distinguished men who had visited Egypt and Arabia. Taking into consideration the great extent of the empire during the period of its grandeur, and the fertility and wealth of some of its provinces, which caused gold dust at that time to be brought to market here in considerable quantity, it cannot be doubted that this capital contained a great deal of barbaric magnificence, and even a certain degree of civilization, much more so than is at present to be found in this country; and it is certainly a speculation not devoid of interest to imagine, in this town of Negroland, a splendid court, with a considerable number of learned and intelligent men gathering round their sovereign, and a priest writing down the history of the glorious achievements of his master, and thus securing them from oblivion. Pity that he was not aware that his work might fall into the hands of people from quite another part of the world, and of so different a stage of civilization, language, and learning! else he would certainly not have failed to have given to posterity a more distinct clue to the chronology of the history of his native country.

It is remarkable that the area of the town, although thickly overgrown with rank grass, is quite bare of trees, while the wall is closely hemmed in by a dense forest; and when I entered the ruins, I found them to be the haunt of a couple of tall ostriches, the only present possessors of this once animated ground: but on the south-west corner, at some distance from the wall, there was a small hamlet.

## THE MANGA DISTRICT

*December* 4. Here we entered that part of the province of Manga which is governed by Kashélla Belál; and the difference in the character of this tract from the province of Koyám, which we had just left behind, was remarkable, the country being undulated in downs of red sand, famous for the cultivation of ground-nuts and beans, both of which constitute a large proportion of the food of the inhabitants, so that millet and beans are generally sown on the same field, the latter ripening later and constituting the richest pasture for cattle and camels. Of grain, Negro millet (*Pennisetum typhoïdeum*) is the species almost exclusively cultivated in the country of Manga, sorghum not being adapted for this dry ground.

The same difference was to be observed in the architecture of the native dwellings, — the corn stacks which impart so decided a character of peace and repose to the villages of Háusa, but which are sought for in vain in the whole of Bórnu Proper, here again making their appearance. The Manga call them 'sébe' or 'gúsi'. The cottages themselves, although they were not remarkable for their cleanliness, presented rather a cheerful aspect, the thatch being thickly interwoven with and enlivened by the creepers of various cucurbitaceæ, but especially the favourite kobéwa or *Melopepo*. The same difference which was exhibited in the nature of the country and the dwellings of the natives, appeared also in the character of the latter, the Kanúri horseman or the Koyám camel-breeder being here supplanted by the Manga footman, with his leather apron, his bow and arrow, and his battle-axe, while the more slender Manga girl, scarcely peeping forth from under her black veil, with which she bashfully hid her face, had succeeded to the Bórnu female, with her square figure, her broad features, and her open and ill-covered breast. I have observed elsewhere that, although the Manga evidently form a very considerable element in the formation of the Bórnu nation, their name as such does not occur in the early annals of the empire, and we therefore can only presume that they owe their origin to a mixture of tribes.

## THE TOWN OF BORSARI

*December* 6. On reaching the town of Borzári, I preferred encamping outside, although there was not the least shade; my heavy luggage and my numerous party rendering quarters inside the town rather inconvenient. The governor, to whom I sent a small present, treated me very hospitably, sending me a heifer, a large provision of rice, several dishes of prepared food, and two large bowls of milk. This excellent man, whose name is Kashélla Manzo, besides the government of his province, had to regulate the whole intercourse along this road, being instructed at the time especially to prevent the exportation of horses from the Bórnu territory into the Háusa states.

The town, which is surrounded with a low crenellated wall and a ditch in good repair, is of considerable size and well built, and may contain from 7000 to 8000 inhabitants; but there is no great industry to be seen, nor is there a good market. The wells measure ten fathoms in depth.

## THE BEDDE COUNTRY

*December* 7. The Bedde, according to their language, are closely related to the Manga, but, as far as I had an opportunity of judging, are much inferior to them in bodily development, being not at all distinguished for their stature; but it is very probable that the inhabitants of these places in the border district, who come into continual contact with their masters the Bórnu people, are more degenerate than those in the interior, who, protected by the several branches of the komádugu and the swamps and forests connected with them, keep up a spirit of national independence, possessing even a considerable number of a small breed of horses, which they ride without saddle or harness.

*December* 8. Three miles further on, turning a little more southward from our westerly direction, we reached the town of Géshiya, once a strong place and surrounded by a clay wall, but at present in a state of great decay, although it is still tolerably peopled, the groups of conical huts being separated by fences of matting into several quarters. Here we encamped on the north side, near a fine tamarind tree, where millet was grown to a great extent. The south and west sides were surrounded by an extensive swamp or swampy watercourse fed by the komádugu, and, with its dense forest, affording to the inhabitants a safe retreat in case of an attack from their enemies. All the towns of the Bedde are situated in similar positions; and hence the precarious allegiance of the people (who indulge in rapacious habits) to the ruler of Bórnu. The inhabitants of Géshiya, indeed, have very thievish propensities; and as we had neglected to fire a few shots in the evening, a couple of daring men succeeded, during the night, in carrying away the woollen blanket in which my companion the Méjebrí merchant 'Alí el A'geren was sleeping at the side of his horse. Although he was a man of hardihood and experience, he was dragged or carried along to a considerable distance, until he was forced to let go his blanket; and, threatening him with their spear in case he should cry out, they managed this affair so cleverly and with such dispatch, that they were off in the dark before we were up to pursue them. It was a pity that these daring rascals escaped with their spoil; but in order to prevent any further depredations of this kind, we fired several shots, and, with a large accordion, upon which I played the rest of the night, I frightened the people to such a degree, that they thought every moment we were about to ransack the town.

Leaving the boundaries of modern Bornu, Barth made for Zinder, then 'the capital of the westernmost province of the Bornu empire'. He reached this 'gate of Sudan' on Christmas Day, 1852 — 'an important station for me, as I had here to wait for new supplies, without which I could scarcely hope to penetrate any great distance westward'. In the New Year he received 1000 dollars in specie, 'packed very cleverly in two boxes of sugar so that scarcely anybody became aware that I had received money'. On January 30 he departed from Zinder 'in the best spirits, having at length succeeded, during my prolonged stay there, in getting rid of the disease in my feet which had annoyed me ever since my return from Baghírmi to Kúkawa.' Regretfully having to avoid historic Daura because of its knavish governor, whose predatoriness was more to be feared than the attacks of his own robber bands, Barth took the Gazawa route to Katsina and Kano.

## KATSINA AGAIN

*February* 3. I then rode to Sadíku, the son of the famous Mállem 'Omáro, or Ghomáro, who had been eight years governor of Kátsena, after the death of his father, till having excited the fear or wrath of his liege lord, in consequence of calumnies representing him as endeavouring to make himself independent, he was deposed by 'Alíyu the second successor of Bello, and obliged to seek safety among the enemies of his nation. Sadíku was a stately person, of tall figure, a serious expression of countenance, and a high, powerful chest, such as I have rarely seen in Negroland, and still less among the tribe of the Fúlbe. However, he is not a pure Púllo, being the offspring of a Bórnu female slave. He had something melancholy about him; and this was very natural, as he could not well be sincerely beloved by those among whom he was obliged to live, and in whose company he carried on a relentless war against his kinsmen. Sadíku's house, which was in the utmost decay, was a convincing proof, either that he was in reality miserably off, or that he felt obliged to pretend poverty and misery. He understood Arabic tolerably well, although he only spoke very little. He expressed much regret on hearing of the death of Mr. Overweg, whom he had known during his residence in Marádi; but having heard how strictly Europeans adhere to their promise, he expressed his astonishment that he had never received an Arabic New Testament, which Mr. Overweg had promised him. But I was glad to be able to inform him that it was not the fault of my late lamented companion, who, I knew, had forwarded a copy to him, by way of Zínder, immediately after his arrival in Kúkawa. Fortunately I had a copy or two of the New Testament with me, and therefore made him very happy by adding this book to the other little presents which I gave him. When I left the company of this man, I was obliged to take a drink of fúra with Serkí-n-turáwa — however, not as a proof of sincere hospitality, but as a means of begging some further things from me; and I was glad at length to get rid of this troublesome young fellow.

*February* 4. It was with a peculiar feeling that I pitched my tent a few hundred yards from the gate (kófa-n-samrí) of this town, by the governor of which I had been so greatly annoyed on my first entering this country.

I staid outside the town until the following morning, while my quarters in the town were preparing. There was an animated intercourse along my place of encampment, between the old capital and the new place Wagóje, which the governor had founded two years before; and I received the compliments of several active Fúlbe, whose expressive countenances bore suffi- cient evidence of the fact that their habits were not yet spoiled by the influence of the softer manners of the subjected tribe, although such an amalgamation has already begun to take place in many parts of Háusa.

The house which was assigned to me inside the town was spacious, but rather old, and so full of ants that I was obliged to take the greatest care to protect not only my luggage, but my person from these voracious insects. They not only destroyed everything that was suspended on pegs from the walls, but while sitting one day for an hour or so on a clay bank in my room I found, when I got up, a large hole in my tobe, — these clever and industrious miners having made their way through the clay walls to the spot where I was sitting, successfully constructed their covered walks, and voraciously attacked my shirt, all in an hour's time.

My present to the governor consisted of a very fine blue bernús, a kaftan of fine red cloth, a small pocket pistol, two muslin turbans, a red cap, two loaves of sugar, and some smaller articles. The eccentric man received me with undisguised pleasure as an old acquaintance; but being aware that I had a tolerable supply of handsome articles with me, he wanted to induce me to sell to him all the fine things I possessed: but I cut the matter short by telling him, once for all, that I was not a merchant, and did not engage in any commerce. On the whole, he was well pleased with his presents; but he wanted me to give him another small pistol, and, in the course of my stay here, I was obliged to comply with his request. He had a cover made for the pair, and used to carry them constantly about his person, frightening everybody by firing off the caps into their faces.

It was, no doubt, a very favourable circumstance for me that the ghaladíma of Sókoto was at this time staying here; for under the protection of the unscrupulous governor of Kátsena, I should scarcely have reached the residence of the emír el Múmenín in safety. The ghaladíma, who was the inspector of Kátsena as well as of Zánfara, had collected the tribute of both provinces, and was soon to start, with his treasure and the articles he had purchased there, on his home journey, so that there did not seem to be time enough for sending some of my people to Kanó to make there the necessary purchases; but circumstances, which I shall soon mention, delayed us so much that there would have been ample opportunity for doing so, and thus saving a considerable sum of money. The ghaladíma was a simple straightforward man, not very intelligent, certainly, nor generous, but good-natured and sociable. Born of a female slave, he had very little about him of the general characteristics of the Fúlbe, being tall and broad-shouldered, with a large head, broad features and tolerably dark complexion.

I made some considerable purchases in this place, amounting altogether to 1,308,000 shells, employing the greatest part of my cash in providing myself with the cotton and silk manufactures of Kanó and Núpe, in order to pave my way, by means of these favourite articles, through the countries on the middle course of the Niger, where nothing is esteemed more highly than these native manufactures. But, as I afterwards found out, I sustained a considerable loss in buying the Núpe tobes here, at least 20 per cent. dearer than I should have been able to do in Gando; but this I could not possibly know beforehand, nor was it my previous intention to make any stay in that place, where large parcels of these articles are never brought into the market. I also added to my store a few more articles of Arab manufacture, there having arrived, on the 5th of March, a very numerous caravan of Ghádamsi and other people from the north, with not less than from 400 to 500 camels, but without bringing me even a single line, either from my friends in Europe or even from those in Africa. Having likewise arranged with 'Alí el A'geren the Méjebrí who had accompanied me from Kúkawa, buying from him what little merchandise he had, and taking him into my service for nine dollars a month, I prepared everything for my journey; and I was extremely anxious to be gone, as the rainy season was fast approaching. On the 26th of February evident signs were observed of the approach of the wet season, — the whole southern quarter of the heavens being thickly overcast with clouds, while the air also was extremely damp, just as after a shower. Mounting on horseback, in order to observe better these forerunners of the 'dámana', I clearly distinguished that it was raining in the direction of Záriya and Núpe; and even in our immediate neighbourhood a few drops fell. In the course of the evening the freshness and coolness of the air was most delicious, just as is the case after a fall of rain; and summer lightning was flashing through the southern sky.

The ghaladíma also was very anxious to be gone; but the army of the Góberáwa being ready to start on an expedition, on a grand scale, against the territory of the Fúlbe, we could not leave the place before we knew exactly what direction the hostile army would take. They having at length set out on their foray, on the 7th of March, we began to watch their movements very anxiously, each of these two powers, — the independent pagans as well as the conquering Fúlbe, — having in their pay numbers of spies in the towns of their enemies. Only two days before the Góberáwa left their home, they killed Bú-Bakr the chief spy whom 'Alíyu, the sultan of Sókoto, entertained in their town.

In the company of the ghaladíma there was a younger brother of his, of the name of Al-háttu, who had lost the better portion of the character of a free man by a mixture of slave-blood, and behaved, at times, like the most intolerable beggar; but he proved of great service to me in my endeavour to become acquainted with all the characteristic features of the country and its inhabitants.

Besides this man, my principal acquaintance during my stay in Kátsena this time was a Tawáti of the name of 'Abd e' Rahmán, a very amiable and social man, and, as a fáki, possessing a certain degree of learning. He had been a great friend of the sultan Bello, and expatiated with the greatest enthusiasm on the qualities and achievements of this distinguished ruler of Negroland. He also gave me the first hints of some of the most important subjects relating to the geography and history of Western Negroland, and called my attention particularly to a man whom he represented as the most learned of the present generation of the inhabitants of Sókoto, and from whom, he assured me, I should not fail to obtain what information I wanted. This man was 'Abd el Káder dan Taffa (meaning, the son of Mústapha), on whose stores of knowledge I drew largely. My intercourse with 'Abd e' Rahmán was occasionally interrupted by an amicable tilt at our respective creeds. On one occasion, when my learned friend was endeavouring to convince me of the propriety of polygamy, he adduced as an illustration, that in matters of the table we did not confine ourselves to a single dish, but took a little fowl, a little fish, and a little roast beef; and how absurd, he argued, was it, to restrict ourselves, in the intercourse with the other sex, to only one wife. It was during my second stay in Kátsena that I collected most of the information which I have communicated on a former occasion with regard to the history of Háusa.

Besides this kind of occupation, my dealings with the governor, and an occasional ride which I took through and outside the town, I had a great deal to do in order to satisfy the claims of the inhabitants upon my very small stock of medicinal knowledge.

Living in Kátsena is not so cheap as in most other places of

Negroland — at least we thought so at the time, but we afterwards found Sókoto, and many places between that and
Timbúktu, much dearer; but the character of dearth in
Kátsena is increased by the scarcity of shells in the market,
which form the standard currency, and, especially after I had
circulated a couple of hundred dollars, I was often obliged to
change a dollar for 2300 shells instead of 2500.

## DEPARTURE FROM KATSINA

*March* 21. The whole town was in motion when we left; for the
governor himself was to accompany us for some days' journey,
as the whole country was exposed to the most imminent danger,
and further on he was to send a numerous escort along with us.
It was a fine morning, and, though the rainy season had not
yet set in in this province, many of the trees were clad already
in a new dress, as if in anticipation of the fertilizing power of
the more favoured season.

The first day we made only a short march of about three
miles, to a village called Kabakáwa, where the ghaladíma had
taken up his quarters. I had scarcely dismounted, under a tree
at the side of the village, when my protector called upon me,
and in a very friendly manner invited me, urgently, to take up
my quarters inside the village, stating that the neighbourhood
was not quite safe, as the Góberáwa had carried away three
women from this very village the preceding day. I, however,
preferred my tent and the open air, and felt very little inclination to confide my valuable property, on which depended
entirely the success of my enterprise, to the frail huts, which
are apt to catch fire at any moment; for while I could not
combat against nature, I had confidence enough in my arms,
and in my watchfulness, not to be afraid of thieves and robbers.

In the afternoon the ghaladíma came out of the hamlet, and
took his seat under a neighbouring tree, when I returned his
visit of the morning, and endeavoured to open with him and
his companions a free and unrestrained intercourse; for I was
only too happy to get out of the hands of the lawless governor

of Kátsena, who, I felt convinced, would not have been deterred by any scruples from possessing himself of my riches: indeed he had gone so far as to tell me that, if I possessed anything of value, such as pistols handsomely mounted, I should give them to him rather than to the sultan of Sókoto, for that he himself was the emír el Múmenín; nay, he even told me that his liege lord was alarmed at the sight of a pistol.

*March* 22. In order to avoid the enemy, we were obliged, instead of following a westerly direction, to keep at first directly southward. The country through which our road lay was very beautiful. The dorówa, which, the preceding day, had formed the principal ornament of the landscape, in the first part of this day's march gave place entirely to other trees, such as the tall rími or bentang tree, the kúka or monkey-bread tree, and the deléb palm or gigiña (*Borassus flabelliformis*?); but beyond the village of Dóka, the dorówa, which is the principal tree of the provinces of Kátsena and Záriya, again came prominently forward, while the kadéña also, or butter tree, and the alléluba, afforded a greater variety to the vegetation. The alléluba (which, on my second stay at Kanó, I saw in full blossom) bears a small fruit, which the natives eat, but which I never tried myself. Even the dúm palm, with its fan-shaped yellow-coloured foliage, gave occasionally greater relief to the fresher vegetation around. The country was populous and well cultivated; and extensive tobacco-grounds and large fields of yams or gwáza were seen, — both objects being almost a new sight to me; for tobacco, which I had been so much surprised to see cultivated to such an extent in the country of the pagan Músgu, is scarcely grown at all in Bórnu, with the exception of Zínder, and I had first observed it largely cultivated near the town of Kátsena, while yams, as I have already had repeatedly occasion to mention, are not raised at all in Central Negroland. Numerous herds of cattle were seen dotting the landscape, and contributed largely to the interest of the scenery. But the district of Máje especially, which we traversed after a march of about seven miles, impressed me with the highest opinion of the fertility and beauty of this country.

## CHAPTER 9

# SOKOTO (1853)

## THE ZAMFARA REGION

*March* 26. We here separated from most of our companions, —
the governor of Kátsena, as well as the people from Kanó and
Záriya, who were carrying tribute to the sultan of Sókoto,
remaining behind, and only an escort or 'rékkia' of fifty horsemen continuing in our company. The hostile army of the
Góberáwa being in this neighbourhood, the danger of the road
further on was very considerable; and the Kanáwa and Zozáwa
or Zegézegé, of whom the latter carried 2,000,000 shells, 500
tobes, and 30 horses, as tribute, were too much afraid of their
property to accompany us. There had also arrived a troop of
about 100 fatáki with asses laden entirely with the famous
dodówa cakes; but they also remained behind.
*March* 28. Zýrmi is an important town even at present, but,
being under the dominion of the Fúlbe, is only capable of
preserving its existence by a constant struggle with Góber and
Marádi. However, the governor of this town is not now master
of the whole of Zánfara, as he was in the time of Captain
Clapperton, who visited it on his journey to Sókoto, the Fúlbe,
or Féllani, having found it more conducive to their policy to
place each governor of a walled town in this province, under
the direct allegiance of Sókoto, in order to prevent the loss of
the whole country by the rebellion of a single man. Some ninety
or one hundred years ago, before the destruction of the capital,
this province was almost the most flourishing country of
Negroland; but it is at present divided into a number of petty
states, each of which follows a different policy; hence it is

difficult to know which towns are still dependent upon the dominion of Sókoto, and which adhere to their enemies the Góberáwa.

When we again reached the direct road, the neighbourhood of our friends was distinctly indicated by a very strong and not quite aromatic smell, which proceeded from the luggage of those of the caravan of native traders (or fatáki) who had attached themselves to our troop in Zékka, leaving their more cautious brethren behind. The merchandize of these small traders consisted, for the most part, of those vegetable cakes, called dodówa which constitute an important article of trade, as the dorówa or *Parkia*, from the fruit of which those cakes are made, thrives in great abundance in the province of Zegzeg, while it is comparatively rare in the provinces of Kébbi and Góber. Three thousand of these cakes constitute an ass-load, and each of them in general is sold in Sókoto for five kurdí, having been bought on the spot for one urí; so that the profit, being not less than 500 per cent., makes this commerce attractive for poor people, notwithstanding the dangerous state to which this road is at present reduced. The return freight which these petty merchants bring back from Sókoto, generally consists of the salt of Fógha.

*March* 29. From hence, along a path filled with market people, we reached the walled town of Badaráwa, which, like most of the towns of Zánfara, is surrounded on all sides with a dense border of timber, affording to the archers, who form the strength of the natives, great advantage in a defence, and making any attack, in the present condition of the strategetical art in this country, very difficult. In the midst of this dense body of trees there was a very considerable market, attended by nearly 10,000 people, and well supplied with cotton, which seemed to be the staple commodity, while Indian millet (sorghum) also was in abundance. A great number of cattle were slaughtered in the market, and the meat retailed in small quantities. There was also a good supply of fresh butter (which is rarely seen in Negroland), formed in large lumps, cleanly prepared, and swimming in water; they were sold for 500 kurdí each.

Neither was there any scarcity of onions, a vegetable which is extensively cultivated in the province of Zánfara, the smaller ones being sold for one urí, the larger ones for two kurdí each. These onions are mostly cultivated round a large tebki, about half a mile to the west of the town, which even at the present season was still of considerable size. Instead of entering the narrow streets of the town, I pitched my tent in the open fields, at a considerable distance from the wall; for I was the more in want of fresh air, as I was suffering greatly from headache. The consequence was that I could not even indulge in the simple luxuries of the market, but had recourse to my common medicine of tamarind water.

While endeavouring to recruit myself by rest and simple diet, I received a visit from an intelligent and well-behaved young fáki, Mállem Dádi, who belonged to the suite of the ghaladíma, and whose company was always agreeable to me. He informed me that the Zánfaráwa and the Góberáwa had regarded each other with violent hatred from ancient times, — Babári, the founder of Kaláwa, or Alkaláwa, the former capital of Góber, having based the strength and well-being of his own country on the destruction of the old capital of Zánfara, ninety-seven years previously. Hence the people of Zánfara embarked heart and soul in the religious and political rising of the sheikh 'Othmán against his liege lord the ruler of Góber. I learned also that the same amount of tribute, which I have before mentioned as carried on this occasion by the messengers of Záriya to the emír el Múmenín, was paid almost every second month, while from Kátsena it was very difficult to obtain a regular tribute, the governor of that town generally not paying more than 400,000 kurdí and forty articles, such as bernúses, kaftans, etc., annually. It was only an exceptional case, arising from the exertions of the ghaladíma as I was told, that he had sent, this year, 800,000 shells, besides a horse of Tárki breed, of the nominal value of 700,000 kurdí.

*March* 30. I observed the first rúdu, a sort of light hut consisting of nothing but a thatched roof raised upon four poles from eight to ten feet in height, and affording a safe retreat to the inhabitants, during their night's rest, against the swarms of mosquitoes which infest the whole region along the swampy creeks of the Niger, the people entering these elevated bed-rooms from below, and shutting the entrance behind them.

Thus we reached, a little past noon, the town Sansánne 'Aísa, which was originally a mere fortified encampment or 'sansánne'. But its advanced and in some respects isolated position, as an outlying post against the Góberáwa and Mariyadáwa, rendered it essential that it should be strong enough by its own resources to offer a long resistance; and it has in consequence become a walled town of considerable importance, so that travellers generally take this roundabout way, with a strong northerly deviation. Here also the wall is surrounded with a dense forest, affording a sort of natural fortification.

When I had made myself comfortable, I received a visit from the ghaladíma of the town; he brought me the compliments of the governor, who was a man of rather noble birth, being nobody else but 'Alí Káramí, the eldest son and presumed successor of 'Alíyu the emír el Múmenín. He bears the pompous title of serkí-n-Góber, 'lord of Góber', although almost the whole of that country is in the hands of the enemy. Having taken his leave, the messenger soon returned accompanied by Alháttu, the younger brother of the ghaladíma of Sókoto, who was anxious to show his importance, bringing me a fat sheep as a present, which I acknowledged by the gift of a fine heláli bernús, besides a red cap and turban; and the governor expressed his satisfaction at my present by sending me also corn for my horses, and a half a dozen fowls. In the evening we had a short but violent tornado, which usually indicates the approach of the rainy season; but no rain fell, and we passed the night very comfortably in our open encampment, without any accident.

## THE FOREST OF GUNDUMI

*March* 31. We had a very difficult day's march before us, — the passage of the wilderness of Gúndumi, — which can only be traversed by a forced march, and which, even upon a man of

Captain Clapperton's energies, had left the impression of the most wearisome journey he had ever performed in his life.

The beginning of our march, after we had watered our animals and filled our water-skins, was rather inauspicious, our companions missing their way and with their bugles calling me and my people, who were pursuing the right track, far to the south, till, after endeavouring in vain to make our way through an impervious thicket, and after a considerable loss of time, anything but agreeable at the beginning of a desperate march of nearly thirty hours, we at length with the assistance of a Púllo shepherd regained the right track. We then pursued our march, travelling without any halt the whole day and the whole night through the dense forest, leaving the pond called tebki-n-Gúndumi at some distance on our left, and not meeting with any signs of cultivation till a quarter before eleven the next morning, when, wearied in the extreme and scarcely able to keep up, we were met by some horsemen, who had been sent out from the camp at Gáwasú to meet us, provided with water-skins in order to bring up the stragglers who had lagged behind from fatigue and thirst. And there were many who needed their assistance — one woman had even succumbed to exhaustion in the course of the night; for such a forced march is the more fatiguing and exhausting as the dangers from a lurking enemy make the greatest possible silence and quiet indispensable, instead of the spirits being kept up with cheerful songs as is usually the case. But having once reached the cultivated grounds, after a march of two miles and a half more we arrived at the first gáwasú trees which surround the village which is named after them, 'Gáwasú'. In the fields or 'kárkará' adjoin-this village, 'Alíyu the emír el Múmenín had taken up his camping-ground, and was preparing himself for setting out upon an expedition against the Góber people.

# AUDIENCE WITH THE SULTAN OF SOKOTO

*March* 31. It was well that we had arrived, having been incessantly marching for the last twenty-six hours, without taking into account the first part of the journey from the town to the pond, for I had never seen my horse in such a state of total exhaustion, while my people also fell down immediately they arrived. As for myself, kept up by the excitement of my situation, I did not feel much fatigued, but, on the contrary, felt strong enough to search without delay through the whole of my luggage, in order to select the choicest presents for the great prince of Sókoto, who was to set out the following morning, and upon whose reception depended a good deal of the success of my undertaking. The afternoon wore on without my being called into the presence of the sultan, and I scarcely expected that I should see him that day; but suddenly, after the evening prayer, Alháttu made his appearance with some messengers of the chief, not in order to hasten my present, but first to give me a proof of their own hospitality, and bringing me a very respectable present consisting of an ox, four fat sheep, and two large straw sacks or tákrufa containing about four hundred pounds weight of rice, with an intimation, at the same time, that 'Alíyu wished to see me, but that I was not now to take my present with me. I therefore prepared myself immediately; and on going to the sultan's we passed by the ghaladíma, who had been lodged in a courtyard of the village, and who accompanied us.

We found 'Alíyu in the northern part of the village, sitting under a tree in front of his quarters, on a raised platform of clay. He received me with the utmost kindness and good-humour, shaking hands with me, and begging me to take a seat just in front of him. Having paid my compliments to him on behalf of the Queen of England, I told him that it had been my intention to have paid him a visit two years previously, but that the losses which we had met with in the first part of our journey had prevented me from carrying out my design. I had scarcely finished my speech, when he himself assured me that at the right time he had received the letter which I had addressed to him through the sultan of A'gades (informing him of the reason why we could not then go directly to pay him our compliments), and that from that moment up to the present time he had followed our proceedings, and especially my own, with the greatest interest, having even heard at the time a report of my journey to A′damáwa.

I then informed him that in coming to pay him my compliments I had principally two objects in view, one of which was that he might give me a letter of franchise guaranteeing to all British merchants entire security for themselves and their property in visiting his dominions for trading purposes; and the second, that he might allow me to proceed to Timbúktu, and facilitate my journey to that place (which was greatly obstructed at the present moment by the rebellion of the province of Kebbi) by his own paramount authority. Without reserve he acceded to both requests in the most cheerful and assuring manner, saying that it would be his greatest pleasure to assist me in my enterprise to the utmost of his power, as it had only humane objects in view, and could not but tend to draw nations together that were widely separated from each other. At the same time he expressed, in a very feeling way, his regret with regard to 'Abd Allah (Capt. Clapperton), whose name I had incidentally mentioned, intimating that the then state of war, or 'gába,' between Bello and the sheikh el Kánemí, the ruler of Bórnu, had disturbed their amicable relations with that eminent officer, whom in such a conjuncture they had not felt justified in allowing to proceed on his errand to their enemy. In order to give him an example how, in the case of foreign visitors or messengers, such circumstances ought not to be taken into account, I took this opportunity to show him that the ruler of Bórnu, although in open hostility with the most powerful of his ('Alíyu's) governors, nevertheless had allowed me, at the present conjuncture, to proceed on my journey to them without the slightest obstacle. He then concluded our conversation by observing that it had been his express wish to see me the very day of my arrival, in order to assure me that I was heartily welcome, and to set my mind at rest as to the fate of Clapperton, which he was well aware could not fail to inspire Europeans with some diffidence in the proceedings of the rulers of Sókoto.

With a mind greatly relieved I returned to my tent from

this audience. The dusk of the evening, darkened by thick thunder-clouds, with the thunder rolling uninterruptedly, and lighted up only by the numerous fires which were burning round about in the fields where the troops had encamped under the trees, gave to the place a peculiar and solemn interest, making me fully aware of the momentous nature of my situation. The thunder continued rolling all night long, plainly announcing the approach of the rainy season, though there was no rain at the time. Meanwhile I was pondering over the present which I was to give to this mighty potentate, who had treated me with so much kindness and regard on the first interview, and on whose friendship and protection depended, in a great measure, the result of my proceedings; and thinking that what I had selected might not prove sufficient to answer fully his expectation, in the morning, when I arose, I still added a few things more, so that my present consisted of the following articles: a pair of pistols, richly ornamented with silver, in velvet holsters; a rich bernús (Arab cloak with hood) of red satin, lined with yellow satin; a bernús of yellow cloth; a bernús of brown cloth; a white heláli bernús of the finest quality; a red cloth kaftan embroidered with gold; a pair of red cloth trowsers; a Stambúli carpet; three loaves of sugar; three turbans and a red cap; two pairs of razors; half a dozen large looking-glasses, cloves and benzoin.

Having tied up these presents in five smart handkerchiefs and taking another bernús of red cloth with me for the ghaladíma, I proceeded first to the latter, who received his present with acknowledgements, and surveyed those destined for his master with extreme delight and satisfaction. We then went together to 'Alíyu, and found him in a room built of reeds, sitting on a divan made of the light wood of the tukkurúwa, and it was then for the first time that I obtained a distinct view of this chief, for on my interview the preceding night it had been so dark that I was not enabled to distinguish his features accurately. I found him a stout middle-sized man, with a round fat face, exhibiting evidently rather the features of his mother, a Háusa slave, than those of his father Mohammed Bello a free and

noble Púllo, but full of cheerfulness and good humour. His
dress also was extremely simple, and at the same time likewise
bore evidence of the pure Púllo character having been aban-
doned; for while it consisted of scarcely anything else but a tobe
of grayish colour, his face was uncovered, while his father Bello,
even in his private dwelling, at least before a stranger, never
failed to cover his mouth.

He received me this time with the same remarkable kindness
which he had exhibited the preceding evening, and repeated
his full consent to both my requests, which I then stated more
explicitly, requesting at the same time that a letter of franchise
might be written at once, before his setting out on his expedition.
This he agreed to, but he positively refused to allow me to
proceed on my journey before his return from the expedition,
which he said would not be long; and, acquainted as I was
with the etiquette of these African courts, I could scarcely
expect anything else from the beginning. He then surveyed the
presents, and expressed his satisfaction repeatedly; but when
he beheld the pistols, which I had purposely kept till the last,
he gave vent to his feelings in the most undisguised manner,
and pressing my hands repeatedly, he said 'nagóde, nagóde,
barka, 'Abd el Kerím, barka' — 'I thank you, God bless
you, 'Abd el Kerím, God bless you.' He had evidently
never seen before anything like these richly-mounted pistols,
which had been selected in Tripoli by the connoisseur eyes of
Mr. Warrington, and surveyed the present on all sides. It was
to these very pistols that I was in a great measure indebted for
the friendly disposition of that prince, while the unscrupulous
governor of Kátsena, who had heard some report about them,
advised me by all means to sell them to himself, as his liege
lord would not only not value them at all, but would even be
afraid of them.

Soon after I had returned to my tent, the ghaladíma arrived,
bringing me from his master 100,000 kurdí, to defray the expenses
of my household during his absence; and I had afterwards the
more reason to feel grateful for this kind attention, although the
sum did not exceed forty Spanish dollars, as I became aware,

during my stay in Wurno, how difficult it would have been for me to have changed my dollars into kurdí.

*April* 3. The sultan was kind enough, before he left in the afternoon, to send me word that I might come and take leave of him; and I wished him, with all my heart success in his expedition, as the success of my own undertaking, namely, my journey towards the west, depended upon his vanquishing his enemies. Giving vent to his approval of my wishes by repeating that important and highly significant word, not more peculiar to the Christian than to the Mohammedan creed, 'Amín, amín', he took leave of me in order to start on his expedition, accompanied only by a small detachment of cavalry, most of the troops having already gone on in advance. I had also forwarded a present to Hámmedu, the son of 'Atíku, an elder brother and predecessor of Bello; but he sent it back to me, begging me to keep it until after his return from the expedition. The ghaladíma also, who was to accompany the sultan, called before his departure, in order that I might wind round his head, a turban of gaudy colours, such as I then possessed, as an omen of success.

## HISTORY OF THE FULANI OF SOKOTO

There is no doubt that, if any African tribe deserves the full attention of the learned European, it is that of the Fúlbe (*sing.* Púllo), or Fúla, as they are called by the Mandingoes; Féllani (*sing.* Baféllanchi), by the Háusa people; Felláta, by the Kanúri; and Fullán, by the Arabs. In their appearance, their history, and the peculiar character of their language, they present numerous anomalies to the inhabitants of the adjacent countries. No doubt they are the most intelligent of all the African tribes, although in bodily development they cannot be said to exhibit the most perfect specimens, and probably are surpassed in this respect by the Jolof. But it is their superior intelligence which gives their chief expression to the Fúlbe, and prevents their features from presenting that regularity which we find in other tribes, while the spare diet of a large portion of that tribe does not impart to their limbs all the development of which they are capable, most of them being distinguished by the smallness of their limbs and the slender growth of their bodies. But as to their outward appearance, which presents various contrasts in complexion as well as in bodily development, we must first take into account that the Fúlbe, as a conquering tribe, sweeping over a wide expanse of provinces, have absorbed and incorporated with themselves different and quite distinct national elements, which have given to their community a rather varying and undecided character.

Moreover, besides such tribes as have been entirely absorbed, and whose origin has even been referred to the supposed ancestors of the whole nation, there are others which, although their pedigree is not brought into so close a connexion with that of the Fúlbe, nevertheless are so intermingled with them, that they have quite forgotten their native idiom, and might be confounded with the former by any traveller who is not distinctly aware of the fact.

On the other hand, foremost among those tribes who have been entirely absorbed by the community of the Fúlbe are the Toróde or Torunkáwa, who, although they are considered as the most noble portion of the population in most of the kingdoms founded by the Fúlbe, yet evidently owe their origin to a mixture of the Jolof element with the ruling tribe, and in such a manner that, in point of numbers, the former enjoyed full superiority in the amalgamation; but it is quite evident that, even if we do not take into account the Toróde, the Jolof have entered into the formation of the remarkable tribe of the Fúlbe or Fúla, in a very strong proportion, although the languages of these two tribes at present are so distinct, especially as far as regards grammatical structure; and it is highly interesting that A'hmed Bábá (who, by occasional hints, allows us to form a much better idea of the progress of that tribe, in its spreading over tracts so immense, than we were able to obtain before we became acquainted with his history of Súdán) intimates distinctly that he regards the Jolof as belonging to the great stock of the Fullán or Fúlbe, although at the present time the terms 'Jolof' and 'Púllo' seem to be used in opposition, the one meaning a person of black, the other an individual of red complexion.

It is this element of the Toróde in particular which causes such a great variety in the type of the Fúlbe community, the Toróde being in general of tall stature and strong frame, large features, and of very black complexion, while the other sections of that tribe are always distinguished by a tinge of red or copper colour.

A new epoch for this wide-spread tribe did not open till the beginning of this century, when, in the year 1802, Báwa the ruler of Góber summoned to his presence the sheikh 'Othmán, together with the other chiefs of the tribe, and severely reprimanded them on account of the pretensions which they were beginning to put forward. It was then that 'Othmán, who, being settled in the village Dághel, performed the office of imám to his countrymen, and had begun to give them a new religious impulse, which raised them above their petty interests, filled with indignation at the manner in which he, the great Moslim, was treated by those pagans, was roused to the attempt of making himself and his tribe independent of the will of the native ruler of the country, and having assembled his countrymen, who now conferred upon him the dignity and authority of a sheikh, raised the standard of revolt; but his proceedings, at least as far as regarded Góber and the capital Alkaláwa, were far from proving successful at the beginning, he being vanquished in almost every encounter: but the fanatical zeal of his followers, whom he continually inspired with fresh energy by his religious songs, was so great that gradually he overcame all these obstacles, and at length succeeded in laying the foundation of a vast empire, being greatly assisted in his career by his brother 'Abd Alláhi, who, although his senior, had been the first to pay him homage, and by his son Mohammed Bello. He took up his residence first at Gando, where he was besieged for a long time, and afterwards at Sifáwa, till, as described by Captain Clapperton in the excellent and concise account of this struggle which he has given in the report of his second journey, Othmán ended his life in a sort of fanatical ecstasy or madness.

He was followed by Mohammed Bello, who endeavoured to introduce more order into the empire thus consolidated, and who, on the whole, must rank high among the African princes, being distinguished not less by his great love of learning and science than by his warlike spirit, although his military achievements were far from being always successful. But he has had the misfortune, after enjoying a great name in Europe, for a short time, for the kind and generous spirit in which he received Captain Clapperton on his first journey, to incur the severest condemnation on account of the manner in which he treated that same enterprising traveller on his second journey. No doubt he was a distinguished ruler; but he must not be judged according to European ideas. He had to struggle hard, not less against the native tribes anxious to assert their independence, than against his great rival Mohammed el Kánemí the king of Bórnu, who, just at the time of Clapperton's second stay, pressed him very closely, and having successfully overrun the eastern provinces of the Fulfúlde or Felláta empire, threatened Kanó. Hence this political position, together with the instigations of the Arabs, who feared for their commerce with Negroland if the road from the south should be opened, will account in some measure for his treatment of the English traveller, who perhaps urged his going to the sheikh of Bórnu with too much energy. However, there is no doubt that Bello's successor and brother, 'Atíku, who ruled from the year 1832 till 1837, would have weakened the interest of the European public in the example which Bello gave of an energetic and generous ruler in those distant and out-of-the-way regions, if his career had become known to them; for he seems to have fully belied the expectation, of 'a mean prince', which he raised when still living in his retirement, as a jealous king's brother, without power and influence. But his reign was too short for consolidating sufficiently the loosely-connected empire, although, as long as he lived, full security is said to have reigned. The spirit of independence broke out more strongly under his successor 'Alíyu, a son of Bello by a female slave, who, save a well-meaning and cheerful disposition, does not appear to have inherited many of the noble qualities of his father, and least of all his warlike spirit; and hence the lamentable condition in which I found this extensive kingdom, while there is scarcely any hope that affairs will assume a more consolidated character before another more energetic ruler succeeds to ʿAlíyu. Nevertheless the kingdom or empire, even at the present time, still comprises the same provinces which it did at its most flourishing period, with the exception of Khadéja, the governor of which has made himself independent; but the military strength of these provinces, especially as regards cavalry, as well as the amount of revenue, is greatly impaired, although the latter, collected from all the provinces together, certainly exceeds one hundred millions of shells, or about 10,000 *l.* sterling, besides an equal value in slaves and native cloth, or articles of foreign produce. The whole strength of the empire, if the distracted state of each province allowed its quota to be withdrawn from thence, would certainly still form an imposing force, — viz., the cavalry of the seat of government, together with the subjected parts of Kébbi and Zánfara, about 5000; the cavalry of Kanó, from 5000 to 7000; that of Baúchi, from 1500 to 2000; that of Zégzeg, 3000; Aʼdamáwa, 2000; Kátsena and Mésaw, each about 1000; Katágum, 1200; Marmar and Shéra, each 500; Bobéru, 600; Dáura, 400; Kazáure, about 200. But we have seen to what a state Zánfara is at present reduced, while the curious manner in which Kébbi is portioned out between the rulers of Sókoto and Gando cannot fail to cause a great deal of jealousy and controversy between the two courts, at the very centre of power; and as for Aʼdamáwa, there are still so many hostile elements in the interior of that half-subdued province, that it is impossible to withdraw from thence a particle of its home force; nay, even the province of Kanó is so harassed and distracted by the continual inroads of the governor of Khadéja, that the ruler of that province is scarcely able to send a few hundred horsemen to join the army of his liege lord.

## DESCRIPTION OF WURNO

*April* 4. The principal apartment of this clay hall, supported by two massive columns, with an average temperature of 94°, was

an excellent abode during the hottest part of the day, when it
felt very cool and pleasant; but it was rather oppressive in the
morning and evening, when the air outside was so much cooler.
But in the courtyard there was not the slightest shade, all the
trees in this quarter of the town, as well as the huts consisting
of reed, having been swept away by a great conflagration the
preceding year, a young kórna tree, which had been planted
at a later period, only just beginning to put forth its foliage.
The whole courtyard, also, was in a most filthy state, characteristic of the manners of the natives in their present degraded
moral and political situation. The first thing, therefore, that I
had to do, in order to make myself tolerably comfortable, was
to cleanse out this Augean stable, to build a hut for my servants,
and a shady retreat for myself. I was well aware that the latter,
which it was not easy to make water-tight, would become useless
with the first considerable fall of rain; but I entertained the hope
that, before that time, I should be able to set out on my journey.

It was market-day, there being a market held here every
Monday and Friday, although the great market of Sókoto,
which is much more important, even in the present reduced
condition of that place, still serves to supply the wants of the
inhabitants of all the neighbouring towns and villages at large.
Sending, therefore, into the market in order to supply my most
urgent wants, I found that corn, as well as meat, was even
dearer here than in Kátsena, — 100 shells scarcely sufficing for
the daily maintenance of one horse, and 800 shells buying no
more corn than 500 would have done in Kátsena, while an ox
for slaughtering cost 7000 shells, and I bought two milking-
goats, in order to enjoy the luxury of a little milk for my tea, for
2700 shells. The only article which was at all cheap was onions.
The market is held on a natural platform spreading out in
front of the north-western gate, and surrounded and fortified
by a ditch, as, in the present weak state of the Fúlbe, the market
people are liable to be suddenly attacked by the enemy. This
place, as well as the whole of the town, I visited the following
day, in company with my friend Alháttu, who, in acknowledgement of the present I had given him in Gáwasú, and in expecta-

tion of more, took me under his special protection; but in
crossing the town, in a westerly direction from our quarters, I
was surprised at its neglected and dirty appearance, — a small
ravine which intersects the town forming a most disgusting
spectacle, even worse than the most filthy places of any of the
deserted capitals of Italy. Emerging then by the western gate
(the kófa-n-sábuwa), through which leads the road to Sókoto,
and which was just being repaired by the people of the
ghaladíma, in order to make it capable of withstanding the
effects of the rainy season, we turned northwards round the
town. In front of each gate, on the slope of the rocky eminence
on which the town is built, there is a group of wells, each with
a little round clay house, where the proprietor of the well has
his usual residence, levying on each jar of water a small contri-
bution of five shells; but there are also a great number of wells
facing the north-western gate, close to the market.

After the luxuriant vegetation of other parts of Negroland,
I was astonished at the naked appearance of the country around
the capital, only a few kúka or monkey-bread trees being seen;
but the country presented a very different aspect on my return
journey the next year, at the end of the rainy season. Góber is
distinguished for its general dryness, and for this very reason is
esteemed exceedingly well adapted for cattle-breeding. The
frontiers of the three different provinces or territories (viz.
Kebbi, Góber, and A'dar) join in this corner; and this is the
reason that, while Sókoto is regarded as lying within the borders
of the province of Kebbi, Wurno is considered as belonging to
the conquered territory of the province of Góber; while just
beyond the gulbi-n-ríma, in a northerly direction, the province
of A'dar or Tadlar commences.

Meanwhile the town became more and more deserted; and
on the 7th of April, Alháttu and 'Omár, or Ghomáro, the two
brothers of the ghaladíma, with numbers of other people, went
to join the expedition: but these fighting men, with a few
exceptions, care only about their bodily comfort, and for a few
'goríye' or Kóla nuts would be willing to sell the whole of their
military accoutrements. It was a great matter with these

warriors, that, while the old goríye were nearly finished, the new ones, which were just then brought into the market, were sold for the high price of 120 shells each. In scarcely any place of Negroland did I observe so little true military spirit as in Wurno; and almost all the leading men seem to be imbued with the melancholy conviction that their rule in these quarters is drawing to an end.

*April* 8. It was again market-day, and I made sundry purchases, including a small ox, for almsgiving, as I had made it a rule, in every large town where I stayed any considerable time, to distribute alms amongst the poor. I was astonished at the great quantity of cotton which was brought into the market, and

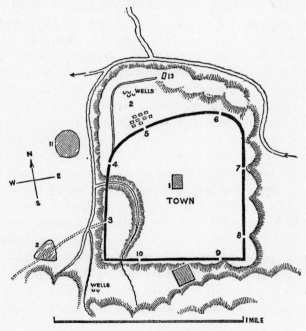

FIG. 6.   The City of Wurno

| | | | |
|---|---|---|---|
| 1. | Residence of Alíyu. | 7. | K. Kúrremi. |
| 2. | Market-place. | 8. | K. Ráha. |
| 3. | Kófa-n-Sábuwa. | 9. | K. Ríma. |
| 4. | K. Serkí-n-A'gades. | 10. | K. Ghaladámchi. |
| 5. | K. Kásuwa. | 11. | Gída-n-Serkí-n-A'gades. |
| 6. | K. Máleki. | 12. | Suburb. |

which showed what these fine vales are capable of producing, if the inhabitants, instead of being plunged in apathy and exposed to the daily incursions of a relentless enemy, were protected by a strong government.

But the whole condition of the country, to the west as well as to the east, was most deplorable; and three native merchants, of the Zoromáwa or Zoghorán, when speaking about my projected journey towards the Niger, and beyond that river westward, told me in the most positive manner, 'bábo haña', 'there is no road'; that is to say, 'the country is closed to you, and you cannot proceed in that direction'. And taking into consideration the low ebb of courage and enterprise among the natives — the weakness and unwarlike spirit of 'Alíyu — the complete nullity of Khalílu — the vigour of the young and warlike Mádemé the rebel chief of Kebbi, who, starting from his residence Argúngo, distant only a couple of hours' march from that of Khalílu, was carrying the flame of destruction in every direction — the revolted province of Zabérma, with an equally young and energetic ruler, Dáúd the son of Hammam Jýmma — the province of Déndina in open revolt and cutting off all access to the river,— all these circumstances rendered the prospect of my accomplishing this journey very doubtful. Moreover, besides the weakness of the two rulers of the Fúlbe dominions, there is evidently a feeling of jealousy between the courts of Sókoto and Gando; and here we find the spectacle of two weak powers weakening each other still more, instead of uniting most cordially in an energetic opposition against the common foe. For instance, the young chief of Kebbi, who at present caused them so much trouble, had been previously a prisoner in Wurno; but when Khalílu wanted to take his life, 'Alíyu procured his liberty, and gave him a splendid charger to boot.

## ENTRY INTO SOKOTO

*April* 20. Ascending then the slope of the eminence on which the town is built, and which rises to about one hundred feet, and leaving a spacious 'máriná' or dyeing-place on the slope of the hill on our left, we entered the walls of Sókoto by the kófa-n-rími; and although the interior did not at present exhibit that crowded appearance which made such a pleasing impression upon Clapperton, the part nearest the wall being rather thinly inhabited, and the people being evidently reduced to a state of great poverty and misery, it made a cheerful impression on me, on account of the number of dúm palms and kórna trees by which it is adorned.

Orders having been sent beforehand, I was quartered without delay in the house of the ghaladíma — a clay dwelling in tolerable repair, but full of white ants, so that I was glad to find there a 'gadó' or couch of reeds, where I was able to rest myself and put away my small effects, without being continually exposed to the insidious attacks of these voracious insects. Having thus made myself comfortable, my first visit the following morning was to Módibo 'Alí, who had already testified his friendship for me by sending me a fat sheep to Wurno. Differing entirely from the present generation of beggars, whose ignoble habits make a long stay in Wurno or Sókoto intolerable, he is a cheerful old man of noble demeanour, and with pure Fúlbe features, with which his middle height and rather spare growth exactly corresponded. He was simply but neatly dressed in a white shirt and a shawl of the same colour. Módibo 'Alí is the oldest member of the family of the Reformer still alive, being the son of 'Alí an elder brother of 'Othmán the Jehádi, and about seventy-five years of age. He was seated in the antechamber of his house, before the door of which his little herd of milch cows were assembled; and he received me with unaffected kindness. I immediately saluted him as an old friend and acquaintance, and we had a very pleasant and cheerful conversation, after which I delivered to him my present, consisting of a heláli bernús, a piece of white muslin, a high red cap or 'mátri', a small flask of 'óttár' of roses, two razors, a pound of cloves, a loaf of sugar, and a looking-glass; and he was particularly delighted with some of these articles, which, on account of the insecurity of the road at the present time, are imported more rarely even from Kanó. In former times a great many Arabs used to visit this place, partly for purposes of trade, partly in order to obtain a present from the sultan; but the danger of the communication in the present reduced state of the empire is so great that not a single Arab merchant visits the town. This circumstance cannot fail to render the conquering tribe more favourably disposed towards opening an intercourse with the English, or Europeans in general, by way of the Niger. At present almost the whole traffic in foreign merchandise is in the hands of the people of Ghát and A'gades, especially in those of Mohammed Bóro, my friend the fugger of A'gades, who, being a native of A'dar, and having a numerous host of full-grown sons, exercises a great influence upon commercial and even political affairs in these quarters.

Having thus commenced an acquaintance with the most respectable man in the town, I made a longer promenade through its interior, when I found the chief quarter, which had been the residence of Bello, greatly dilapidated, and the royal mansion itself in a state of the utmost decay.

*April* 22. It was the great market-day, which was of some importance to me, as I had to buy a good many things, so that I was obliged to send there a sum of 70,000 shells; but the market did not become well-frequented or well-stocked till between two and three o'clock in the afternoon, when I myself proceeded thither. I had taken a ride in the morning through the south-eastern quarter of the town, proceeding through the kófa-n-'Atíku, thence along the wall, towards the west, and re-entered the town by the kófa-n-'Alí Jédu, where the whole quarter is very desolate, even the wall being in a state of decay, and the fine mosque, built by the gedádo during Clapperton's stay here, fallen entirely to ruins. But, even in the present reduced condition of the place, the market still presented a very interesting sight, the numerous groups of people, buyers as well as sellers, and the animals of various descriptions, being picturesquely scattered over the rocky slope. The market was tolerably well attended, and well supplied, there being about thirty horses, three hundred head of cattle for slaughtering, fifty takérkere, or oxen of burden, and a great quantity of

leather articles (this being the most celebrated branch of manufacture in Sókoto), especially leather bags, cushions, and
similar articles, the leather dressed and prepared here being
very soft and beautiful. There were more than a hundred
bridles for sale, the workmanship of which is very famous
throughout all this part of Negroland; but especially a large
quantity of iron was exposed for sale, the iron of Sókoto being
of excellent quality and much sought for, while that of Kanó is
of bad quality. A good many slaves were exhibited, and fetched
a higher price than might be supposed, — a lad of very indifferent appearance being sold for 33,000 shells; I myself
bought a pony for 30,000. It being just about the period when
the salt-caravan visits these parts, dates also, which usually
form a small addition to the principal merchandise of those
traders of the desert, were to be had; and I filled a leather bag,
for some 2000 shells, in order to give a little more variety to
my food on the long road which lay before me.

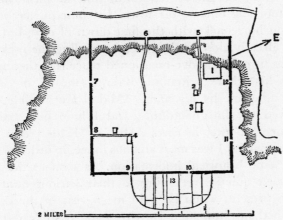

FIG. 7.   The City of Sokoto

1. Market-place.
2. House of Gedádo, at present 'Abdú.
3. House of Bello, now of 'Alíyu, very much in decay.
4. House of 'Atíku, at present Hámedu, and close to it the mosque built by Gedádo, now in ruins.
5. Kófa-n-Koré.
6. Kófa-n-Dúnday.
7. Kófa-n-Kadé.
8. Kófa-n-'Alí Jédu.
9. Kófa-n-'Atíku.
10. Kófa-n-Tarámnia.
11. Kófa-n-Rími.
12. Kófa-n-Marké.
13. Suburb.

## RETURN TO WURNO

*April* 24. Altogether my visit to Sókoto formed a most interesting intermezzo to my involuntary stay in the capital, although it could not fail to give me a further insight into the frail character of the dominion of the Fúlbe over these regions; and during my stay here I certainly had no cause to complain of inhospitable treatment, as my friend Módibo 'Alí sent me, every day, a large basin of furá, the favourite drink of ghussub water, two dishes of hasty pudding, and two bowls of milk. Having given, by this excursion to the former capital, fresh energy to my spirits, I returned to my quarters in Wurnó on the 24th, accomplishing the distance in little more than four hours; and it was time that I returned, for in the evening of that same day the joyful news arrived that the sultan had reached Gándi. However, he did not enter Wurnó till the 23rd,[1] having forwarded a message to me the preceding evening from Yan-serkí, in the territory of Rába, requesting me to meet him the following morning outside the town. In consequence of this I mounted on horseback with the first dawn of day, but found the sultan already close to the gate, descending the rocky path which leads from the above-mentioned place. He then made a halt, with his whole suite, and saluted me in the kindest manner, calling me by my name, 'Abd el Kerím. The sultan was followed by the ghaladíma; and I here first made the acquaintance of the learned 'Abd el Káder dan Taffa (Mustapha), whom I was most anxious to see, in order to obtain from him some historical information. As soon as the people had dispersed quietly, returning to their various quarters, I sent him a present, when he paid me a visit in the evening, and furnished me immediately with some positive data with regard to the history of the dynasty of the Asáki, or A'skia, the rulers of Songhay, which he had perfectly in his head, and which were of the greatest importance in giving me an insight into the historical relation of the western countries of these regions with that of Central Negroland.

[1] Barth is clearly wrong with this date. The German text gives 28 April, evidently the correct one.

In the forenoon I went to 'Alíyu, in order to pay my compliments to him upon his safe return from this expedition, which, although not very glorious, had yet proved not quite unprofitable, he having reduced to subjection the poor little hamlets of the rocky district of Kotórkoshé, the inhabitants of which had previously placed themselves under the protection of the enemy; but even this insignificant victory he had only achieved through the bravery of the horsemen from Kátsena, while his own men had, as usual, exhibited the greatest cowardice. As long as the Fúlbe do not defeat the host of the Góberáwa, who take the field every year and offer them battle, the state of this empire will become daily worse and worse, while at present each of the two parties, the indigenous inhabitants as well as the conquerors, do nothing but accelerate the ruin of the country, without dealing a decided blow.

Although I had made the chief a very respectable present on my first arrival, I thought it well to give greater impulse to his friendly disposition towards me, by adding something also this time, presenting him with a cloth waistcoat and several smaller articles, besides a musical box, with the performance of which he was extremely pleased; but unfortunately, when, anxious to impart his delight to his greatest friend and principal minister, 'Abdú the son of Gedádo, he had called the latter to witness this wonder, the mysterious box, affected by the change of climate and the jolting of the long journey, was silent for a moment, and would not play. I may observe here, that I think it better for travellers not to make such presents as musical boxes, which so easily get out of order. The sultan fully granted my request for a speedy departure, promising also to assist me in my dangerous undertaking with a small 'rékkia' or escort; and it was very essential to me to hasten my proceedings, as the following day brought the first evident proof of the approach of the rainy season.

I was sitting, one day, in the entrance-hall of my house, in the company of some of these sons of the desert, when Góme, the brother of the sultan 'Abd el Káder, from A'gades, who had lately been dethroned in order to make way for a new chief,

A'hmed e' Rufáy, called upon me, and, with a very important and mysterious air, requested me to give him a private audience. After I had dismissed my other visitors, he began by reminding me of the kind manner in which his brother had received me, and finished by urgently begging me to use my influence in order to restore 'Abd el Káder to his former dignity. I had great difficulty in convincing him that I had very little influence with the emír el Múmenín, and that I was afraid my intercession would have little or no effect, although, as well by way of private acknowledgement for the kindness of my host in that place, where I began to acquire more confidence in the success of my proceedings, as from a persuasion of the influence which a great service rendered by me to this man would have upon my future prospects, I should have desired nothing better than to be the means of reinstating him in his former position.

Among the people who sought my acquaintance there was also Khalílu dan Hassan, one of the presumptive heirs to the royal power — Hassan being a younger brother of Bello — a young man of gentlemanly manners, but not of a very generous disposition, as he plainly evinced on my home journey the following year, when he wanted to oblige me to send him, after my safe return home, a pair of pistols in exchange for a black shirt scarcely worth 5000 shells, or two dollars.

All this time, I had employed my leisure hours in reading a manuscript work which had given me the first insight into the history of the western portion of these Féllani dominions. It had been composed by 'Abd Alláhi, the brother of 'Othmán the Reformer, to whom the western portion of the conquered region was awarded as his share. But although this work, the title of which is 'Tezén el aúrekát', contained, besides a great deal of theological matter, some important historical data, it did not satisfy my curiosity; and I had been endeavouring in vain to obtain the work of Bello, entitled 'Infák el misúrí fi fat-há el Tekrúri', which had been earnestly recommended to me by my friend the fáki 'Abd el Káder in Kátsena; but I did not succeed in getting it into my hands till a few days before I left this place, when I found that the greater part of its contents, which had any geographical or historical importance, were identical with those documents brought back by Captain Clapperton, on his first journey.

## DEPARTURE FROM WURNO FOR TIMBUKTU

*May* 8. But strongly reminded of the effects of the rainy season, by a heavy shower which fell on the 6th, driving me out of my cool shed, I urged my departure, and in the afternoon of the 8th took leave of 'Alíyu with a cheerful spirit, it being evident to me, not only that he entertained not the slightest mistrust of my future proceedings, but on the contrary even took considerable interest in me, as he found that it was my earnest desire to become well acquainted with the country and the people, and that I was anxious to establish friendly relations with the most distinguished and learned among them. But he gave me repeatedly to understand that he wished me not to go to Hamdalláhi, to present my compliments to their countrymen and coreligionists there and their chief or his successor, we having just received a few days previously the news of the death of Shékho A'hmedu, while he had not the slightest objection to my going to Timbúktu, and paying a visit to the sheikh el Bakáy, who had spent some time in Sókoto and was on friendly terms with the family of Fódiye.

At length I was able to pursue my journey, which now, as soon as I had passed Sókoto, was to lead me into almost unknown regions, never trodden by European foot.

I was escorted out of the town, in grand style, by the ghaladíma with six horsemen, and then pursued my former track to Sókoto.

*May* 14. There had been so heavy a shower the preceding afternoon, that a large stream broke through the roof of my dwelling and placed my whole room several inches under water. I passed, therefore, a most uncomfortable night, and when I got up in the morning I had a very bad headache. Every thing also, was extremely wet, so that it took us a long time to get ready our camels, and it was eight o'clock when we left the kófa-n-Tarámnia, which, though the widest of the gates of the town, did not allow my two largest boxes to pass without damage.

## ENTRY INTO GWANDU

*May* 15. We left on our right, the town of Sifáwa or Shifáwa, an important place in the history of the Púllo reformer 'Othmán dan Fódiye, but at present almost desolate and reduced to great misery, presenting a fair specimen of the state of the province of Gando, which we here entered.

*May* 17. As we approached the town of Gando, I could not help wondering how the people had been led to choose this locality as the seat of a large empire, commanded as it was by hilly chains all around, while the rising ground would have offered a far more suitable locality. But the situation of the town is on a par with the character of its dominion — without commanding strength, and quite incapable of keeping together that large agglomeration of provinces which have gathered around it. However, for a provincial town, the interior is very pleasant and animated, being adorned with a variety of trees, among which the banana is prominent.

Having sent a messenger in advance, I soon obtained quarters in the house of El Khassa, the chief eunuch of the court; but they were extremely narrow and unpleasant, although I had a very good clay house for myself.

Thus I had entered the residence of another very important Púllo chief, whose dominion extended several hundred miles over the country which I had to traverse, and whose friendship it was of the utmost importance for me to secure, as his provinces inclose both banks of the Niger, while the dominion of the sultan of Sókoto does not reach the principal branch at all. It was the more unfavourable that the present ruler of this very extensive kingdom should be a man without energy, and most inaccessible to a European and a Christian. His name is Khalílu, and he is the son of 'Abd Alláhi, the brother of the great Reformer 'Othmán, to whom that remarkable man, at his death, gave the western part of his vast domains, while he installed the celebrated Sultan Bello over the eastern portion. Khalílu succeeded to his brother Mohammed Wáni about seventeen years ago, and has since lived in a state of the greatest seclusion, well fitted for a monk, but by no means suited to the ruler of a vast empire, employing one of his brothers in order to keep up a certain show of imperial dignity where it was absolutely necessary. Thus, during the first few years of his reign, he had employed 'Abd el Kádiri, and was now employing Halíru, or, as the name is written, Hadhíru. Even by Mohammedans he is scarcely ever to be seen except on Fridays. It appeared, from my first arrival, extremely doubtful whether he would allow me to see his holy face; and after a vain struggle, merely in order that, by an untimely obstinacy in matters of form, I might not frustrate all my schemes of discovery, I agreed at length to deliver my present to the messengers of the sultan, in his palace, without seeing him. This present consisted of almost the same number of articles as I had given to the emír of Sókoto, with the exception of the silver-mounted pistols. I gave him three bernúses — one of yellow, one of red cloth, and the third of the kind called heláli; a háík or jeríd of the finest quality, a Stambúli carpet, two entire pieces of muslin, a red cap, four loaves of sugar, three phials of rose oil, a pair of razors, five looking-glasses, a pound of cloves, and another of benzoin.

My present to the sultan himself seemed at first to have given great satisfaction; but after a few days, matters assumed a different aspect, and I was told that the pistols which I had given to 'Alíyu were of more value than the whole of the presents which Khalílu had received from me, while the empire of the latter extended over a larger tract of country than that of the former; and I was clearly given to understand that it was not in my power either to proceed or even to retrace my steps, unless I gave much larger presents.

Notwithstanding all this disagreeable business, which occasionally cost me much bitter reflection, greatly enhanced by the advance of the season, the month of May being at an end, and

that of June having set in with violent rains, I passed the time
during my residence in this place not quite uselessly, especially
as I was so fortunate as to obtain here from a learned man of the
name of Bokhári, a son of the late Mohammed Wáni, a copy of
that most valuable historical work of A'hmed Bábá,[2] to which
my friend ʿAbd el Káder, in Sókoto, had first called my attention, but without being able to satisfy my curiosity; and I spent
three or four days most pleasantly in extracting the more important historical data of this work, which opened to me quite a
new insight into the history of the regions on the middle course
of the Niger, whither I was bending my steps, exciting in me a
far more lively interest than I had previously felt in a kingdom
the great power of which, in former times, I here found set
forth in very clear and distinct outlines, and I only lamented
that I had not time enough to copy the whole.

As for the town of Gando itself, there was not much to be
seen; and the situation of the place, hemmed in as it is in a
narrow valley, did not admit of long excursions; moreover, the
insecurity of the neighbourhood was so great that it was not
possible, at least in a northerly direction, to proceed many yards
from the wall.

The interior of the place was not quite without its charms,
the whole of the town being intersected, from north to south,
by the broad and shallow bed of a torrent, which exhibited
fine pasture-grounds of fresh succulent herbage, while it was
skirted on both sides by a dense border of exuberant vegetation,
which altogether is much richer in this place than either in
Sókoto or Wurno, being surpassed only by the fine vegetable
ornament of Kanó. The rains are extremely plentiful in Gando,
causing here quite an exceptional state in the productive power
of the soil; and to this circumstance we have partly to ascribe
the fact that very fine bananas are grown here in considerable
quantity: and the fruit being just ripe at the time, formed a
very pleasant variation to my usual food. The onion of Gando
is remarkable for its size and quality, compared with that of all
the neighbouring districts; and it is well for the traveller, in

[2] *Tarikh-es-Soudan.*

whatever direction he may intend to go, to lay in a supply of this wholesome article. But the place is extremely dull, and the market very insignificant — a fact easily to be explained by the desperate state of the provinces around, although the situation of the capital, as a central place for commerce, is rather favourable. But the town of Jéga has not yet lost, in this respect, the whole of its former importance, and is still the great entrepôt for that coarse kind of coloured silk which is imported from the north, and which, notwithstanding its very inferior character, is nevertheless so greatly sought after by the natives for adorning their leatherwork. It is, perhaps, in consequence of the little trade which is carried on, that the people of Gando have applied themselves with more industry to supplying their own want of cotton cloth — and no one can deny that their cotton strips are of first-rate quality: their dyeing, on the contrary, is very coarse, and they seem quite unable to give to the dyed cloth that lustre which so eminently distinguishes the manufactures of Núpe and Kanó; but nevertheless this cloth of Gando is in great demand as far as Libtáko.

The kingdom or empire of Gando, according to its titles, comprises a number of wealthy provinces, all lying along that great West-African river which opens such an easy access into this continent, or on its branches; although nobody who stays in the capital for any length of time would suppose that it holds such a preeminent rank.

## THE KEBBI COUNTRY

*June* 4. It was almost eleven o'clock when we at length left the western gate of the town, or the kófa-n-Jéga, and entered the open fields, where the crop was already shooting forth. Keeping along the rocky ground bordering the valley on the north side, we soon had a specimen of the swamps which during the rainy season are formed in these deep valleys of Kebbi, while we beheld here also extensive rice-grounds, the first which I saw under actual cultivation. But the guide, who was to accompany me to the very western extremity of the territory of Khalílu,

having not yet arrived, we made only a short march of about
six miles, and took up our quarters in a comfortable hut lying
outside the walls of Kámbasa, which, by a separate wall, is
divided into two distinct quarters.

This town lies on the north side of a large swamp, which fills
the bottom of the fáddama, and affords excellent grounds for
the cultivation of rice. The governor treated me hospitably,
sending me everything that was wanted for a good African
dinner, from a sheep down to a bit of salt and a few cakes of
dodówa; and I made him a suitable present in return. During
the night we suffered greatly from mosquitoes, giving us a fair
idea of what we were to expect on our journey through these
swampy valleys.

*June* 5. Proceeding then through a very rich country, we
reached, after a march of about two miles, the town of
Gúlumbé, situated close to the southern border of the valley,
and exhibiting extensive fields cultivated with yams and cotton.
The banana constituted the chief ornament of the narrow
border inclosed between the fáddama on one side, and the wall
of the town on the other, and the gónda or *Erica Papaya*, raising
its feathery foliage on its slender, virginlike stem, towered
proudly over the wall. The town was walled, of considerable
size, and densely inhabited; but nevertheless the people were
in such dread of the enemy, that they kept up a continual
beating of drums; and although, on account of the smallness
of the gate, we encamped outside, in a courtyard situated
between the wall and the border of the fáddama, we thought
it prudent to fire a few shots, in order to apprize the people
around that we were well prepared to receive them, to the
great relief of the inhabitants of the town, who, delighted at
the unexpected addition to their strength, treated us in a
very hospitable manner. The only disturbance to our night's
rest was caused by the mosquitoes, which harassed us
greatly and drove most of my people into the rúdu, that kind
of raised hut which I have described on a former occasion,
and which forms the most essential part of even the poorest
dwelling in the province of Kebbi.

*June* 6. After a thunder-storm accompanied by a few drops of rain, the night was succeeded by a beautiful morning; and I felt great pleasure in surveying the interesting landscape, only regretting that the insecure state of the country did not allow the natives to enjoy it in tranquillity, the war having driven thousands of people from their homes, and as many more into captivity. The fields on this side of the town, as well as on the other, where we had approached it the day before, were fenced with great care, while horses and asses were grazing on the rich pasture-grounds. After a little more than a mile and a half, we passed, on our left, a farming-village called I'gené, after its master, a cheerful Púllo of advanced age, who was just inspecting the labour of his slaves in the fields. The crops hereabouts were already more than a foot above the ground; and a little further on they reached a height of two feet. Besides sorghum, yams were cultivated to a great extent; but nevertheless, on account of the insecurity of the country, dearth and famine everywhere prevailed.

A little further on we passed, on our left, a considerable sheet of water, with plenty of dorówa, large kadé, and sycamores. The deléb palms had ceased just beyond I'gené. A broad flat-topped mountain, called Hamári, at the eastern foot of which lies the town of Zóro, broke the uniform surface of the country.

Proceeding through this rich but distracted and unsafe district, I was greatly delighted when, near the walled town of Kardi, I fell in with a solitary and courageous pilgrim, a Jolof, from the shores of the Atlantic, carrying his little luggage on his head, and seemingly well prepared to defend it with his double-barrelled gun which he carried on his shoulder, and a short sword hanging at his side, while his shirt was tossed gallantly up, and tied over the shoulder, behind the neck. In my joy at the sight of this enterprising native traveller, I could not forbear making him a small present, in order to assist him in his arduous undertaking.

We then traversed a wooded tract adorned with a violet *liliacea* and with the bush tsáda or bidér, the delicious cherrylike fruit of which I have mentioned repeatedly, and, slightly ascending, reached, a little before eleven o'clock, the beautiful site of the former more extensive wall of the large town of Bírni-n-Kebbi. It was founded in this commanding position by the dynasty of the Kanta, at the time when the rival Songhay empire was dashed to pieces and became the prey of foreigners and of a number of small tribes, who had once been kept in a state of insignificance and subjection.

Under such circumstances Kebbi, besides being the seat of a powerful kingdom, became also the centre of a considerable trade even in gold, till it was destroyed by the Fúlbe under 'Abd Alláhi, in the year of the Hejra 1221, when a great deal of gold and silver is said to have been found among the ruins. The royal palace, however (the ruins of which I visited), does not seem to have been very extensive; but this in part may be attributed to the fact that a great portion of the residence consisted of straw huts for the female department and the followers. The walls of the present town are almost a mile distant from those of the old one, lying close to the steep slope which, with a descent of about 250 feet, goes down here into the large green valley or fáddama which intersects the whole of Kebbi from E.N.E. to W.S.W., and is at this part almost three miles in breadth, affording the richest ground for cultivation, but at present plunged in a state of the utmost insecurity. Even then it was full of cattle, at least its southerly part; but they had to be carefully watched by the natives from above the slope, for the whole of the country on the other side, the hilly chains and cones of which are clearly seen, is in the hands of the A'zena, that is to say, those native inhabitants of Kebbi who, since the death of the more energetic 'Atíku, are successfully struggling for their religious and political independence. On the very brink of the slope a market was held, where we bought some necessaries before entering the town; and I willingly lingered a few moments, as the whole presented a very novel sight, increased by a picturesque spur or promontory which juts out into the valley a few miles to the west, and is a remarkable feature in the landscape. We then entered the town, which is rather thickly inhabited, but it is far from presenting that cheerful aspect which is peculiar to most of the towns in these regions, as it is almost bare of trees. I myself was quartered in an excellent hut, belonging to a newly-married couple, and possessing all the comforts of which these simple dwellings are capable,— the floor and walls of the hut being neatly polished, and the background or 'nanne' being newly sprinkled with snow-white sand; but the whole of the courtyard was extremely narrow, and scarcely afforded space for my horses and camels.

There are two great men in the town, 'Othmán Lowel and 'Othmán Záki; but the former is the real governor of the place, bearing the pompous but rather precarious title of serkí-n-Kebbi — for even he, at the present time, possesses such limited authority, that it was rather out of my respect for historical connections than for his real power, that I made him a considerable present. He is a man of simple manners, without pretensions, and almost blind. His residence was distinguished by its neatness. The other great man, 'Othmán Záki, who was many years ago governor of Núpe, and knew Clapperton, although I did not pay him a visit, showed his friendship for me by very hospitable treatment. He has since returned to Núpe, and is rebuilding Rabba.

## APPROACHING THE RIVER NIGER

*June* 7. Thus we reached the foot of a rocky eminence, on the top of which the walled town of Kóla is situated in a very strong position, commanding the whole passage of the valley. It is the seat of a governor who bears the title of serkí-n-Záromé, and who is said to have as many as seventy musketeers under his command; so that, as he was an officer of much importance in this turbulent country, it did not seem advisable to pass him unnoticed, and we therefore determined to take up our quarters here, although it was still early in the morning. He has a large house or palace, but it is somewhat in decay. Having made him a small present, I was hospitably treated both by himself and his sister, who sent me an excellent goose, which afforded a very pleasant change in my diet. He accompanied me the following morning to the boundary of his little territory.

Leaving the walled town of Júggurú (surrounded by a good many monkey-bread trees) on the hills to our left, we reached, after a march of about five miles along the border of the valley, and only once crossing a romantic rocky defile, the considerable town of Diggi; and here I had the satisfaction of being officially received by three sons of the governor of Zogírma, who quite unexpectedly came galloping up to the front and saluted me, wishing me all possible success on my dangerous undertaking, and bidding me welcome to the province of their father. The eldest of the three was a very handsome young man, and splendidly mounted upon a tall grey horse. Pursuing then our march in their company, we immediately entered the wide fáddama which separated us from Zogírma; and it took us more than three hours to cross this shallow swampy valley, the whole of which at the end of the rainy season is filled with water, but which at present was only intersected by two broken sheets of stagnant water, while I endeavoured in vain to make out, at this spot, an uninterrupted channel of the gulbi: and yet, in the month of September, the whole valley is flooded by a river of considerable breadth.

The town, which was surrounded by a clay wall in good repair, impressed me as being more considerable than I had supposed it to be. We were led immediately to our quarters, and were here treated with very good tíggera, or prepared millet and sour milk; after which a large calabash full of rice, and, a short time after, a heifer, were brought me as a present. Later in the afternoon I went to pay my respects to the governor, Hámed Búrtu, and found him a very decent-looking man of from fifty to sixty years of age, with almost European features, but with rather a melancholy expression of countenance. His residence had a very stately appearance, and surprised me not a little by its style of architecture, which approached to the Gothic, although the fine and well-ornamented clay walls were only loosely held together by a framework of boards and branches. Presenting to him a red bernús of middling quality, a piece of muslin, a pair of razors, and some other trifles, I delivered to him the letter with which Khalílu had furnished me, and explained to him how the ruler of Gando had given me hopes of his being able to conduct me safe to Fógha; for the two horsemen whom I had with me, one from Gando and the other from Sókoto, were only of service as long as there was anything to eat and while there was no great danger. He received my address in the most cheerful manner, and informed me that there were two roads, one of them leading straight on through the midst of the forest from Zogírma to the town of Kallílul. This he said was the safest, though it was probably too difficult for my heavily-laden camels. The other, he added, was more convenient but very unsafe. He promised, however, that he would find trustworthy men to escort me.

Zogírma may contain from 7000 to 8000 inhabitants; but at that time it was suffering greatly from famine, on account of the war which had been raging for the last two years, between the Fúlbe conquerors of the country and the native inhabitants the Dendi, who, favoured by the weakness of the government of their oppressors, had risen to assert their independence; and I could scarcely feel dissatisfied with my host when, after the first signs of hospitality which he had shown me, he left us to provide for our own wants, although we had some difficulty in procuring a sufficient supply of corn. I was very sorry that, owing to the unfavourable circumstances of the whole country, I was prevented from visiting the town of Bunza (which is situated south from Zogírma), on account of its interesting and important situation as regards the intercourse with Núpe on the lower part of the gulbi, where it is still navigable, and the number of deléb palms which are said to adorn it. There was also residing in this place a man whom I should like to have visited, inasmuch as he is reported to possess a great knowledge of the history of the Kanta, and of the relations of the province of Kebbi to the neighbouring countries. His name is Mállem Mahamúdu.

*June* 9. It was thus deemed sufficient to give me for companions only two horsemen; but fortunately they were of such a character that I preferred them to at least a dozen other people, both of them being experienced old warriors and most respectable men, one of them having been till lately the governor of the town of Débe, which was now deserted, and the site of which we had to pass on our road. I was heartily glad to get rid of my two former effeminate companions, Lowel, the servant of the governor of Gando, and Beshír, an attendant of the ghaladíma in Sókoto, as they had been of scarcely any use to me on my way hither, except, perhaps, in procuring me a better reception from the governors of the towns and villages; and I gladly complied with the demands of my new companions, by giving to each of them a new black 'lithám' or 'ráwani bakí' for themselves, a flask of rose oil for their wives, and one thousand shells for the expenses of their households during their absence.

*June* 19. We were now close to the Niger; and I was justified in indulging in the hope that I might the next day behold with my own eyes that great river of Western Africa, which has caused such intense curiosity in Europe, and the upper part of the large eastern branch of which I had myself discovered.

*June* 20. Elated with such feelings, I set out the next morning, at an early hour; and after a march of a little less than two hours, through a rocky wilderness covered with dense bushes, I obtained the first sight of the river, and in less than an hour more, during which I was in constant sight of this noble spectacle, I reached the place of embarkation, opposite the town of Say.

In a noble unbroken stream, though here, where it has become contracted, only about 700 yards broad, hemmed in on this side by a rocky bank of from twenty to thirty feet in elevation, the great river of Western Africa (whose name, under whatever form it may appear, whether Dhiúlibá, Máyo, Eghírrëu, I'sa, Kwára, or Báki-n-rúwa, means nothing but 'the river', and which therefore may well continue to be called the Niger) was gliding along, in a N.N.E. and S.S.W. direction, with a moderate current of about three miles an hour.

## CHAPTER 10

# FROM SOKOTO TO BORNU
## (1854–1855)

On 24 June 1853, Barth set out from Say. 'I now left the Great River behind me, which formed the link between the tolerably well-known regions of Central Negroland and the totally unexplored country on the south-western side of its course.' Travelling through Gurma, Libtako, Hombori and Kabara, he reached Timbuktu, 'the object of my arduous undertaking', on 7 September. There he spent more than six months, unable to leave the city for fear of being murdered and saved from assassination within its walls only by the loyal friendship of Sheikh El Bakay.

Barth eventually succeeded in obtaining a safe conduct back to Nigeria in May 1854. Passing through Gao, he crossed the Niger at Say and re-entered the domains of the Sokoto-Gwandu empire in August.

*August* 2. The evening was beautiful, and the scenery of the river, with the feathery dúm-palms on the opposite shore, was lovely in the extreme, and well adapted to leave on my mind a lasting impression of the magnificent watery highroad which Nature has opened into the heart of this continent. Thus I took leave of the Niger.

## RETURN TO BIRNIN KEBBI

*August* 14. We had heard already on our journey that we had arrived at the very latest time in order to cross, with any degree of safety, the swampy fáddama of the gúlbi-n-Sókoto, which a little later in the season is extremely difficult to pass. At all events it was very fortunate that no rain had fallen for the last few days, or we should have experienced considerable difficulty in crossing this swampy ground.

## GWANDU AGAIN

*August* 17. A little further on I met with one of those incidents which, although simple and unimportant in their character, yet often serve to cheer the solitary traveller in foreign countries, more than the most brilliant reception. After having crossed a valley, we were ascending the last rocky passage before coming to Gando, when we met here a troop of men, and as soon as one of them saw me in the distance, he broke out into the cheering exclamation, 'Márhaba, márhaba, 'Abd el Kerím'. It was highly gratifying to me when returning after a long absence to a place where I had resided for so short a time, to be recognized immediately and saluted in so hearty a manner, although my stay in Gando was connected with many a melancholy reminiscence.

Here, on the top of the rocky eminence, we obtained a view of the valley of Gando, and, descending, soon reached the gate of the town, and straightway rode to the house of the monkish prince, where we were soon surrounded by a number of people, who congratulated me on my fortunate return.

The town was no better off now than it had been a year before, the expedition against Argúngo, of which I had heard on the road as being undertaken by 'Alíyu, having turned out a mere sham, and in consequence the pagan rebels being stronger and more daring than ever; and, just as was the case during my former residence, there was an expedition on a small scale every Tuesday and Thursday, made by the old people and the women, in order to collect wood with some degree of security. On the whole, there was nothing of interest to record, except the remarkable quantity of rain which fell during my stay, and which was said to have fallen before my arrival, confirming the impression already previously received in my mind, that Gando was one of those places most abundantly supplied with the watery element; and it was highly interesting for me to learn from the people on this occasion, that, as a general rule, they reckon upon ninety-two rainy days annually. I am quite sure that the average rain-fall in this place is certainly not less than sixty inches; but it is probably more than eighty, and perhaps even one hundred.

*August* 23. I was heartily glad when I left this town, where I had experienced a great deal of trouble, although I could not but acknowledge, that if I had not succeeded in some degree in securing the friendship of the ruling men in this place, it would not have fallen to my lot to have reached even the banks of the Niger.

It is to be hoped that Khalílu will soon be succeeded by a more energetic prince, who will restore peace and security to the extensive dominions of which Gando is the capital. Under such circumstances this town, on account of its mercantile connections with the provinces along the Niger, could hardly fail to become a place of the greatest interest.

## BACK TO SOKOTO

*August* 24. At the present day, at the outskirts of almost all the larger towns of Negroland, Fúlbe families are established, who rear cattle for the express purpose of supplying milk for the daily wants of the inhabitants; and these people gladly provide travellers with that most desirable article when they are well paid for it; but having degenerated to mere tradesmen, they, of course, possess little hospitable feeling.

The whole country which we traversed on our next day's march, was clothed with the richest vegetation, the crops being almost ripe, but cattle and horses being very scanty. Thus, after a good march, we reached the town of Bodínga, having lost another of our camels on the road, which, in crossing one of the swampy valleys in which this part of Negroland abounds, had fallen backwards with his load, and died on the spot. But the quantity of water that we had to sustain from above and below, was not only destructive to animals, but likewise to men, and I myself felt most cheerless, weak, and without appetite, bearing already within me the germs of dysentery, which soon were to develop themselves, and undermine my health in the most serious way.

*August* 26. The whole town, suburbs, wall, cottages, and gardens, were now enveloped in one dense mass of vegetation, through which it was difficult to make one's way, and recognise places well known from former visits. Scarcely had I been quartered in a comfortable hut, when my friend 'Abd el Káder Dan-Taffa, sent his compliments to me, and shortly after made his appearance himself, expressing the liveliest satisfaction at seeing me again, and sincere compassion for the reduced state of my health. Not less encouraging was the reception I met with from my old friend Módibo 'Alí. When I made him a small present, regretting that after the long time I had been without supplies I was not able to make him a better one, he was so kind as to express his astonishment that I had anything left at all. He also begged me not to go on at once to Wurnó, but to stay a day in this place, and to write to 'Alíyu, informing him of my safe return, and how much I stood in need of his aid. I made use of this opportunity of at once requesting the emír El Múmenín to forward me with as little delay as possible on my journey, hinting, at the same time, that I should feel very grateful to him, if he would assist me with horses and camels. I intimated also, that as I myself, on account of the reduced state of my health, was anxious to reach home by the most direct road, I had to beg for permission for a countryman of mine, who had just come to Bórnu, meaning Mr. Vogel, to visit the south-eastern provinces of his kingdom. The following evening, a messenger arrived from the vizier 'Abdú, son of Gedádo, informing me that we were to start on the succeeding day, and that we should find camels on the other side of the river. The river, as I had already learned, was very much swollen, and extremely difficult to cross.

While my Mohammedan and black friends thus behaved towards me in the kindest and most hospitable manner, the way in which I felt myself treated by my friends in Europe, was not at all encouraging, and little adapted to raise my failing spirits; for it was only by accident, through a liberated female slave from Stambúl, who called upon me soon after my arrival, that I obtained information of the important fact, that five Christians had arrived in Kúkawa, with a train of forty camels. While I endeavoured to identify the individuals of whom this person gave me some account from a very selfish point of view, with the particulars contained in Lord Russell's despatch, which I had received near Timbúktu, about the members of an auxiliary expedition to be sent out to join me, I was greatly astonished that, for myself, there was not a single line from those gentlemen, although I felt still authorized to consider myself the director of the African Expedition; and I could only conclude from all this, that something was wrong. I had not yet any direct intimation of the rumour which was spread abroad with regard to my death: and taking everything into consideration, it was certainly a want of circumspection in Mr. Vogel, notwithstanding the rumours which were current in Bórnu, not to endeavour to place himself in communication with me in the event of my being still alive.

## WURNO AGAIN

*August* 30. After an agreeable march of about six miles, it being a fine clear day, we reached Wurnó, the residence of 'Alíyu. Here we were lodged in our old quarters, where, however, the frail building of the hut had disappeared, and nothing remained but the clay house. I was received by the court of the emír El Múmenín also with great kindness, and, curious as it may appear to Europeans, my hostile relations with the Fúlbe of Hamda-Alláhi seemed only to have increased my esteem in the eyes of these people. 'Alíyu had even heard of the un-generous conduct of the Sheikh el Bakáy's younger brother towards me; and while he greatly praised the straightforward behaviour of the former he did not fail to reproach Sídi A'lawáte with meanness. He treated me very hospitably, although I was not able to enjoy greatly the more luxurious kind of food which was here offered to me, for luxurious it seemed after my poor diet in the famished and distracted region near the Niger. It was only by the strictest diet, especially by keeping to sour milk, together with repose, that I succeeded, after a great deal of suffering, in keeping under the disease. However, my recovery in the beginning was only temporary, and on the 13th of the following month dysentery broke out with considerable violence, and caused me a total loss of strength; but, after a severe crisis, it was overcome by the use of Dover's powders, although even then a simple diet was the most effectual remedy, my food consisting of nothing but pounded rice, mixed with curdled milk, and the seeds of the *Mimosa Nilotica*. At length, on the 22nd of September, I was again enabled to move about a little on horseback, and from that day forward, my health continued to improve.

*September*. During this my second stay in the capital of this extensive empire, I had again full opportunity of observing the extreme weakness and want of energy which prevails in its very centre; although I could not but acknowledge the feeling of justice which animates the ruler himself, notwithstanding his want of spirit. In proof of this I may relate that being informed one day that five young sons of his had committed acts of injustice in the market, he became greatly enraged, and immediately sent his two chief courtiers, 'Abdu and the ghaladíma, with positive orders to seize and imprison the offenders; and when the young outlaws succeeded in escaping and hiding themselves for a day or two, he had the chief slave, who had been with them, executed. But the cowardice of his people, and their oppression of the weak and unprotected, became fully apparent.

*October* 4. Having at length overcome the laziness of my companions, I had the satisfaction of seeing my departure finally arranged for the 5th October. The ghaladíma, in whose company on my outward journey I had come from Kátsena, was again to be my fellow traveller on my return eastward. I therefore completed my preparations, and, on the 4th October, I had my final leave-taking, or, as the Háusa people say, the babankwána, when I took the opportunity of excusing myself to 'Alíyu for having been this year a little troublesome, after the fashion of those Arab sherífs who used to visit him, stating at the same time, that if my means had not been almost exhausted, I should have preferred buying a horse for myself. Having made this prelude, I endeavoured to impress upon him the dangerous state of the road, when he made use of the expression common in Háusa, 'Alla shibúdeta!' ('God may open it!'); but I protested against such an excess of reliance upon the Divine intervention, and exhorted him to employ his own strength and power for such a purpose, for without security of roads, I assured him there could be no intercourse nor traffic. He either was, or seemed to be, very desirous that the English should open trading relations with him; and I even touched on the circumstance, that in order to facilitate such an intercourse, it would be best to blow up certain rocks, which most obstructed the navigation between Yáuri and Búsa, but of such an undertaking I convinced myself that it was better not to say too much at once, as that ought to be an affair of time.

Altogether, 'Alíyu had entered into the most cheerful conversation with me on all occasions, and had questioned me upon every subject without reserve. He also furnished me with four letters of recommendation, one to the governor of Kanó, one to that of Bauchi, one to that of A'damáwa, and one in a more general sense, addressed to all the governors of the different provinces in his empire. Thus I took leave of him and his court, probably never to see that region again, and lamenting that this extensive empire, which is so advantageously situated for a steady intercourse with Europeans, was not in the hands of an energetic chieftain, who would be able to give stability to conquest, and to organise the government of these provinces, so richly endowed by nature, with a strong hand.

*October* 5. It was about three o'clock in the afternoon when I took my final leave of Wurnó. I had twice resided in this capital for some length of time, experiencing, on the whole, much kindness. On my outward journey I had been furnished on my dangerous undertaking with a strong and powerful recommendation; and on my return, although I had come into hostile contact with another section of the same tribe to which the inhabitants of this country belong, I had been again received without the least suspicion, had been treated with great regard, notwithstanding the exhausted state of my finances, and allowed to pursue my home journey as soon as the season re-opened the communication with the neighbouring province.

## RETURN TO KANO

*October* 17. On my arrival in Kanó, I found everything prepared, and took up my quarters in a house provided for me; but I was greatly disappointed in finding neither letters nor supplies; being entirely destitute of means, and having several debts to pay in this place,— amongst others, the money due to my servants, to whom I had paid nothing during the whole journey from Kúkawa to Timbúktu, and back. I was scarcely able to explain how all this could have happened; having fully relied upon finding here everything I wanted, together with satisfactory information with regard to the proceedings of Mr. Vogel and his companions, whose arrival in Kúkawa I had as yet only accidentally learned from a liberated slave in Sókoto.

Barth now sent his faithful servant, Muhammed el Gatroni, 'upon whom I could fully rely', to Zinder to collect the money and goods that he had left there on his way from Kuka to Katsina in early 1853. In the meantime, as always, Barth refused to waste his days.

Meanwhile, till the return of this messenger, I endeavoured to pass my time as usefully as possible, by completing a survey of the town which I had begun during my former residence, but was far from having finished. At the same time the state of my health, on account of the close quarters in which I was here lodged, after having roved about in the open air for so long a time, required uninterrupted exercise. Owing to the change in my mode of living, severe fits of fever attacked me repeatedly.

Kanó will always remain one of the most unfavourable localities for Europeans in this region; and it was well that Mr. Vogel, for the first year after his arrival in Negroland, purposely avoided this spot. Even my animals did not escape the malignant effect of the climate. Three of my horses were seized, one after the other, with a contagious disease, commencing with a swelling of the thighs, and from thence spreading to the breast and the head, and generally proving fatal in six or eight days. In this way I lost two out of my three horses, including my old companion, who had carried me through so many dangerous campaigns, and who had shared all my fatigues and sufferings for nearly three years; but the small and ugly, but strong horse which the Sultan of Sókoto had made me a present of, escaped with its life. This disease which attacked my horses, of course, interfered greatly with my excursions, and took away almost all the pleasure which they would otherwise have afforded, as I was reduced to the necessity of making use of very indifferent animals.

Besides my own private concerns, and the anxiety produced by the urgency of my debts and the uncertainty with regard to the property left by me in Zínder, there were two objects which attracted my whole attention and caused me a good deal of perplexity and hesitation. The first of these was the expedition sent by the English government up the river Bénuwé, of which I had not the slightest idea at the time when it was carried out, for the despatches which I had received in Timbúktu, after so much delay, did not contain a word about such a proceeding; and the letters which were forwarded afterwards to my address, informing me that such an expedition was to be undertaken, remained in Kúkawa, and I did not get them until my arrival in that place at the end of December. Thus it was not until the 29th October that, just in the same manner as I had heard accidentally in Sókoto of the arrival of Mr. Vogel in Kúkawa, I was informed here, by the report of the natives, of such an expedition having taken place. I at first thought that it was undertaken by Captain M'Leod, of whose proposal to ascend the Niger I had accidentally gleaned some information through a number of the Galignani,[1] and it was not until the 13th November that I succeeded in meeting the person who had seen the expedition with his own eyes. This man informed me that the expedition consisted of one large boat,[2] he did not know whether

---

[1] The news-sheet from Malta.        [2] The *Pleiad*.

of iron or of wood, and two smaller ones, containing altogether seven gentlemen and seventy slaves, he of course taking the Kroomen for slaves. Moreover, I learned from him that the members of this expedition had not gone as far as Yóla, the capital of A'damáwa, as the governor of Hamárruwa had warned them not to go up to that place with their steamer, on account of the narrow passage between the mountains. He also informed me, that they had been expected, and that he himself, having proceeded to Yákoba[3] in order to procure more ivory for them, had found them gone on his return.

The other circumstance which greatly occupied my mind at this time, was the state of affairs in Kúkawa. For in the beginning, on the first news of the revolution in Bórnu, and of the Sheikh 'Omár being dethroned and his vizier slain, I had given up my project of returning by Bórnu, intending to try again the difficult road by A'ír. At a later season, however, when I heard on the road that 'Omár was again installed, I cherished the hope that it might be possible to take the safer route by the Tebu country, especially as I received the news of a most sanguinary struggle having taken place between the Kél-owí and the Kél-gerés. In this struggle a great many of the noblest men of the former were said to have fallen, together with several hundred of the common people on both sides. I was sorry to hear that in this struggle my best friends had succumbed.

## DIFFICULTIES IN KANO

Mohammed el Gatroni returned on 18 October with the news that, since it was widely believed that Barth had perished on his Timbuktu expedition, his belongings had been sent for by Vogel at Kukawa. Luckily, as a result of winning a civil suit against a Ghadames merchant in Kano — a case heard in public by the ghaladima — Barth was able to raise credit of 500,000 cowry shells. With this loan he set about re-equipping his party.

*November* 10. The difficulty which I had in supplying my wants, and purchasing the articles that in my opinion were necessary for my outfit, was the greater, as everything was very dear at the time, the merchants being of opinion, on account of the

[3] Bauchi.

turbulent state of the road, that no caravan from the north would arrive that year. Camels especially were exceedingly dear, seven fine animals which Khweldi had sent from Zínder, being sold for 60,000 shells each, a very high price for a camel. I deemed myself therefore very fortunate in being able to purchase a she-camel of inferior quality for 45,000. I also was so lucky as to buy an excellent mare for 70,000 shells, or less than thirty dollars. Having thus at length provided for all my wants, I got everything ready for starting on the 21st; and heartily glad I was when I was fairly embarked on this the last stage of my journeying in Negroland, with the prospect before me, that, in six months or so, I might again breathe the invigorating air of the north.

## INCIDENT AT GERKI

*November* 25. Passing then through a dense forest, I reached the well in front of the town of Gérki. My people had already arrived, but had not yet succeeded in obtaining the smallest quantity of water, the well, although not very deep, being rather poor, considering the number of people which it had to supply. I had, in consequence, to pay 300 shells for supplying the wants of myself and my animals. Not feeling any greater inclination this time to encamp inside Gérki than I had done on my former journey, I chose my own camping-ground on the north side of the town. It was a pleasant spot; but, unfortunately, it was too near a large monkey-bread tree, which in the course of the night afforded to an audacious thief an excellent cover, under which to proceed twice to a very clever performance of his art. I would strongly advise any future traveller in these districts, the inhabitants of which are very expert thieves, to take care not to pitch his tent too near a large tree. As it was, to my great disgust, the fellow succeeded in carrying away, first the tobe, and then the trowsers, belonging to one of my servants; but I strongly suspected one of the inhabitants of Hóbiri, from whom I had bought, the previous evening, an ox of burden for 9000 shells, to be the culprit. Gérki is famous on account of the many thefts which are committed in its neighbourhood.

## MEETING WITH VOGEL

*December* 1. I had scarcely proceeded three miles when I saw advancing towards me a person of strange aspect,— a young man of very fair complexion, dressed in a tobe like the one I wore myself, and with a white turban wound thickly round his head. He was accompanied by two or three blacks, likewise on horseback. One of them I recognised as my servant Mádi, whom, on setting out from Kúkawa, I had left in the house as a guardian. As soon as he saw me, he told the young man that I was 'Abd el Kerím, in consequence of which, Mr. Vogel (for he it was) rushed forward, and taken, by surprise as both of us were, we gave each other a hearty reception from horseback. As for myself, I had not had the remotest idea of meeting him; and he, on his part, had only a short time before received the intelligence of my safe return from the west. Not having the slightest notion that I was alive, and judging from its Arab address that the letter which I forwarded to him from Kanó was a letter from some Arab, he had put it by without opening it, waiting till he might meet with a person who should be able to read it.

In the midst of this inhospitable forest, we dismounted and sat down together on the ground; and my camels having arrived, I took out my small bag of provisions, and had some coffee boiled, so that we were quite at home. It was with great amazement that I heard from my young friend that there were no supplies in Kúkawa; that what he had brought with him had been spent; and that the usurper 'Abd e' Rahmán had treated him very badly, having even taken possession of the property which I had left in Zínder. He moreover informed me that he himself was on his way to that place, in order to see whether fresh supplies had not arrived, being also anxious to determine the position of that important town by an astronomical observation, and thus to give a firmer basis to my own labours. But the news of the want of pecuniary supplies did not cause me so much surprise as the report which I received from him, that he did not possess a single bottle of wine. For having now been for more than three years without a drop of any stimulant except coffee, and having suffered severely from frequent attacks of fever and dysentery, I had an insuperable longing for the juice of the grape, of which former experience had taught me the benefit. On my former journey through Asia Minor, I had contracted a serious fever in the swamps of Lycia, and quickly regained my strength by the use of good French wine. I could not help reproaching my friend for having too hastily believed the news of my death before he had made all possible inquiries; but as he was a new comer into this country, and did not possess a knowledge of the language, I could easily perceive that he had no means of ascertaining the truth or falsehood of those reports.

I also learned from him, that there were despatches for me in Kúkawa, informing me of the expedition sent up the river Tsadda, or Bénuwé. With regard to his own proceedings, he informed me that his sole object in going to Mándará had been to join that expedition, having been misled by the opinion of my friends in Europe, who thought that I had gone to A'damáwa by way of Mándará, and that when once in Morá he had become aware of the mistake he had committed when too late, and had endeavoured in vain to retrieve his error by going from that place to Ujé, from whence the overthrow of the usurper 'Abd e' Rahmán, and the return of his brother 'Omár to power, had obliged him to return to Kúkawa.

While we were thus conversing together, the other members of the caravan in whose company Mr. Vogel was travelling arrived, and expressed their astonishment and surprise at my sitting quietly here in the midst of the forest, talking with my friend, while the whole district was infested by hostile men.


## RETURN TO BORNU

*December* 11. In order to procure myself a good reception from the ruler of Bórnu, after the great political disturbances which had taken place, I thought it prudent to send a messenger to him to announce my arrival. I only needed to give full expression to my real feelings in order to render my letter acceptable to my former protector, for my delight had been extreme, after the news which I had received of 'Abd e' Rahmán having usurped the supreme power, on hearing that the just and lawful Sheikh 'Omár had once more regained possession of the royal authority. The consequence was, that when, after having traversed the district of Koyám, with its straggling villages, its fine herds of camels, and its deep wells, some of them more than forty fathoms in depth, I approached the town on the 11th December, I found 'Abd e' Nebí, the chief eunuch of the Sheikh, with thirty horsemen posted at the village of Kalíluwá, where a market was just held, in order to give me a honourable reception. Thus I re-entered the town of Kúkawa, whence I had set out on my dangerous journey to the west, in stately procession. On entering my quarters, I was agreeably surprised at finding the two sappers, Corporal Church and private Macguire, who had been sent out from England to accompany Mr. Vogel, and to join me, if possible, in my proceedings.

On reaching safely the town of Kúkawa, which had been my head-quarters for so long a period, and from whence I had first commenced my journeys of exploration in Negroland, it might seem that I had overcome all the difficulties in the way of complete success, and that I could now enjoy a short stay in the same place before traversing the last stage of my homeward journey. Such however was not the case, and it was my lot to pass four months in this town under rather unpleasant circumstances.

Another circumstance which contributed to render my situation in this place still more uncomfortable, was the relation which existed between Mr. Vogel and Corporal Church, one of the sappers who had come with him from England; and I was sorry that the praiseworthy and generous intention of the Government in sending out these two useful persons, should not be carried out to the fullest extent, but, on the contrary, should be baffled by private animosity. In this respect I had already been greatly disappointed and grieved, on hearing from

Mr. Vogel, when I met him on the road, that he had gone alone to Mándará, without making any use of the services of his companions. I did all in my power to convince the two sappers that under the circumstances in which they were placed, they ought to forget petty jealousies, as it was only by a mutual good understanding that complete success in such undertakings could be secured. I succeeded in convincing Macguire, although I was less successful with Corporal Church.

Meanwhile I spent my time in a tolerably useful manner, looking over some of the books which Mr. Vogel had brought with him, especially M. Jomard's introduction to the translation of the 'Voyage au Waday', by M. Perron, and the 'Flora Nigritia' of Sir William Hooker. I was also considerably interested by the perusal of a packet of letters which had been conveyed in the very box that had been plundered, and which, although dating back as late as December, 1851, afforded me a great deal of pleasure. Partly in order to fulfil a vow which I had made, and partly to obtain a more secure hold upon the friendly dispositions of the natives, I made a present to the inhabitants of the capital, on Christmas-day, of fourteen oxen, not forgetting either rich or poor, blind or fókara, nor even the Arab strangers.

My residence in the town became infinitely more cheerful, in consequence of the arrival of Mr. Vogel, on the 29th December, when I spent a period of twenty days most pleasantly in the company of this enterprising and courageous young traveller, who, with surprising facility, accustomed himself to all the relations of this strange life. But while borne away by the impulse of his own enthusiasm, and giving up all pretensions to the comforts of life, he unfortunately committed the mistake of expecting that his companions, recently arrived from Europe, and whose ideas were less elevated, should do the same, and this had given rise to a lamentable quarrel, which frustrated in a great measure the intentions of the Government who had sent out the party. Exchanging opinions with regard to countries which we had both of us traversed, and planning schemes as to the future course which Mr. Vogel was to pursue, and especially as to the next journey which he was to undertake towards Yákoba and A'damáwa, we passed our time very agreeably. I communicated to him, as far as it was possible in so short a space of time, all the information which I had collected during my extensive wanderings, and called his attention to various points which I begged him to clear up, especially with regard to some remarkable specimens of the vegetable kingdom, and the famous mermaid of the Bénuwé, the 'ayú'.[4] It was rather unfortunate that no copy of the map which had been constructed from the materials which I had sent home had reached him, so that he remained in the dark with regard to many points which I had already cleared up. I also delivered to Mr. Vogel those letters of introduction which I had received from the ruler of Sókoto, addressed to the various governors of the provinces in this part of his empire, so that he had a fair prospect before him of being well received. We, moreover, lost no time in obtaining the Sheikh's consent to his journey.

[4] The manatee.

## CHAPTER 11

# THE JOURNEY BACK (1855)

## DEPARTURE FROM KUKAWA

*January* 1. Thus we began cheerfully the year 1855, in which I was to return to Europe, from my long career of hardships and privations, and in which my young friend was to endeavour to complete my discoveries and researches, first in a south-westerly direction, towards the Bénuwé, and then eastwards, in the direction of the Nile. We likewise indulged in the hope that he might succeed, after having explored the provinces of Baúchi and A'damáwa, in penetrating eastward along that highly interesting route which leads from Saráwu to Lóggoné, round the southern border of the mountainous country of Mándará.

Meanwhile some interesting excursions to the shores of the Tsád, formed a pleasant interruption in our course of studies and scientific communications, and these little trips were especially interesting, on account of the extraordinary manner in which the shores of the lake had been changed since I last saw them, on my return from Bagírmi, the water having destroyed almost the whole of the town of Ngórnu, and extending as far as the village of Kúkia, where we had encamped the first night on our expedition to Músgu. There were two subjects which caused me some degree of anxiety with regard to the prospects of this enterprising young traveller,— the first being his want of experience, which could not be otherwise expected in a young man fresh from Europe; and the other, the weakness of his stomach, which made it impossible for him to eat any meat at all. The very sight of a dish of meat made him sick.

*January* 20. Having obtained, with some difficulty, the letter of recommendation from the Sheikh, and prepared everything that Mr. Vogel wanted to take with him, forming a sufficient supply to maintain him for a whole year, I accompanied my young friend out of the town, in the afternoon of the 20th January. But our start was rather unlucky, several things having been left behind; and it was after some delay and uncertainty that we joined the people who had gone on in advance with the camels, at a late hour, at the village of Díggigí. Here we passed a cheerful evening, and drank with spirit to the success of the enterprise upon which my companion was then about to engage. Mr. Vogel had also taken with him all his meteorological instruments, and his luggage being of a manifold description and rather heavy, I foresaw that he would have great trouble in transporting it through the difficult country beyond Yákoba, especially during the rainy season; and indeed it is evident, from the knowledge which we possess of his further proceedings, that he either left his instruments behind in the capital of Baúchi, or that he lost them in crossing a river between that place and Záriya. As for his barometer, which he had transported with great care to Kúkawa, it went out of order the moment it was taken from the wall.

Having borne him company during the following day's march, I left him with the best wishes for his success.

All that now remained for me under the present circumstances was, to resign myself in patience, although the delay pressed upon me with indescribable heaviness, and I had scarcely energy enough to endeavour to employ my time usefully.

*March* 23. A rather pleasant intermezzo occurred, whereby at the same time one of the conditions was fulfilled upon which my own departure was dependent, by the arrival of the Arab caravan from the north; and on the 23rd of March, I went to see them encamped in Dáwerghú, the path being enlivened by all sorts of people going out to meet their friends, and to hear what news had been brought by the new comers.

This caravan also carried 1000 dollars for the mission, but it was not addressed to me, as I had long been consigned to the grave, but to Mr. Vogel, although the chief of the caravan offered to deliver it to me. All this mismanagement, in consequence of the false news of my death, greatly enhanced the unpleasant nature of my situation; for, instead of leaving this country under honourable circumstances, I was considered as almost disgraced by those who had sent me out, the command having been taken from me and given to another. There is no doubt that such an opinion delayed my departure considerably; for, otherwise, the Sheikh would have exerted himself in quite a different manner to see me off, and would have agreed to any sacrifice in order to satisfy my claims.

*April*. Meanwhile I endeavoured to pass my time as well as I could, studying the history of the empire of Bórnu, and entering occasionally into a longer conversation with some of the better instructed of my acquaintances, or making a short excursion; but altogether my usual energy was gone, and my health totally undermined, and the sole object which occupied my thoughts was, to convey my feeble body in safety home. My reduced state of body and mind was aggravated by the weather, as it was extremely hot during this period, the thermometer in the latter part of the month of April, at half-past two o'clock in the afternoon, rising as high as 113°. My exhausted condition had at least this effect upon the people, that it served to hasten my departure, by convincing them that I should not be able to stand this climate any longer.

*May* 4. At length on the 4th of May, I left the town and encamped outside, close in front of the gate. The Sheikh had also given me another camel, and a young and rather weak horse, which did not seem very fit for such a journey, and which in the sequel proved rather a burden than otherwise to me. In this spot I remained some days, waiting for my fellow-traveller Kólo, who was still detained in the town, so that I did not take leave of the Sheikh until the 9th of the month, when he received me with great kindness, but was by no means backward in begging for several articles to be sent to him, especially a small cannon, which was rather out of comparison with the poor present which he had bestowed upon myself. However, he promised me that I should still receive another camel from him, of which I stood greatly in need, although I had made up for one which was lost during my stay before the gate of the town, through the carelessness of A'bbega, by buying a fresh camel at the last moment of my departure. It was for this purpose that I took the sum of thirty dollars from the 1000 dollars brought by the caravan, and which I was anxious to leave behind for the use of Mr. Vogel. Altogether I was extremely unfortunate with my camels, and lost a third one before I had proceeded many miles from the town, so that I was obliged to throw away several things with which my people had overladen my animals.

Our move from Dáwerghú in the afternoon of the 10th was very inauspicious; and while a heavy thunder-storm was raging, enveloping everything in impenetrable darkness, only occasionally illumined by the flashes of lightning, I lost my people, and had great difficulty in joining them again.

## FAREWELL TO NIGERIA[1]

*May* 19. Oppressed as I had been all the time by the apprehension that something might still occur to frustrate my departure, I deemed it one of the happiest moments of my life, when in the afternoon of Saturday the 19th, we at length left our station at this northern frontier of Bórnu, in the present reduced state of that kingdom; and I turned my back with great satisfaction upon these countries where I had spent full five years in incessant toil and exertion. On retracing my steps northwards, I was filled with the hope that a Merciful Providence would allow me to reach home in safety, in order to give a full account of my labours and discoveries; and, if possible, to follow up the connections which I had established with the interior, for opening regular intercourse with that continent.

[1] The reader who has followed Barth's narrative closely will be able to ascribe the note of relief in Barth's *valete* not to any thankfulness at leaving the country (for, as his writings show, he loved Nigeria and its peoples deeply), but to a sense of safety and relaxation that is, after his arduous years in the Western Sudan, fully understandable.

Barth reached Tripoli at the end of August, his caravan having spent three months in crossing the Sahara along the Bilma–Murzuk route. He was met by Warrington.

*August* 28. Having spent a cheerful evening in his company, I set out the following morning on my last march on the African soil, in order to enter the town of Tripoli,[2] and although the impression made upon my mind by the rich vegetation of the gardens which surround the town, after the long journey through the desert waste, was very great, yet infinitely greater was the effect produced upon me by the wide expanse of the sea, which, in the bright sunshine of this intermediate zone, spread out with a tint of the darkest blue. I felt so grateful to Providence for having again reached in safety the border of this Mediterranean basin, the cradle of European civilization, which from an early period had formed the object of my earnest longings and most serious course of studies, that I would fain have alighted from my horse on the sea beach, to offer up a prayer of thanksgiving to the Almighty, who, with the most conspicuous mercy, had led me through the many dangers which surrounded my path.

Thus I closed my long and exhausting career as an African explorer, of which these volumes endeavour to incorporate the results.

After its original leader had succumbed in his arduous task, instead of giving way to despair, I had continued in my career

[2] There is some confusion about Barth's actual dates between reaching Tripoli and landing in England. According to his diary, he entered Tripoli on 28 August and then, 'having stayed four days', he crossed to Malta in a Turkish steamer. This was the *Feizi Bahri* (not referred to in the diary). He 'made only a short stay in the island' before sailing to Marseilles 'in order to reach England by the most direct route'. Declining to pause in Paris, Barth states that he arrived in London on 6 September, 1855. Although this date is repeated in the German edition (thus ruling out the possibility of a misprint) and has been accepted by most authorities, I cannot accept it as correct. I have come across a reference to a telegram dispatched from Marseilles at 11.5 a.m. on 8 September. Again, there is a letter from Barth to Lord Clarendon, advising him of his safe return to England, dated 18 September — a delay of almost a fortnight over such an important matter cannot be reconciled with Barth's methodical and punctilious habits. *The Times* published no report of Barth's return to England, and the nearest certain date in this period is of Barth's arrival in Marseilles on 8 September.

amid great embarrassment, carrying on the exploration of extensive regions almost without any means. And when the leadership of the mission, in consequence of the confidence of Her Majesty's government, was intrusted to me, and I had been deprived of the only European companion who remained with me, I resolved upon undertaking, with a very limited supply of means, a journey to the far west, in order to endeavour to reach Timbúktu, and to explore that part of the Niger which, through the untimely fate of Mungo Park, had remained unknown to the scientific world. In this enterprise I succeeded to my utmost expectation, and not only made known the whole of that vast region, which even to the Arab merchants in general had remained more unknown than any other part of Africa, but I succeeded also in establishing friendly relations with all the most powerful chiefs along the river up to that mysterious city itself.

No doubt, even in the track which I myself pursued I have left a good deal for my successors in this career to improve upon; but I have the satisfaction to feel that I have opened to the view of the scientific public of Europe a most extensive tract of the secluded African world, and not only made it tolerably known, but rendered the opening of a regular intercourse between Europeans and those regions possible.

# INDEX OF NAMES IN BARTH'S DIARY

*(Modern spelling has been adopted)*